People, Planet, Profit.

People, Planet, Profit.

Environmentally and Socially Sustainable Business Strategies

Kit Oung

BEP

BUSINESS EXPERT PRESS

Leader in applied, concise business books

People, Planet, Profit.: Environmentally and Socially Sustainable Business Strategies

First published in 2022 by
Business Expert Press, LLC
222 East 46th Street, New York, NY 10017
www.businessexpertpress.com

ISBN-13: 978-1-63742-181-9 (paperback)
ISBN-13: 978-1-63742-182-6 (e-book)

Business Expert Press Environmental and Social Sustainability for Business Advantage Collection

First edition: 2022

10 9 8 7 6 5 4 3 2 1

Description

When you see or read about excessive corporate profiteering, business malpractices, poor social welfare, and environmental and ecological disasters, do you have an urge to do something? With so many analysis reports, academic journals, news coverage, and documentaries on the subject, why is there so little action?

Most management gurus and executives recognize that it is possible to achieve a triple bottom line—running a business for the benefit of the people, the planet, and profit at the same time. To achieve this, businesses have to solve their internal issues involving the leadership team, the management team, and the technical team.

Drawing from leadership and management practices, practical case studies, and using energy, water, raw material, waste, and its associated environmental impact as examples, *People, Planet, Profit.*, describes the ten internal issues—five technical, two leadership, and three managerial—and solutions to these issues.

A coherent, joined-up, and concerted effort allows responsible businesses to initiate, gain momentum, and achieve success in reducing their environmental impact. The same tools can then be applied to other areas of a triple bottom line.

Keywords

triple bottom line; sustainability; environment; balanced scorecard; strategy-to-execution premium; resource efficiency; energy; water; raw material; waste

Contents

Testimonials

"What stood out for me was the reference to change felt at a deeply personal level. This is key to the commitment needed for change management and hardly anyone talks about it. Unless there is emotion in the will to change—anger, resolve, passion—the solutions attempted will continue to be in the range of 'business as usual.' I feel that leadership that is willing to take hard, tough, unpopular decisions is the key to placing the correct emphasis on people and the planet. Business leaders who dare to be different.

There are about 80 plus individual business tycoons owning 90 percent or more of the world's wealth and the logical progression towards a 'winner takes all' mentality. The way Amazon is behaving, for example, not paying enough taxes, low wages, criminal levels of profit, no respect for people or the planet—is going beyond even the usual cut-throat behavior of capitalism and big business.

I really like the sentence 'turning resource productivity from common sense into common practice.' The meaning of the words effectiveness and efficiency is much broader than the economic context and doing this will mean that conservation, saving water and environment, saving energy, and using less resources will become ends in themselves, instead of the means for supporting profits. It is also important to note that positive advertising, putting minuscule funds into "charity" are not the same as putting people and planet first.

It is very good book and in the simple language that will bring the desired readers. The ten chapters are nicely arranged and the step-wise approach in the last chapter is very practical. I would certainly recommend it to the group I work with the most—non-profit organizations working in the development sectors under corporate-style management, and medium-sized businesses that are mostly part of the value and supply chains of big companies."—**Simi Kamal, Chairperson and CEO, HISAAR Foundation, Pakistan**

"People, Planet, Profit., by Kit Oung is what a good business book should be: a commentary on one of our most urgent and timely topics; a practical guide to read, review, and work with daily; as well as a compendium of comprehensive explanations and cases to educate yourself with.

Focusing on resource productivity as a key focus to create a sustainable organization and business, he provides a 10-Step-Approach to get green topics into the heads of employees and into bottom-line financial profit. Useful in that he builds on known frameworks such as TBL, Balanced Scorecard and established change practices, which make the move to sustainability more familiar than it might otherwise come across.

He builds on this with a Strategy-to-Execution-Premium, which aims to keep the resource productivity 'alive' as a core business practice. The many business cases throughout all chapters are super practical and allow for carrying practices over, as much as using them as food for thought."—**Nicole Keeding-Bensch, Internationale Hochschule Bad Honnef, Germany**

"This book provides a simplified and structured approach to triple bottom line. It is based on the practical experiences of the author. Kit's knowledge underlines the best practices he has applied and contributed over more than two decades. He shows you the real-world solutions that you need to move business toward continual improvement on cost reduction in conjunction with environmental and social commitments."—**Majeed Javdani, Chief Executive Officer, Namdaran El Rayaneh, Iran**

"A must-have addition to anyone who is contemplating understanding and implementing effective management of resources.

It is a balanced mix between well-researched concepts of resource productivity, the drivers for shifting and embracing these concepts, success and distracting factors, and practical and proven examples within various size organizations.

While the concepts are not new as it follows a plan-do-check-act loop, the way they are woven into easily understandable, well explained, and digestible bundles of information are refreshing, facilitating adoption, implementation, and success. I find the case studies included in each chapter educational and priceless. I was impressed as to how innovative his approach is."—**Mary-Rose Agopian Nguyen, Principal, Strategy Advisory LLC, USA**

"People, Planet, Profit., is an insightful look at business strategies, techniques, and methods that can help senior leaders and middle management plan and implement energy and resource effectiveness projects in your organization. It is a remarkable book that can create a valuable understanding of how organizations could reduce their GHG, energy consumption, and environmental footprints, resulting in enhanced financial contributions and positive impacts on people and the planet. Simple and straightforward, I was pleased to read a book that walks through the challenges and potential solutions organizations, leaders, and employees undertake to implement and maintain projects of these scales. Utilizing the Strategy-to-Execution Premium concept presented within could help people identify and resolve possible struggles and focus on their desired outcomes. "—**Argenis José Osorio Pérez, Manager, Quality Assurance & Business Excellence, University of Calgary, Canada**

Foreword

There are times in a professional career that you come across a person that at first seems quiet, but has hidden depths. Kit and I met through an ISO Task Force for revising the *Integrated Use of Management System Standards* handbook in Geneva in January 2016. I was to quickly learn that he was passionate and a true expert in energy and resource productivity. His work in helping the United Kingdom develop the required energy legislation and performance targets was a revelation, and he has a legacy and results that are recognized not only in the United Kingdom but internationally.

Kit has placed a litmus paper on businesses and some national initiatives to use their energy and resources productively. For organizations seeking to achieve energy, resources, and emissions goals will gain deep and science-based evidence to build their business cases for change. This book is providing a different lens, a construct, and a framework of reference for readers to consider and perhaps assist in reframing their thinking and approach.

This book reflects his lived, worked, and academic experience but also the application of his deep knowledge to various government, not-for-profit, utilities (infrastructure), and private organizations. Kit explores the anthesis, well-worn comments, and knee-jerk responses we all hear, but his dialectic and reasoned approach and evidence-based research will better inform executives and policymakers to manage and lead the creation and management of energy and resources.

In an era and postpandemic future we face, there will be a review, revisit, and reassessment of all business strategies. It will be sobering as to whether the scenario planning sessions they may have conducted and filed-away can be taken more seriously.

Firstly, new workers are making decisions to join or not join a firm upon many factors.

Secondly, investment houses, as we see, directly impact and have long-term consequences for Australia and its GDP but also its long-term growth in a zero-carbon economy and more efficient and effective production, storage, distribution, consumption, and renewal of energy and materials. They have already changed their investment decisions and placements.

I suspect this will unfold as Kit describes and some folk will remind "top management" of what they committed to but were not always cognizant. It will place the book as a must-read in readiness for any strategic analysis, stakeholder engagement, and seek sustainable responses for long-term resilience. Perhaps, that suboptimized "Triple Bottom Line" approach that Kit points out will replace the stakeholder top-line approach not only in business but many entities: "top management" must seek optimal outcomes for People, Planet, and Profit for their stakeholders and interested parties.

Finally, there is a management-level roadmap that paves the way for executives to incorporate environmental stewardship and resource-productive operation into their corporate vision. No longer will businesses be forced into environmental compliance as a cost of doing business, but rather can integrate such practices into their culture to achieve reduced operating costs and enhanced environmental stewardship.

—Michael W. McLean, Managing Director, McLean
Management Consultants Pty Ltd, Australia

Acknowledgments

I have an unyielding belief, strong desire, and passion for good governance: the alignment between strategy, management, and execution to bring about good company performance, health and safety, resource productivity, and sustainability. It is not a sexy subject and has no state-of-the-art technology, does not involve any cocktails of leadership jargon, nor the existence of a management cure-all soup. But, the existence, alignment, and execution of all three components are vital if we are to avert the impending climate disaster or survive another round of pandemic or major economic shock.

I didn't discover *Strategy-to-Execution Premium* out of the blue—I had help along the way. Back in the late 1990s, as a young engineer, I thought that I knew everything there is to know and that all my engineering skills are all I needed to save energy and prevent environmental pollution. What became very clear is that I was constantly fighting "management"— be it as a self-assured consulting engineer or as a production engineer— convincing management is rather difficult. The reasons given appear to be a moving feast of "yes, but ..." or outright "no." My then mentors—all formerly Imperial Chemical Industries (ICI) specialists—who became friends shined bright spots where holes exist in my thought processes.

In the late 2000s, as my career progressed into management, I was constantly bombarded by my team with ideas that are often seemingly sensible but are often poorly conceived or have flaws in them that needed ironing out. To be fair, it reminds me of ... me!!! At the same time, I had to juggle multiple company priorities, which at many times meant that trade-offs are very essential as there is only one of me and I have only 24 hours a day. More often than not, the number of add-on "initiatives" is so large, and, amazingly, anything could get done. I began to see that, perhaps, management is not the issue here. After all, management is sandwiched between the "top management" or leaders of the company and the folks at the bottom.

The third part of the jigsaw came in the early 2010s, having spent several short periods of study in business management and leadership in two of the best business schools in the world and sat on two boardrooms. Here, I experienced firsthand the issues leaders faced—the cutting edge of an organization, its strategy, its management, and the consequences of its decisions—the good and the bad—and how it trickles through the whole organization. I remember the three *Harvard Business Review* articles and three business school lectures clicked the three components together very well. I have it in my bag all of the time and it's heavily annotated— Robert Kaplan and David Norton's *Mastering the Management System*, Michael Porter's *The Five Competitive Forces That Shape Strategy*, and John Kotter's *Leading Change: Why Transformation Efforts Fail*. And the three business school lectures were those of Andy Neely, Jonathan Trevor, and Mark de Rond.

All in, the concepts described in this book span 25+ years of experience, but I'm not alone in thinking about and working on *Strategy-to-Execution Premiums*. You might have assumed that having written (and ghostwritten) six books, writing another book is easy and/or straightforward. The reverse is true. As I reviewed and researched the subject matter and many case studies to draw out success factors and to conceptualize the materials for this book, I find that I can never have enough knowledge and skills in every topic there is in this world. For every important aspect of good practice, there is a multitude of nuance and multiple sources of expertise.

I would like to acknowledge the following people who, in the course of a few years, and multiple correspondences, assisted me in solidifying the *Strategy-to-Execution Premium* framework. In particular, I'd like to acknowledge Andy Neely (Pro-Vice-Chancellor for Enterprise and Business Relations, University of Cambridge), Nicholas Bloom (Professor of Economics, Stanford Institute for Economic Policy Research), and Robert Kaplan (Emeritus Professor of Leadership Development, Harvard Business School). They have provided their expertise, inputs, guidance, and including advanced copies of their latest work when developing and formalizing the concepts and frameworks in this book.

I'd also like to thank the following people who have reviewed this book, in part or in full, and in some instances, debated the concepts covered, all with the intent of crafting a message that is clear, concise, consistent, and correct. Some have also signposted additional examples and case studies that could be incorporated into the book:

- David Thorpe. Founder/Director, The One Planet Centre.
- Duncan Giddens. Senior Environmental Specialist, OECD. Former Senior Project Manager at the Environment Agency, UK.
- Mark Apsey. Managing Director, Ameresco.
- Jason Leadbitter. Sustainability and Corporate Social Responsibility Manager, INOVYN.
- Mary-Rose Nguyen. Executive Director, Strategy Advisory.
- Michael McLean. Managing Director, McLean Management Consultants.
- Richard Hadfield. Managing Director, Progressive Certification.
- Roland Risser. Former Deputy Assistant Secretary—Renewable Power, U.S. Department of Energy.
- Steven Fawkes. Managing Partner, EnergyPro.
- Swati Murthy. Practice Head—Sustainability, Tata Consulting Services.

Finally, my gratitude and appreciation also go to my editorial and production team at Exeter Premedia Services, Gunabala Saladi, and Suba Esther Rani.

Introduction

Isn't it true that the hardest part of driving any kind of change is whether the individual—the employee, the citizen—feels the need to change at a deeply personal level? And in hindsight, when the circumstances that cry out for change are gone, when things have returned to "normal"—don't we always wish we had been bolder, more ambitious, gone faster, gone further?

—Sam Palmisano [1]

Before the World Wars, a majority of businesses were local to their geography. Companies used raw materials and energy sourced locally. Laborers were from the local community. Their products were sold locally too. At that time, companies juggled a similar number of issues ranging from health and safety, maintaining their assets, generating good-quality products, using materials responsibly, conducting their business ethically, and taking care of the known environmental impact of the days. Any poor practices would result in dissent from their customers and community which would directly impact the profitability of the business.

After the World Wars, due to a need to rebuild the economy and the infrastructure destroyed during the wars, companies focused on economic growth, building wealth, and creating employment, while governments focused on rebuilding the infrastructure, social needs, and environmental issues. This practice was further solidified by Milton Friedman and The Business Roundtable. In the 1980s, Milton Friedman and his colleagues at the Chicago School of Economics promoted the concept of monetarism and shareholder primacy—a concept that influenced the thinking of many Western economies such as the United States and the United Kingdom.

Founded in 1972, The Business Roundtable is a nonprofit association consisting of the Chief Executive Officers of major U.S. companies who lobby the three U.S. legislative branches in favor of business-friendly policies [2]. In 1997, The Business Roundtable declared that the fiduciary duties of top management were to protect the interest of the stockholders. Due to the economic power of the United States and dominance of the "American Dream" throughout the world, this formed the principles of corporate governance and cemented the practice and behaviors of top management.

> *... In The Business Roundtable's view, the paramount duty of management and boards of directors is to the corporation's stockholders; the interests of other stakeholders are relevant as a derivative of the duty to stockholders. The notion that the board must somehow balance the interests of stockholders against the interests of other stakeholders fundamentally misconstrues the role of directors. It is, moreover, an unworkable notion because it would leave the board with no criterion for resolving conflicts between the interests of stockholders and of other stakeholders or among different groups of stakeholders. ...*
>
> —The Business Roundtable, 1997 [3]

Despite a vast increase in economic growth and incomes, there was a corresponding decline in other elements of business operations ranging from excessive executive compensation, short termism, financial manipulations, and corporate scandals, leading to the 2008 financial crisis. Between 1860 and 1990, a period of 130 years, there were 56 major man-made Health and Safety disasters and 37 major corporate scandals. Between 1990 and 2020, in a span of 40 years, there were 54 major man-made Health and Safety disasters and 182 major corporate scandals.

There are also many and frequent cases of discrimination of all types: gender, age, skin tone, bodily features, language, national origin, physical and mental disability, race, religious beliefs, sexual orientation, family standing, social affiliation, and reprisal for whistleblowing could be found frequently in the media along with pay gap disparities and harassments. In addition to these, issues on climate change, forest fires, hurricanes and typhoons, prolonged droughts, and floods were reported more frequently in the last 20 years.

The list of major corporate scandals and ethical issues include corporate giants, stock market favorites, and family-trusted brands, such as ABN-Amro, AIG, Airbus, BAE Systems, Barings Bank, Boeing, BP,

Bristol-Myers Squibb, Chevron-Texaco, Deutsche Bank, Enron, Freddie Mac, Halliburton, Hewlett-Packard, Lehman Brothers, Merrill Lynch, Monsanto, Nestlé, Olympus Corporation, Petrobras, Royal Bank of Scotland, Royal Dutch Shell, Siemens, Southwest Airlines, Swissair, Tesla, Toshiba, Tyco, Union Carbide, Volkswagen, Wells Fargo, WorldCom, Xerox, 1Malaysia Development Berhad, and 7-Eleven.

Many more major and global companies and brands, while not causing major disasters and scandals, fell short of their declared energy, environmental, and resource consumption objectives. Some of these include Shell [4], BP [4], Total [4], and ConocoPhillips [5] falling short of their net-zero pledges with Shell relying heavily on CO_2 offsets rather than reducing their demand for energy [5]; Starbucks falling short of its 2008 commitment to make 25 percent of its cups reusable by 2015, lowered its target to five percent in 2011, and in 2016 further lowered its target by half to be achieved in 2022 [6]; Coca-Cola and Pepsi falling short on their single-use plastic and plastic recycling targets [7]; Nestlé, and P&G missing their 2020 deforestation goals [8]; and Costco and Netflix did not publish their CO_2 emissions reduction targets despite stating at a high level their commitments to reduce their environmental impact [9]. An analysis by Transition Pathway Initiative showed only 15 percent of businesses have energy and climate commitment that is fully aligned with 1.5°C global warming and 63 percent of commitments are either nonexistent or so vague that it is impossible to decipher [10].

At the same time, 72 percent of the global population earns below the average income levels and lives in areas where the local biodiversity cannot repair itself [14]. There are also examples of companies located in the developed world whose labor practices, employment benefits, and social welfare are worse off than those in developing countries. *The New York Times* reported that the United States is the only advanced nation that does not have national laws covering minimum vacation time (paid or unpaid), sick days, and paid maternity and paternity leave compared to other developed nations. Among the Organization for Economic Cooperation and Development (OECD) countries, the United States also has the highest percentage of low-wage workers and the lowest minimum wage as a percentage of the median wage [11]. There is also evidence that some employees rely on customer tips to survive [12].

While businesses are very successful, many are not paying their fair share of taxes—monies that are essential to finance infrastructure, health, education, and other community services—services that also benefit them. In 2020, 55 companies on the S&P500 or Fortune 500 avoided paying a combined total of $8.5 billion in taxes through a series of complex accounting, reporting structures, and tax rebates. Nike and FedEx reportedly generated $2.8 billion and $1.2 billion in pretax income but have paid no taxes between 2018 and 2020 [13]. During the same period, Amazon reported a pretax income of $45 billion, they paid no taxes in 2018 and a total of $1.9 billion or 4 percent versus 21 percent applicable to other U.S. corporations [14].

As such, the general public and governments are increasingly demanding companies to take a broader view and accountability of their business operations and to take business ethics, health, safety, employee welfare, use of resources, protecting the environment, supplier and societal issues seriously as well as the profitability perspective.

The modern concept of sustainable development was derived from Our Common Future [15] also known as the Brundtland Report in recognition of the Chair of the World Commission on Environment and Development, Gro Harlem Brundtland. The report proposes a model for "sustainable development" balancing the need for economic growth, environmental protection, and social equality.

In 1994, John Elkington coined the phrase *Triple Bottom Line* [16]. Both concepts are generally accepted, and there is a proliferation of measurements, reporting frameworks, and certification schemes for them. Some companies are successful in this endeavor. Many are not and issues such as business ethics, health and safety, responsible use of resources, and environmental impacts are still rampant and trending in the wrong direction. As such, the concept of sustainable development and the triple bottom line are still elusive in businesses, and many still struggle to implement it.

Issues such as quality and asset management are directly related to profitability, and businesses are already proficient in it. Issues like health and safety, business ethics, and employee welfare are also much easier to implement as most are a series of "Do" and "Don't."

Where most businesses struggle with is in energy, water, raw material, waste footprint, and its associated environmental impact. This book focuses on one element of the triple bottom line: the responsible use of resources—raw materials, energy, water, and generation of waste. Businesses can use this as a template to integrate the other elements of triple bottom line into their operations. This can range from quality, health, safety, environmental impacts, and social welfare in the local community. When the business practices become more mature, they may want to consider integrating multiple issues and optimize all of the issues at the same time.

Yes, improvements in resource productivity will nearly always lead to a reduction in the environmental impact of a company. This book focuses on resource productivity instead of the impact of the environment for three reasons: (1) it is instilling the practice of solving the environmental impacts at source rather than an afterthought; (2) some environmental impacts are cumulative over a long time, whereas the resource productivity can be measured in situ; and (3) addressing resource productivity has an impact on the whole supply chain of the raw materials, energy, water, and waste, leading to an overall global change in the supply and demand of resources.

What Is Resource Productivity? Why Resource Productivity as a Basis for the Triple Bottom Line?

Over the last 30 years, there has been a general increase in awareness and knowledge about the impact of human beings and the impact of their activities on their surroundings and planet earth. Coupled with an increase of documentaries on the subject matter, such as *David Attenborough: A Life on Our Planet*, and the rise of climate change activists such as Greta Thunberg and *Extinction Rebellion*, issues such as energy, water, raw material and waste, and climate change are brought to the fore.

For energy, global energy consumption over the last 50 years has grown at a steady pace of 2.5 percent per annum [17]. Over the same period, the convention of referring to "energy savings" changed many times: from energy savings to energy conservation, energy best practice, energy efficiency, energy management, low carbon, net-zero, and so on, without any significant reductions in energy use and energy consumption. The accumulation of CO_2 in the atmosphere is simultaneously making the planet's air and oceans warmer and making the ocean water more acidic. At the same time, three trillion trees (at a rate of 50 billion trees per year) were cut down in name of farming, industrialization, and urbanization [18]; the excessive use of fertilizers and pesticides in farming leached into waterways impacting the aquatic biodiversity [19] and into human health and land-based biodiversity [20].

Cumulatively, a warmer and prolonged climate is thawing the permafrost in Siberia and melting the ice sheets in the Arctic and Antarctic. It is making the forest much easier to catch fire, particularly in the Mediterranean countries, California, and Australia. Warmer ocean slows down the ocean currents that flow from warmer part of the planet to the polar regions and vice versa, impacting the planet's ability to regulate temperatures; and the acidification of the ocean water makes aquatic life form, particularly corals and crustaceans difficult to grow and survive. Research by Johan Rockström and his team suggests that air, ocean, virgin forest, and wildlife (both land and aquatic) are part and parcel of the way planet earth regulates and maintains stable living conditions, are interlinked, and are rapidly and assuredly tipping the scales for life on Earth as we currently know [21], [22]. Even if there is an overwhelming success to limit warming by 1.5°C above preindustrial levels by 2030, approximately five billion people could still be exposed to the climate issues described [23].

A quick survey of the current capabilities for energy efficiency shows that existing energy-saving techniques and technologies can reduce energy consumption by 73 percent [24] and with 25 to 30 percent of the savings without major capital costs and changes to business practices [25]. The Boston Consulting Group [26] further estimates that countries can achieve an 80 percent reduction from its 1990 level greenhouse gases using only proven and accepted technologies available today without harming economic growth—thus meeting the 2°C commitment to Paris Agreement. However, the use and promotion of energy-efficient technologies are only achieving just over one percent savings year on year—a fraction of its true potential [27].

For raw material and waste, many are familiar with reducing packaging waste. Sadly, many organizations in Canada, France, Belgium, Germany, Spain, the Netherlands, the United Kingdom, and the United States operate an "out of sight, out of mind approach"—by shipping their plastic waste to countries like China (now reduced), Turkey, Malaysia, Vietnam, Thailand, Indonesia, and the Philippines—all of which have relatively lower regulatory requirements and environmental standards. These plastic wastes are piling high or are waiting to be incinerated in the open air, causing atmospheric and effluent pollution, related health consequences, and environmental impacts [28], [29]. Research by McKinsey & Company suggests that efforts to reduce packaging waste are concentrated in three areas: emphasis on full recyclability and a higher degree of recycled content (60 percent), reduction of plastics consumption (26 percent), and repurposing plastics after their beneficial use (14 percent) [30].

When it comes to nonpackaging wastes such as end-of-life products, by-products, and graded products, the reusing, recycling, and remanufacturing rates are low [31]. Through better or improved design, a handful of leading companies were able to increase their reuse, recycle, and remanufacture rates to high numbers. Now, some manufacturers sell soaps, shampoos, and disinfectants using recycled plastics. Some airlines have also introduced new blankets made from repurposed waste plastics.

Even in low-tech industries like agriculture and farming, there is a 50 percent excess use of phosphorus-based fertilizers, 60 percent excess use of nitrogen-based fertilizers, and between 30 and 42 percent excess pesticide use [20]. Ironically, while we use excessive energy, water, fertilizers, and herbicides to grow the food, on average, 33 percent of the harvested food does not reach human or animal consumption [32]. This figure is much higher for perishable foods, such as fruits and vegetables, and lower for nonperishable, such as grains. FAO also reports higher food waste in Central and South Asia and Sub-Saharan Africa.

For water, while 75 percent of the planet is water, 97 percent of it is saltwater and 1.7 percent is in inaccessible glaciers, polar ice caps, deep underground caverns, or falls at the wrong time, at the wrong place, or the wrong speeds, leading to floods. The remaining 1.3 percent is shared between agriculture (70 percent), domestic (11 percent), and industrial

(19 percent) use [33]. The increasing numbers of industries, water leakage, unregulated and uncontrolled water extraction, contamination of groundwater, poor water use practices, and rising temperatures in most of the countries are making freshwater a scarce resource.

The acidification of freshwater due to CO_2 in the air and rising air temperatures has reduced the size of freshwater reserves by 80 percent, causing corals bleaching, and melting water stored as ice in the polar caps. Summer sea ice has reduced by 40 percent in 40 years, which will limit the planet to regulate its global temperature [18].

In general, the general public understands the concept of optimizing the consumption of raw materials, energy, and water and minimizing the generation of waste as "resource efficiency." However, as will be described in Chapter 3, efficiency is just one of the different ways to achieve the stated resource goals. The other ways to optimize resources in a business include the concept of use, consumption, yield, and effectiveness. All five concepts offer a comprehensive way to look at optimizing and improving resources deployed. No "one" word or phrase captures all five concepts of using resources optimally. We use the concept of "productivity" to mean consuming resources as efficiently and effectively as possible to reduce or avoid waste. "Resource productivity" captures all of these concepts— use, consumption, yield, efficiency, and effectiveness—from a physical quantity perspective, not from an economic or financial perspective.

Some people are naturally drawn to protect the environment. Some others would continue to deny the relevance of climate change and its impact on the future sustainability of life on the planet. Regardless of what individuals and collective individuals in a business believe about climate change, conservation, and ecosystem, it is no longer acceptable for businesses to operate on a business-as-usual basis—focusing on making products or providing services without consideration of the unintended consequences. They have to juggle many facets of the business environment: sales, profitability, new markets, competition, and regulations and address the issues around environment and sustainability.

Businesses must want to take action on improving their resource productivity, mitigate environmental impact, and improve profitability.

Governments are not best placed to take action due to three compounding reasons.

Firstly, the type of economics that informs Government policy making—macroeconomics—assumes that every person is rational. The "rational" man or woman running a business will always ensure that they are as efficient and effective when utilizing resources. Waste and inefficiencies are a cost that any "rational" man or woman will minimize. As such, when Governments talk about resource productivity and the related environmental impact, they are in effect talking about decarbonization, deforestation, plastic wastes, etc. As can be seen by the statistics earlier, this assumption is wrong!

Secondly, it is not the Government's role to mandate companies to consume less, save money, and increase their profitability. Similarly, suppliers for raw material, energy, and water, waste recycling and waste management companies, equipment manufacturers, consultants, and other service providers want to be supplying their products and services. Businesses reducing their consumption detract from the supplier's interest. Academics, R&D, professional associations, lobby groups, and the media also depend on the continued consumption for them to do their bits.

Thirdly, there are also a lot of professional lobby groups whose aim is to block, delay, modify, and water down policies that promote environmental protection and sustainability in many countries. Some of these lobby groups are allegedly funded by large coal, oil, and gas companies [34] [35] [36] (e.g., BP, Shell, ExxonMobil, Chevron, Total, Santos, Origin Energy, Sunset Power, and Whitehaven Coal), meat and dairy companies [37], and large energy-consuming companies [38] [39] [40] (e.g., Toyota, Apple, Amazon, Microsoft, Walt Disney, Intuit, United Airlines, Air-France, International Airlines Group, Lufthansa, Ryanair, Deloitte, Alphabet (Google's parent company), Bayer, AstraZeneca, Pfizer, FedEx, Verizon, Johnson & Johnson, Dow, Goodyear, and BHP)—many of whom publicly acknowledge the importance of climate change and the need to take action. The five largest oil and gas companies (BP, Shell, ExxonMobil, Chevron, and Total) reportedly spend approximately over $200 million every year lobbying [41] climate change policies globally.

The UN's Conference of the Parties (COP) is evidence of this innate difficulty for Governments to take effective action. From Paris (COP21, 2015), Marrakech (COP22, 2016), Bonn (COP23, 2017), Katowice (COP24, 2018), and Madrid (COP25, 2019) to Glasgow (COP26, 2021), each meeting gains commitments for the fringe issues—reducing deforestation, reducing methane emissions, phasing down coal and fossil fuels—yet passes the baton for the "real deal"—energy demand reduction, finance for decarbonization, and carbon capture—to the next meeting. Ahead of the Glasgow meeting, the oil and gas companies allegedly spent $81.9 million on lobbying [42]. 503 delegates from 27 countries were employed by fossil fuel companies or associated lobbying groups. Collectively, they represent the largest group compared to any other countries represented! [43]

Ultimately, improving resource productivity is for the benefit of the business, and companies have to take it upon themselves to take action. Taking action is also important because it represents 75 percent of the global economy [11]. Moving forward in a postpandemic world: Generation Zs want to work for companies with strong purpose and environment and social performance; customers want to associate with green and socially responsible businesses; financial and insurance institutions want to invest in responsible businesses. The society expectation and regulatory trend are toward a net-zero, circular economy, ethical, and transparent reporting. All in, the importance and call for environmental and social responsibilities in business will increase.

In 2015, 2016, and 2018, I surveyed what businesses were doing in terms of resource productivity, their reasons for addressing these issues, and the barriers they faced. After analyzing all 805 survey responses, more than 70 percent agree their company has a policy and a work program for resource productivity. Among all resource productivity topics, the top three priorities were consuming less energy (33 percent), consuming less raw materials and generating less waste (33 percent), and consuming less water (eight percent). Businesses focus on these areas because of a desire to reduce their operating costs (49 percent) and improve the environment and society (30 percent). The other reasons make up the remaining 21 percent.

A study by the Economist Intelligence Unit reported similar findings and is shown in Figure I.1. Discounting "raising awareness among

Increasing energy efficiency

Reducing waste

Offering more sustainable product or services

Reducing water consumption

Raising awareness on sustainability among customers

Promoting local community initiatives

Purchasing carbon offsets

Sourcing from sustainable sources

Investing in renewable energy

Others

0%   5%   10%   15%   20%   25%

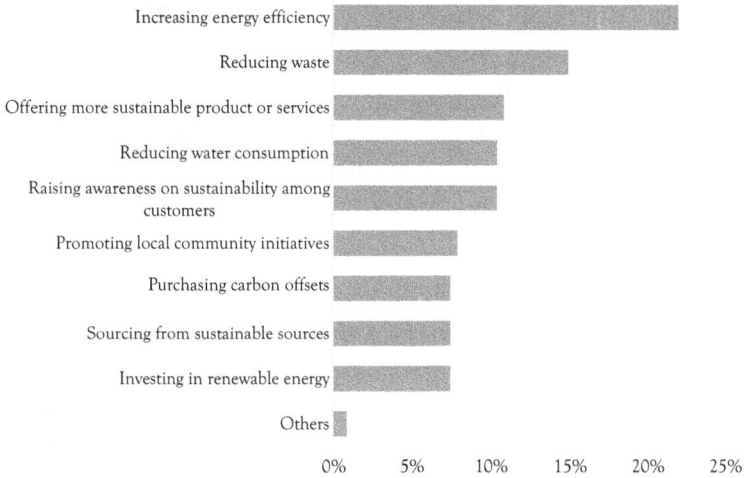

Figure I.1 Top focus areas of leaders and managers in a business

Source: Data adapted from [23]

customers," "purchasing carbon offsets," and "promoting local community initiatives" from Figure I.1 as it does not result in any physical activity to improve resource productivity: working on consuming less energy, using less raw materials (thus generating less waste), consuming less water, and supply chain initiatives make up 70 percent of the focus areas.

All in, we are consuming natural resources 50 percent faster than our planet can regenerate to meet our current consumption needs [44]. Traditionally, each resource is optimized independently of the other. In reality, each resource on this planet is interrelated and balanced within the ecosystem. A study by S&P Dow Jones Indices for over 2,500 companies analyzed between 2009 and 2014 shows a strong correlation between energy, water, raw material, and waste in many agricultural, industrial, and service sectors. As such, activities that increase energy consumption, acidify water sources, and change land use all accelerate the accumulation of greenhouse gases in the atmosphere and push our planet further away from its ability to regenerate [22].

Although technologies and techniques are available to solve (or at least improve) the existing resource productivity situation, their adoption is a huge challenge due to a lack of leadership, vision, and follow-through action. Despite the aspirations of many governments and publicly traded companies to become "more" resource productive, we are slow and far from becoming so. This is not to say that all businesses are bad in resource productivity. S&P Dow Jones Indices found companies that outperform their peers consistently do so over a long time because they are willing to invest in resource productivity and sustainability. The resource productivity of laggards also consistently lags behind their peers [44].

For the significant majority in the middle, anecdotal evidence and hearsay for poor resource productivity point to multiple reasons and range from the fact that: (1) different industries have different requirements that are not replicable or have no commonalities; (2) failure in markets and government policies to expedite the diffusion of new technology; (3) low cost of resources such as raw materials, energy, and water impedes the return on investments; (4) short sightedness requiring immediate returns on investment (ROI); and (5) senior executives having no interest in it or are constantly moving its goalposts. Others claim that they have exploited most (if not all) opportunities to save; thus, there are no opportunities to use less. Other evidence points to the lip service paid by the largest corporations in the world on resource productivity, with little to show [45].

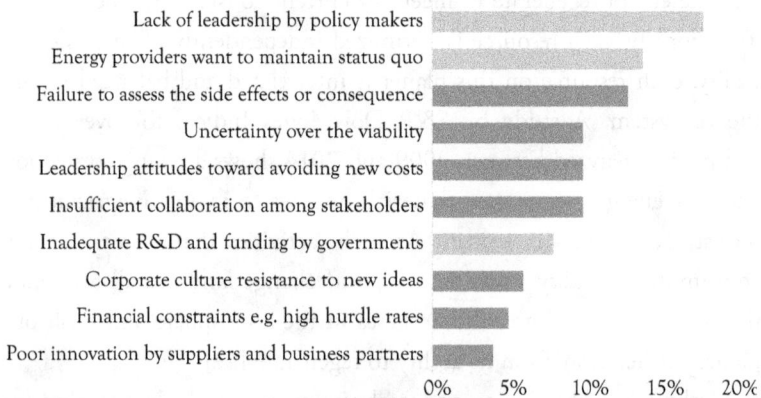

Lack of leadership by policy makers
Energy providers want to maintain status quo
Failure to assess the side effects or consequence
Uncertainty over the viability
Leadership attitudes toward avoiding new costs
Insufficient collaboration among stakeholders
Inadequate R&D and funding by governments
Corporate culture resistance to new ideas
Financial constraints e.g. high hurdle rates
Poor innovation by suppliers and business partners

0%   5%   10%   15%   20%

Figure I.2 Top 10 reasons companies are not investing in energy savings according to Harvard Business Review

Source: Data adapted from [46]

Rather interestingly, all of the above are not the true cause of inaction. Even the cause of each business being different from its competition is not a valid response. Energy is energy. Water is water. Whether the company is a premiership football club (a luxury hotel or luxury department store) or those lower down the league doesn't matter. This is because while the specific details and application might differ, the principles and methods of incorporating sustainability as part of the business strategy are the same.

Peer-reviewed journals and published information offer a more realistic insight and reason for the slow response. A *Harvard Business Review* survey [46] shows that seven of the top 10 reasons frequently cited by senior executives for inaction have nothing to do with government policies, costs, or external interested parties (Figure I.2). Together with similar studies by the Economist Intelligence Unit [23] and *Financial Times* [47] highlighted the real culprit for ineffective action by companies: poor levels of leadership and management engagements, and willingness to make it happen as the root cause. My surveys from 2015, 2016, and 2018 yielded a similar split between internal and external barriers.

The effect of this is, for businesses that care about resource productivity, many implement projects and initiatives in an ad hoc manner and treat it as a discreet activity independent from its processes and strategy. Eighty to ninety percent of them do not plan or implement their plans as planned [48]. More than 51 percent of senior sustainability and environmental managers admitted to having realized less than 33 percent of technically feasible and economically viable opportunities [49]. A Green Monday survey reported less than nine percent of businesses implemented more than 66 percent of its opportunities that are feasible and viable.

The discrete nature of projects makes it vulnerable for de-prioritization compared to other strategic initiatives and conflicting priorities within the company. They also tend to pigeonhole resource productivity issues into one department, independent from the day-to-day operations and core process(es). This act encourages silo thinking on resource productivity and sustainability.

As such, when we talk about energy savings, water savings, waste reduction, or climate change, we care about the planet and know what must be done. When the topic changes, especially in "business as usual" discussions, or when facing an impending or unfolding crisis such as short-term business issues, or the Covid-19 pandemic in 2020, the intention to save resources disappears from conscious thought and is relegated to the background. To improve resource productivity and minimize the environmental impact, we need to resolve the internal issues in each company.

10 Steps Toward Becoming a Responsible Business

The good news … the issues surrounding resource productivity, environmental impacts, and social issues can be solved. In the 1970s, researchers found that widely used substances such as chlorofluorocarbons (CFCs), aerosols, and solvents accelerated the thinning of ozone in the Antarctic region. There was a rapid and concerted effort to stop using and eliminating ozone-depleting substances. By 2018, the thinning of ozone declined [50]. The Covid-19 pandemic also showed that when there is a will and a need, governments, companies, and people will find a way to make our planet and world safe. Specifically, to avoid the tipping point, all businesses need to target a seven percent year-on-year energy and CO_2 emissions reduction, accelerate the move toward a closed-loop economy, and move on to a diet that consists of more plants and fruits [19].

The second good news … awareness is in abundance on issues like climate change, loss of biodiversity, and ecosystem, and the impact of human beings' unfettered consumption of resources on sustainability.

The third good news … there are a lot of discipline-specific experts to address these issues. The scientists are calling for more urgent action based on scientific data. NGOs and activists are calling for more action by governments. The economists are calling for industrywide reforms and a different interpretation of capitalism. Governments are creating more (or optimizing) policy instruments. Academics are researching more novel ideas. Technologists are creating more technology. Rating agencies are calling for more reporting. Consultants are creating more detailed and complex methodologies, and so on.

Unfortunately, the experts are addressing the issue from within their pigeonhole and are unknowingly solving the wrong problem! If we look closely, the experts are spending time and effort to solve fringe issues related to resource productivity. They are not addressing the root cause—the apparent lack of will, ad hoc, sluggish, and discrete nature of resource productivity in companies. The problem that needed to be solved is, "Why are businesses still so slow in adopting resource-productive practices? Why is the planet still tunneling down the rabbit hole?" Tackling the root cause requires looking at how businesses operate, embedding resource productivity into their *Strategic* intent, using appropriate data and *Technical* analysis to inform decision making, and active *Management* so that resource productivity is part and parcel of its operations.

Resource productivity rooted only in technical analysis lacks the buy-in and interest of the leadership and management team. One that is purely rooted in leadership risks having undeliverable projects or competing priorities in the company. One that is driven purely by management drives the wrong projects to deliver overall good and conflicts with the strategic direction. Even when any two are present but not the third, the initiative still slows down and stalls (Figure I.3). The technical analysis also need not be complex and difficult—in fact, the complexity often hinders the effective use of resources. If anything, stripping out the jargon-laden and high-accuracy analysis in favor of understandable and intuitively meaningful outputs is needed.

> *... CEOs remain convinced that sustainability will transform their industries; that leadership can bring competitive advantage, and that sustainability can be a route to new waves of growth and innovation. But beneath this commitment, frustration is evident: business leaders are in many cases unable to locate and quantify the business value of sustainability, and see market failure hindering the business effort to tackle global challenges. ...*
> —UN Global Compact–Accenture CEO Study on
> Sustainability 2013 [51]

It is the synergy of *Strategy*, *Management*, and *Technical* that matters. Companies that have a defined strategy, use data analysis to inform decision making, and can manage their interdepartmental issues are the ones that improve their deployed resources and do so in a systematic

No buy in from stakeholders,
leading to no interest

Poorly resourced /
implemented, and/or
late

Difficulty getting approvals
and buy in of top
management

Technical
analysis

Strategic
alignment

Active
management

Objective not based on
deliverable projects

Benefits of energy reduction
poorly quantified and/or processes

Wrong project implemented
and/or in conflict with
strategic direction

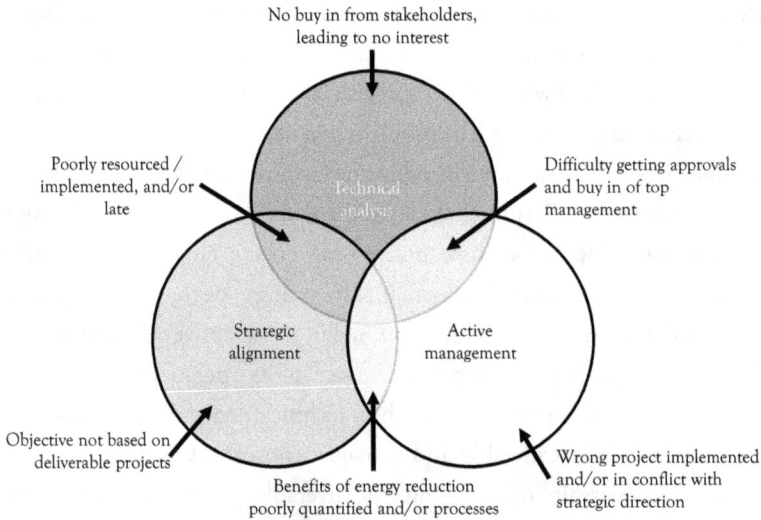

Figure I.3 Three perspectives of a Strategy-to-Execution Premium

and sustained way. It is what good leaders and responsible managers do. Leaders and managers recognize this [52], but not many achieve it.

Nicholas Bloom and his colleagues studied the UK manufacturing sectors and found a correlation between the level of energy savings and management practices. Specifically, they reported that companies with good management practices consume, on average, 17 percent less energy and produce 3.7 percent more products when compared with badly managed manufacturing companies [53].

Evidence from the United Nations Industrial Development Organization (UNIDO) indicates that companies with a good energy management system can achieve two to three percent energy savings against one percent business as usual [54] and most companies have a return on their investments within two years by implementing good management [55].

Now, how does a business embed resource productivity into its *Strategic* intent, use *Technical* analysis to inform decisions, and put in place an actively *Managed* program? There are many management models available to help companies improve their leadership and management practices. These models exist because only eight percent of people are naturally capable to design great strategies, can translate that strategy into action, and can achieve sustained and long-term performance improvements on their own [56]. For the remaining 92 percent, using a management model will help.

Some of the more popular models used are Robert Kaplan and David Norton's *Balanced Scorecard* and *Execution Premium*; John Kotter's *Leading Change*; Scott Keller and Colin Price's *Beyond Performance*; Alexander Osterwalder's *Business Model Canvas*; a host of discipline-specific International Standardization for Organization's (ISO) management systems; B Corporation frameworks, and regional-specific models such as the Baldrige Excellence Framework and EFQM.

Regardless of the specific reasons for implementation, the many models described share the same three perspectives: a clear and deliberate *Strategy* led by the leadership team; using data and *Technical* analysis to identify a series of improvement opportunities; and the relentless *Management* and execution of projects to achieve the desired outcome.

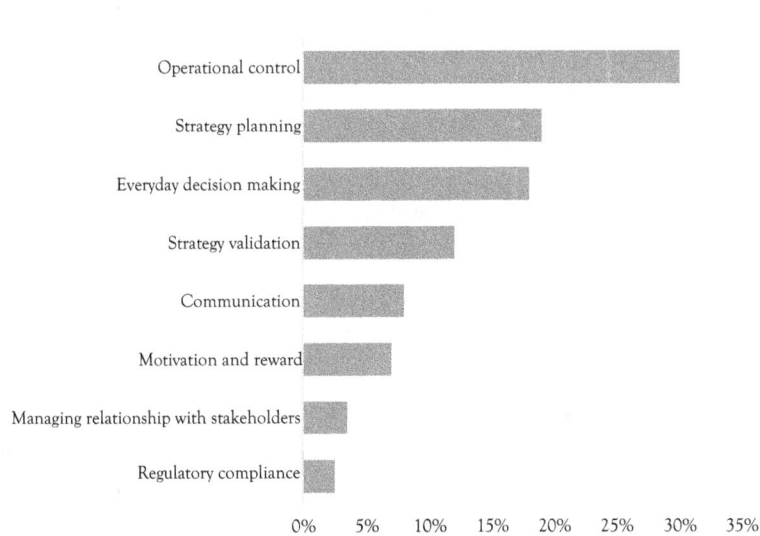

Figure I.4 Reasons a business implements a Strategy-to-Execution Premium

Source: Data adapted from [57]

These three, when working together, predictively indicate success. Those that are adept at understanding and doing them have a higher probability of success (or premiums) than those that do not.

The return *on* investment for good leadership and management practices can be measured in multiple ways and is shown in Figure I.4. The S&P Dow Jones Indices study [44] also reports companies that are consistently good at resource productivity also have a financial performance that is twice that of their peers.

We use the generic term *Strategy-to-Execution Premium* to describe the *Strategy aligned, actively Managed,* and *Analysis driven* resource productivity initiative—by embedding the initiative into the strategic intent of your company and aligning the whole company's resources to drive toward success. There are 10 elements (or leverage points) making up the *Strategy-to-Execution Premium* and can be summarized as follows:

- Chapter 1: Embed resource productivity into the company's strategy
- Chapter 2: Gain and keep leadership commitment
- Chapter 3: Define an appropriate scope and boundaries
- Chapter 4: Measure and benchmark resource productivity
- Chapter 5 (first half): Make resource consumption visible
- Chapter 5 (second half): Set science-led improvement baselines
- Chapter 6: Identify improvement opportunities
- Chapter 7: Overcome inertia and resistance to change
- Chapter 8: Manage the implementation program
- Chapter 9: Celebrate, learn and repeat

Figure I.5 shows how the 10 elements are structured in Chapters 1 to 9 with an implementation plan in Chapter 10. These 10 elements are symbiotic by nature, and each relies on the others for the initiative to sustain itself. Quoting the Musketeers, "One for all, all for one"! Any weak link within the chain will be where bottlenecks occur and/or the point(s) of failure. Take one or more elements out from the equation; the whole initiative crumbles [58].

Different companies will exhibit different bottlenecks or weak links, so to speak. One company may be strong in leadership but weak in management or the technical elements. Others may be strong on the technical elements but weak in the leadership or managerial elements,

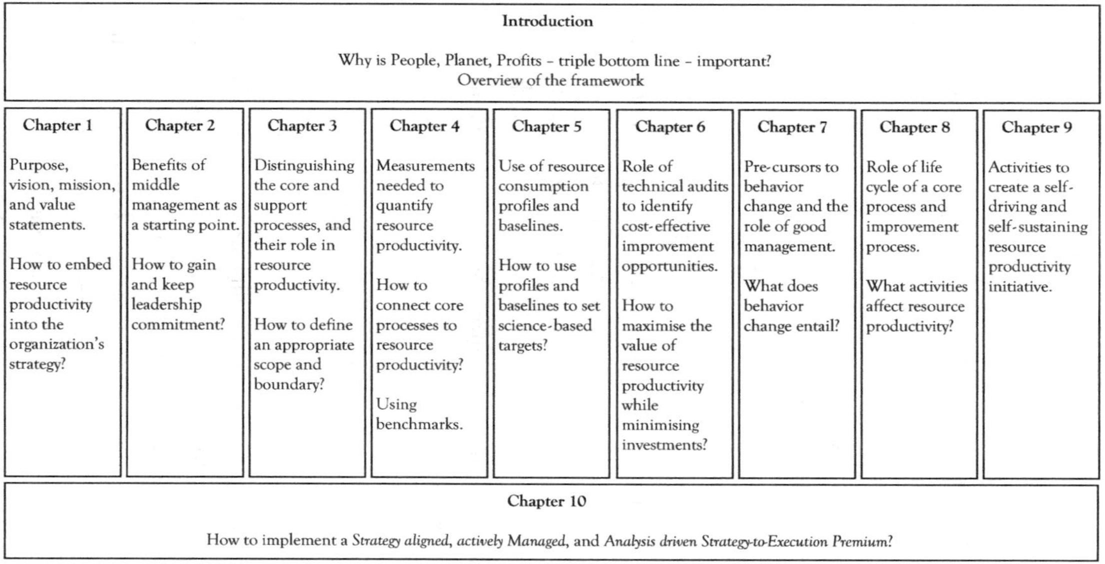

Introduction								
Why is People, Planet, Profits - triple bottom line - important? Overview of the framework								
Chapter 1	Chapter 2	Chapter 3	Chapter 4	Chapter 5	Chapter 6	Chapter 7	Chapter 8	Chapter 9
Purpose, vision, mission, and value statements. How to embed resource productivity into the organization's strategy?	Benefits of middle management as a starting point. How to gain and keep leadership commitment?	Distinguishing the core and support processes, and their role in resource productivity. How to define an appropriate scope and boundary?	Measurements needed to quantify resource productivity. How to connect core processes to resource productivity? Using benchmarks.	Use of resource consumption profiles and baselines. How to use profiles and baselines to set science-based targets?	Role of technical audits to identify cost-effective improvement opportunities. How to maximise the value of resource productivity while minimising investments?	Pre-cursors to behavior change and the role of good management. What does behavior change entail?	Role of life cycle of a core process and improvement process. What activities affect resource productivity?	Activities to create a self-driving and self-sustaining resource productivity initiative.
Chapter 10								
How to implement a Strategy aligned, actively Managed, and Analysis driven Strategy-to-Execution Premium?								

Figure I.5 Components of a Strategy-to-Execution Premium and layout of this book

vice versa. It is important to recognize each element in the chain and its contribution toward resource productivity. You can then identify the areas for improvement and work on the areas. It is also important to distinguish the difference between repairing a weak link versus gold-plating an element. Creating the "perfect element" means other elements will become the weak link in the chain. When all elements are functioning, improvements should occur on all elements so that all elements are of equal strength.

Also, rather interestingly, *Selective Attention Deficit* leads people to remember and acknowledge the activities that they did differently before achieving success. This is why you will find different people and businesses accrediting their success to different elements of the *Strategy-to-Execution Premium* rather than all of the elements involved. They forget that the other elements exist and are at play.

An effective *Strategy-to-Execution Premium* gives companies a systematic approach to improve resource productivity—one that is centered on the strategy of the business, based on data, and actively managed to achieve long-lasting results. Businesses move away from an ad hoc initiative to one that is embedded in the company ethos and continually looking for and driving improvements. Companies can become leaner, resilient, more competitive, and profitable. In addition, successful resource productivity also enables businesses and nations to meet their overall environmental impacts and climate change commitments.

What Is This Book About?

While people know about the *why* and *what* they want to do, and there are many books written about specific elements of resource productivity, their mission is bogged down by *how* to do it in a functioning corporation. Within the resource productivity and sustainability discipline, there are no tools and techniques to address "organizational" issues, thus enabling and accelerating actions to address resource productivity. Fortunately, for all of the problems we faced, there is a solution somewhere and in some other disciplines. It's a matter of finding them and highlighting them. This is the purpose of this book—bringing them together to turn resource productivity from common sense into common practice.

This book gives resource productivity and sustainability champions a framework to optimize a single resource, or multiple resources simultaneously, to bring about sustainable and lasting benefits. It describes 10 essential activities, along with the evidence related to that element from management science, that must be present for businesses to use resources efficiently and effectively. Chapters 1 to 9 focus on the salient features and activities, and Chapter 10 brings all 10 elements into an implementation plan.

The issues and tools described apply to everyone and every industry—commercial, manufacturing, and industry. This book also purposefully shies away from prescribing specific best practices, frameworks, models, tools, techniques, and procedures. All know-how, tools, and techniques available also are constantly evolving. Existing ones are continually refined, new ones emerge, and obsolete ones fade away. Naturally, some companies will be eyeing and implementing these new methods and innovations. Taking a statistical distribution of companies in the world, and according to the diffusion of innovations theory popularized by Everett Rogers [59], 2.5 percent of companies will apply them very early on and another 2.5 percent will never adopt them. This book is aimed at those in the middle—companies who want to incorporate resource productivity into their practice but do so cautiously so as not to affect present-day performance demands and needs.

Real-world companies do not always have the luxury to start from scratch every time they want to introduce a new strategy or initiative. They trade off and adapt without sacrificing existing performance and meeting future needs. For each initiative to succeed, it requires inputs and involvement of many stakeholders, all having their challenges. The *Strategy-to-Execution Premium* framework can be used to add and incorporate an infinite number of topics ranging from health and safety, quality, environmental management, social, ethics, and other topics of interest to the company.

Like resource productivity, engineering, management, and leadership are also littered with jargon. Individuals trained in the said field would be very comfortable with the terms but means little or difficult to be understood by others. We use more generic terms for the technical and managerial language and wrote it in a manner that is sufficiently general to be accessible to all disciplines and apply to a wide range of businesses.

Ascribing *Strategy-to-Execution Premium* as a best practice often means that businesses copy and seek out a "fill in the blanks" template rather than understand the principles behind the framework. As the saying goes, you can lead a horse to water, but you cannot make it drink. No amount of copying and emulating best practice aligns the productive use of resources to strategy, makes leaders and managers take an active interest, or analyzes data in a manner that maximizes overall benefits while minimizing costs. Those that see this as a "best practice" pigeonhole the activities and the same issues continue as before.

Furthermore, 85 percent of executives and investors want fewer prescriptions but have the flexibility to obtain results via their own "responsible" business processes [60]. As such, describing the 10 elements in generic terms will enable leaders and managers to integrate resource productivity into whatever management models the company uses, come up with solutions that fit their situation, or replace the existing model.

This book gives leadership, management, and technical topics roughly an equal emphasis and balanced coverage. Each reader will find some topics familiar while others less so if not outright alien. This has to do with each reader's education and their role and responsibilities in the business. All are essential elements of a *Strategy-to-Execution Premium* and exist in all businesses. Don't give up—you do not need to master all 10 elements, but to understand and implement all of them. What will become clear is that each business, as a whole collective, has all the essential knowledge and skill to effect large-scale resource productivity improvements. Readers may see and can influence (or find ways to seek participation and engagement from) various parts of the business on good governance—one that continually drives and improves their sustainability. If necessary, external technical expertise is available.

This book is not written for experts in the field. Each of the experts is very knowledgeable in what they do, they are very skilled, and experienced at it. Rather interestingly, they each believe their subject matter is the keystone to solving resource productivity issues and are interested in moving their area of expertise forward. However, none of them will be able to act in the overall interest of your company. None of them can make you and your company become resource productive. You are in the driver's seat to ensure the long-term success of your business. This book gives you the necessary tools, ideas, and curated success stories to champion, motivate, and inspire everyone through the use of factual data and insights.

This book is also not written for individuals and communities who believe resource productivity is *not their job*, is the *responsibility of others* (typically higher up the company or government), *detracts from the company's purpose*, or is *far too complex* for one company or one person to champion. There are indeed many actors in the field. Resource productivity can be started and driven by any actors in the industry—that can just as easily be companies themselves.

While the book is written in the sequence shown in Figure I.5, you can choose to read the chapters in many sequences based on your needs. You could read the chapters following the sequence it is written. You could also choose to read the leadership topics (1–2) and management topics (7–10) before the technical topics (3–6). Some may find reading Chapters 1 and 3 first, followed by 2 and 7, 3 to 6, and 8 to 10 useful. The choices are endless.

As mentioned earlier, there are many examples and case studies of how not to do things, and there are bad examples in the print media and on the Internet. Good examples are rather hard to come by. In this book, we summarized many good examples from publicly available sources. Their energy savings, water savings, raw material savings, waste reduction, and social and environmental governance were chosen to illustrate a certain point, to give additional insight into what works in their company. It works for them because it fits their specific context and needs. They are, by no means, the only way for doing things, nor does it imply the case study companies exhibit mastery in all of the 10 elements.

No one business exhibits mastery in all 10 elements, although every one of them strives to become better in all areas. In addition, no companies and no leadership and management initiatives are perfect by design. Businesses tweak their processes and initiatives as they move along. "Perfection" only exists in hindsight when all the planning, execution, monitoring came together with a large pinch of luck, sweat, and the occasional tears.

Launch your resource productivity initiative when you have thought about and developed a coherent and complete *Strategy-to-Execution Premium*, and continually improve from it. No doubt, you won't hesitate to grab free money that is freely available. So, why wait to save money and resources, and positively impact the planet and the communities in the sphere of your influence?

CHAPTER 1

Embed Resource Productivity Into the Company's Strategy

I will build a motor car for the great multitude ... It will be so low in price that no man making good wages will be unable to own one and to enjoy with his family the blessings of hours of pleasure in God's great open spaces ... When I'm through, everyone will be able to afford one, and everyone will have one.

—Henry Ford, quoted in [61]

To make resource productivity a reality, there is a need to put an implementation program together, organize resources, and implement the opportunities. Logically, gaining top management commitment is an important first step. This is where most people get stuck.

Why? Many people have an impression that businesses are only after one thing—maximum profits. Anything that detracts the focus of top managers and others from generating profits is wasting their time. There simply will be no interests. Perhaps, this impression is exacerbated by the many Hollywood blockbusters such as *The Wolf of Wall Street* and reality shows such as *Dragons Den* and *The Apprentice* portraying successful businesses driven by men and women with aggressive, narcissistic, money spenders, high-risk takers, high sex drive alphas with a single-track mind.

The sad reality is that there are big businesses that are operating badly—chasing from short-term profits to the next, constantly staying just ahead of the next crisis. The news media loves to find and report about these and they do so often. However, this is not representative of the true picture! An Internet search will reveal many small to medium, and some large businesses implement initiatives to use their resources productively but choose to remain "under the radar" of the news media.

While profits are essential, it is not the purpose for companies to exist. Entrepreneurs do not start their business purely to generate profits; they start the business to serve specific customer needs in a marketplace. Rather interestingly, business schools also do not teach or preach about operating the business for short-term profits. There is a long tradition, mentioned in the *Introduction*, where businesses balance the needs and interests of multiple stakeholders over the long term. Many Asian and Continental European countries still practice this.

In 2019, The Business Roundtable reverted its stance on top management fiduciary duties (mentioned in the Introduction) to the 1981 version [62]—one that includes all stakeholders, placing the needs of customers, employees, suppliers, communities, and the environment before long-term value for shareholders. Short-term profits and shareholder value are no longer the only raison d'etre for companies.

> *We commit to: (1) Delivering value to our customers. ... (2) Investing in our employees. ... (3) Dealing fairly and ethically with our suppliers. ... (4) We respect the people in our communities and protect the environment by embracing sustainable practices across our businesses. ... and (5) Generating long-term value for shareholders. ... Each of our stakeholders is essential. We commit to deliver value to all of them, for the future success of our companies, our communities, and our country.*
>
> —The Business Roundtable, 2019 [63]

Since the late-1970s and early 1980s, there is an increasing body of evidence from studies by Charles Handy [64], Marc Orlitzky et al. [65], Robert Kaplan and David Norton [66], Scott Keller and Colin Price [67] which found that companies purely focusing on generating financial returns do not last [75] and companies taking into account wider interests have better financial performance than those focused on profits and capitalist agenda. Data suggest that 74 percent of businesses that focus purely on profits and cost-cutting measures are not able to sustain the strategy for more than three years [68].

More recent data show that a whopping 93 percent of Fortune 500 CEOs believe that their companies should also focus on goals other than profits [69]. Another recent study over 18 years shows high-purpose companies outperforming their competition by 50 percent [70]. Those that don't will face an inevitable blowback ranging from being shunned by investors, customers, to employee walkout and public outcry on social media [71].

So, there is no imperative for a business to maximize profits at the expense of others. Perhaps, to get top management commitment for resource productivity, it is prudent to put aside the preconceived notion and define or rediscover the strategic intent of your company and its business.

Understanding the Strategic Intent of a Business

At the heart of every company are four very important concepts that bind all of its business activities, customers, employees, machinery it deploys, and the decisions it makes. The four important concepts are its purpose, vision, mission, and value statements. These four concepts form what is known as the "strategic intent" of a company. All the decisions made are on this basis. All of the products or services sold are on this basis. All of the machinery and equipment used are on this basis. And, all of the employees and specialists are brought together on this same basis.

All business owners, entrepreneurs, and managers who have gone to business school would have learned them. Those that did not would derive them even if they did not associate it with the words used in business school. It is what Cynthia Montgomery calls, the "ongoing job of company leaders and the crowning responsibility of CEOs" [72].

At the root of the strategic intent is its purpose—the ultimate aspiration of the company's existence. It answers the question, "why it produces the product and/or services for its customer." Thus, it becomes the map the business charts its journey—its "true north" or "guiding star" that fuels passion in what it does. It is important to distinguish between making a profit with the purpose of a business. All healthy companies must *make a profit*. Without it, the business would not exist for long. Seymour Tilles frames the purpose of a company succinctly.

... For far too many companies, what little thinking goes on about the future is done primarily in money terms. There is nothing wrong with financial planning. Most companies should do more of it. But there is a basic fallacy in confusing a financial plan with thinking about the kind of company you want yours to become. It is like saying, "When I'm 40, I'm going to be rich." It leaves too many basic questions unanswered. Rich in what way? Rich doing what? ...

—Seymour Tilles, 1963 [73]

Another good explanation on purpose was by David Packard:

I want to discuss why a company exists in the first place. In other words, why are we here? I think many people assume, wrongly, that a company exists simply to make money. While this is an important result of a company's existence, we have to go deeper and find the real reasons for our being. ... Purpose (which should last at least 100 years) should not be confused with specific goals or business strategies (which should change many times in 100 years). Whereas you might achieve a goal or complete a strategy, you cannot fulfill a purpose; it's like a guiding star on the horizon—forever pursued but never reached. Yet although purpose itself does not change, it does inspire change. The very fact that purpose can never be fully realized means that an organization can never stop stimulating change and progress.

—David Packard, 1960 [74]

The second concept is the company's vision—a future that your company wants to create when delivering its purpose. The most frequently cited vision includes improving the health and wellbeing of employees, addressing environmental concerns such as climate change or water pollution, community and other social projects, and so on.

The third concept is the company's mission—the type of activities the business will do to achieve its purpose and its vision. Equally as important are those that it would not. It describes what the company does, why it is different or better than its competition, and why the customer buys (and continues to buy) from the company. A business that tries to be all things to everyone will achieve very little. Some form of trade-offs will be required to be successful.

Finally, the last concept is the company's values—the type of attitudes, behaviors, and practices it will adopt, thus enabling the company to fulfill its purpose, vision, and mission [76]. Having the right set of compatible values accelerates the company's activities and results toward its intended purpose, vision, and mission. Culture—a collection of people working together, exhibiting similar attitudes and behaviors, and carrying out consistent practices—can, according to James Heskett, account for 20 to 30 percent of a company's success. This is why you will find that most of the people who work in the same company think alike!

All businesses, for-profit or nonprofit operating in a competitive market, will have a purpose, vision, mission, and values. Having a clear, aligned, and "living" strategic intent is key. It works for four reasons:

1. *It is a profound understanding of the competitive environment.* When developed based on objective appraisal, the deep and insightful appreciation of the marketplace allows the leadership team to establish a very specific, defined, and balanced game plan/strategy/ goals and how the business will maneuver into a position of competitive advantage, thus be successful over a long term. Resource productivity can feature on its own as a defined goal or part of another goal. As long as the relationship is clear, it is acceptable.

2. *It allows the leadership and management teams to invest for the long term.* Companies with a strong purpose, vision, mission, and values think about the short- and long-term success of the business. Where necessary, their "true north" compels them to make long-term investments in its offering, its people, and its machinery. As mentioned earlier, these companies outperform and outlive their competition. If the activities of the business are not performing or not complementing the strategic intent, leaders and managers change the methods, work organization, or even its business models to keep the company in its strategic direction.

3. *It is a great source of intrinsic motivation for employees.* When employees can see a direct commitment from the leadership and management teams on a balanced set of goals, can see that the goal

is realistic, can see that they are actively taking actions, it is a source of motivation money cannot buy—employees come together with a strong belief that they are contributing to something bigger than they are; knowing that their work is valued, and able to see their efforts come to fruition.

4. *It rallies and builds an unswerving customer loyalty.* Customers buy and continue to buy from a certain company because they believe in the product and/or services and the company's vision, relate to and value the company's purpose, message, and brand image. This is one of the reason companies with environmentally friendly, sustainable sourcing, and so on are thriving even though there may be a higher price tag. During times of economic downturns, you may even see the loyal customers, and even the local community, chipping in to smooth out temporary hardships.

Case Study: Dŵr Cymru Welsh Water

Operating from 4,200 sites, Dŵr Cymru Welsh Water provides 24/7 water and sewerage services to more than three million people in Wales, Herefordshire, and Deeside in the United Kingdom. Unlike many water and wastewater companies, Dŵr Cymru Welsh Water is a not-for-profit company that is limited by guarantee, that is, it has no shareholders, which allows its strategic and operational plan to be driven entirely by the needs and preferences of its customers and other stakeholders.

By utilizing a not-for-profit business model, Welsh Water did not have to chase after short-term financial gains and focuses on the long term by driving down debt (from 93 percent debt in 2001), maintaining its networks of water mains and sewers, upgrading and rebuilding its treatment works while keeping its energy costs below inflation for more than nine years in a row [77], providing a reduction in household water bills [78], and performing in the top quartile of the water regulators' league table [79].

Welsh Water plans to reduce its energy consumption by five percent between 2012 and 2020 and increase its renewably generated energy from 15 percent in 2015 to 25 percent in 2020 (and meeting all of its energy needs by 2050) [80]. A good example for meeting its energy objective comes from its Five Fords Energy Park in Wrexham—a £36 million energy park that integrates several of its effluent treatment processes with anaerobic digestion, combined heat and power (CHP), and solar photovoltaic with further plans to extend its photovoltaic capacity, wind turbine, and battery storage by 2020 [77].

For resource productivity to thrive, that is, getting resource productivity projects into gear and off the ground, maximizing the improvement potential for the business, and benefiting from it, requires a home for resource productivity in the strategic intent. Employees and managers can then align their business cases to that of the leadership teams' interest. Without the explicit alignment at this strategic level, resource productivity becomes an operational benefit, which will be changed, modified, or deferred in preference for items that attract the leadership teams' interest.

The problem is while up to 90 percent of businesses have a strategic intent [82], a surprisingly large number of senior management and employees are not aware of it [83], or they are confused by the company's purpose, vision, mission, and value statements. Confusion of the strategic intent is usually caused by a combination of things: (1) the statements are vague and (2) the statements contradict what the business does. In Fortune 100 companies alone, more than 80 percent have vague, confusing, unhelpful, bland, toothless, and sometimes outright dishonest and destructive strategic intent [84].

Examples of poorly developed strategic intent are easy to locate and identify. Some of these are superficial slogans and eye-catching phrases that can be applied to any company. Some are inauthentic or do not reflect their business activities and values. Others have well-articulated strategic intent but are not fully embraced by every level in the business. Some bad examples are:

The purpose of ABC Co. is to protect and maximize the interests of our stockholders, by providing quality [product/service] at minimum cost and maximum price point.

It is our priority to achieve profitable growth and customer satisfaction by becoming No. 1 or No. 2 supplier of choice for the superior [product/service] we supply.

An "empty" strategic intent creates a disconnect between leadership, management, and the rest in the business, thus enabling different and competing interests to appear. At best, the strategic intent is not complementing the operating plans and activities of the management team. Worst, it creates a war between the leadership team or management team, each constantly questioning and blocking the others' activities.

An absence of alignment with the strategic intent also allows fiefdoms to flourish—each focused on promoting their interests rather than the overall interest of the business. This is also known as silo thinking and a fertile ground for company politics to flourish. Each manager becomes interested in only the performance of his/her area. When it comes to common issues such as resource productivity, each manager either (1) optimizes their department leading to poor overall company performance, or (2) take the "I lose, you lose" attitude and no one takes action.

As a result, there is a constant shift in "goalpost" and a limited number of activities are achieved. Many would have heard, or have said it themselves, that their management is not interested or not engaged in energy savings, water savings, and so on. That is the symptom of poor alignment and disconnect between the leadership, management, and employees. Over time, cynicism, dispirited, overworked, and burnout employees start to creep in due to the constant focus on crisis management of multiple financial and poor performance issues.

The Role of Top Management in Driving Resource Productivity

There is some good news. Firstly, defining a company's strategic intent, fitting the intent with the operating environment, and aligning resource productivity with it is a learnable skill. Secondly, McKinsey & Company reports an increasing number of companies (nearly 6 in 10) are beginning to engage in resource productivity initiatives due to the company's vision, mission, and values [85]. Over time, you can become very good at defining your company's strategic intent.

As mentioned earlier, these are typically enshrined in the purpose vision, mission, and value statements. If your company's strategic intent is not written, it can be discovered. If it is written, test if your business is doing what it says on the sheet of paper! Test also, if resource productivity is featured in the strategic intent.

In summary, you can define the purpose of the company based on what your core process (Chapter 3) does. Then, analyze the external environment (or issues) affecting its performance and internal capabilities (or issues) to deliver the desired performance. It answers the question, "If my vision is to succeed, what aspects in my company do we need to do better and/or do differently?" Then, you look at the things your company must do to compete and surpass the competition. You, then, use this information to define a set of goals (or high-level objectives), high-level performance indicators, and a high-level action plan to be cascaded down the company.

There are many tools and techniques available to help a company analyze its external environment. They are rooted in the study of business strategy and include *Political stability, Economic conditions, Societal expectations, Technology innovation, Legal requirements, and Environmental protection (PESTLE) analysis, 5-forces analysis, competitor profiling, mind mapping, stakeholder analysis, horizon scanning, focused workshops*, the OT portion of *Strength, Weakness, Opportunity and Threats (SWOT) analysis, Blue Ocean thinking*, and *scenario analysis*. Of these techniques, the most commonly used are *PESTLE* and *SWOT* analysis.

Similarly, there are also many tools available to help a company analyze its internal capability to deliver its strategic intent. Again, they are rooted in the study of business strategy and include *value chain analysis*, the SW portion of *SWOT analysis, 7S analysis, core competence, benchmarking*, and many proprietary capability assessments and maturity matrixes. Of these, the most commonly used are *core competence* and *SWOT analysis*.

Here is a brief overview of how to analyze the external (*PESTLE*) and internal (*SWOT*) issues that set up your teams and company for success.

1. *Analyze the value of resource productivity for the company.* The very first port of call is to appraise the value of resource productivity to the company. Sum up the quantities and cost of raw materials, energy, water, wastewater, rework, and waste. Calculate the rough savings if you can reduce raw materials and water consumption, and wastewater by 10 percent, energy consumption by 50 percent, rework and waste to zero. This forms the basics to start thinking about resource productivity. Projecting this cost into the future may be a little tricky because as raw materials, energy, and water become scarcer, the costs will increase. Similarly, the cost of emitting CO_2 is also likely to increase, not decrease, over time.

2. *Assess your external environment using PESTLE analysis.* In addition to the purpose of the business, external issues form an integral part of the company to be successful in the marketplace. A *PESTLE* analysis identifies the external issues that the company must address and will form part of the goals for the business. Arrange a meeting to review and discuss the external issues. A short list of questions that might help structure the *PESTLE* analysis is as follows. Sometimes, it is beneficial to assign specific people or groups of people to analyze these areas before the meeting.

   Political situation: What is the effect of political and policy stability on your business operations? How does the government intervene in the market? What are the enforcement policies? What can the business do to bring about a stable and predictable business environment? What specific practices or contingencies (e.g., investment appraisal practices) are required to counteract these instabilities?

   Economic conditions: What are the customer requirements? How many and how strong is the competition? How does the company's performance compare against the competition? What is the best-in-class performance? Are there any supply chain risks? Who has the biggest purchasing power in the supply chain? Are there any disruptive business models on the horizon? What is the cost of capital and debt? What is the typical inflation rate? If your company takes the first move on resource productivity, how can your company position itself for a favorable tailwind? How would the competition respond? What resources and capabilities does the competition have? How likely will the competition improve their performance? How fast would they do that?

Social expectations: What are the education level, skill, and capability of the workforce? What is the acceptable working condition? What do the customers and local communities expect from the business? How would issues around health, safety, security, and resource productivity be viewed by the local communities? What is the cultural norm in the community? What work-life balance is expected? How would these issues affect the company?

Technology development: What is the current state of technology in the business? How does the deployed technology compare to that of the competition? What are the emerging technologies and/or disruptive innovations? What thing(s), equipment, and process(es), when substituted or replaced, can become a threat to the company? How fast are your competition retrofitting or deploying step changes in technologies?

Legal and other requirements: Are there any legal requirements applicable to the business? Are there any industry standards and/or codes of practice applicable to the business? How are they applicable? Are there any emerging legal and other requirements that may affect the business? How are their development monitored? Is there any tax relief or economic incentives?

Environmental protection: What is the gap between the actual energy and water consumption versus the minimum it needs? How much waste does the business generate? What form of pollution does the business create? How would it affect the employees, the business, the environment, and the local community? Is it "more" economical to avoid and/or minimize the pollution at the source or treat it before discharge? What is or are the acceptable operating limits deemed suitable by the employees, customers, supply chain, regulators, and local communities?

The *PESTLE* description and questions look and sound generic. The demands on a business to manufacture a product or provide a service are voluminous. Most leadership teams have to deal with a broad range of issues, and energy, water, raw material, and waste are some of the many elements. As mentioned in the Introduction, there are many known direct benefits as well as indirect benefits of resource productivity.

Bob Willard, a sustainability champion, estimates that the indirect benefits are in the ballpark of a one percent reduction in recruitment costs, a two percent lower cost of attrition, a five percent reduction in risk of capital, a 10.5 percent increase in employee motivation and productivity, and a five percent increase in market share [86]. To be successful, the leadership team needs to consider the likely results of resource productivity efforts, consider that of their competition, and figure out how the company will use this to benefit the business.

Conventional options include pocketing the "additional" profits; reinvesting the savings toward more resource productivity projects to make it difficult for the competition to catch up; investing in the future products and/or services that clients value; obtaining a green credential and/or other market differentiation that broaden the appeal of products/ services to existing clients; and creating new demand. Strategically and tactically, the options are endless.

The leadership team also needs to keep an eye on both the urgent short-term issues and issues relating to long-term strategic direction. At the end of the *PESTLE* analysis, try to group the identified issues into three to five themes, but no more than seven themes. These themes will become the goals of your business. Using the same information, define the criteria for measuring success in each of the themes. They will become the high-level targets.

There is a reason why businesses should identify three to five goals. In a real and fully operational business, the company will need to meet present-day demands and progress activities that will meet future needs. When the goals are cascaded down, it can become 15 to 25 lower-level objectives that are manageable. Contrast this with some businesses having 25 to 40 goals which when cascaded down becomes 125 to 200 lower-level objectives.

Managing 125 to 200 objectives is very difficult to implement, manage, track, and juggle. If not careful, companies can overcommit the available resources or create conflicting demands on the employees where objectives will never be fully met. A symptom of an overcommitted company is one that frequently under-delivers on its objectives, having employees chasing targets after targets, and from one audit to the next. Eventually, employees burn out, and the business falters.

In addition, amidst all the operational requirements, it is also difficult to remember a large number of initiatives and what is required of them. Experiences from multiple disciplines indicate that three to five objectives with defined targets would be manageable. When the number exceeds seven, progress will become very slow, more akin to start-and-stop.

In general, a balanced set of themes consists of issues that can be grouped into *Positive Outcomes* (financial and nonfinancial outcomes such as safety, health, ethics, resource consumption, and environmental), *Stakeholder Values* (customers, employees, suppliers, etc.), *Critical Processes* (productivity rates, quality measures, timeliness, etc.), and *Key Enablers* (R&D, revenue from new products, etc.) [87]. The trick is to know how resource productivity, that is, energy savings, water savings, raw material savings, and waste minimization, fits into these themes and how it will be measured.

3. *Review internal capabilities using SW analysis (the SW portion of SWOT analysis).* The *PESTLE* analysis will have identified the opportunities and risks (threats) and a shortlist of goals for which the business must do to succeed. The next task is to analyze the internal capability to deliver the identified high-level objectives to the specified high-level targets. This is to ensure that the company is not overcommitting its resources and is capable to deliver the desired objectives. Organize another meeting to review and discuss the internal issues that the business must organize, implement, monitor, and overcome to achieve its goals.

Assessment of internal capabilities usually is limited to resources, competence, awareness, communication, and documentation. A more comprehensive assessment of capabilities also includes organizational structure and reporting lines, organizational culture, shared values, silos and politics, strategic alignment, connectivity with customers and employees, authentic leadership, leadership and functional unity, organizational knowledge, and speed of identifying and resolving conflicts or competing objectives [88].

A critical, honest, and realistic exploration of the internal capability is not a bad thing or some taboo to be hidden away from view—it is the first step toward establishing real and realistic goals and the progress toward them. This assessment needs to be carried out for the entire core and support processes, and at all job roles and functions.

Some questions for consideration include: What are we doing on this goal? What did we do well? What should we stop doing? What can we do better? What and how much tangible and intangible resource is necessary? Should we ring-fence a sum of money? What type of competence is required? Do we have the required competence? How will we acquire and maintain the competence? Where can we draw additional resources? Is our organizational structure hindering the goal? What can we do to detect conflicts? Is our style of communication and management conducive to encouraging everyone towards the goal? What must we as leaders and managers change? How realistic is our SW analysis? Do our customers and employees agree with the strength and weaknesses?

Similar to the *PESTLE* analysis, the list of questions is generic and the onerous is on the leadership team to understand what resources, knowledge, and skills are set aside for resource productivity, and how much communication, awareness training, employee engagement, and documentation are required.

Case Study: ADCO [89] [90]

Abu Dhabi Company for Onshore Oil Operations (ADCO), now part of Abu Dhabi National Oil Company (ADNOC), operates the state-owned onshore and shallow coastal exploration and extraction of oil and gas in the United Arab Emirates of Abu Dhabi. Historically, they have actively implemented many energy savings projects in an ad hoc manner.

In 2009, due to an absence of regional and national targets and low energy and water costs, ADCO used a sustainability charter to integrate economic, environmental, and social issues in order to become a respected contributor to Abu Dhabi's sustainable future through high levels of resource stewardship by operating the assets at the maximum efficiency and optimum cost with minimum impact on the environment and avoiding harm to people.

ADCO translates the vision into five enabling factors for its operations:

- Continuously achieve the highest standards of health, safety, and environmental performance in the industry
- Developing capability and competency to manage an increasingly complex business
- Effectively evaluate and execute optimum reservoir development and management strategies to maximize recovery while minimizing cost
- Adopt and execute proven technologies and strategies that enable the most efficient field development
- Ensure the integrity of assets on a cost-effective basis to optimize systemwide availability

The policy and yardstick to deliver the vision and missions are "to use best available environmental technology and practices; progressively reduce emissions, discharges, and wastes, improve the efficient use of energy and conserve natural resources." Specifically, for energy consumption, ADCO had implemented an energy management program since 2008 to incorporate resource productivity practices into the fabric of its business and operations. Their policy calls for:

- Improving the energy efficiency of existing facilities by 25 percent by 2025 with the base year of 2010
- Increasing the share of renewable energy to two percent of the total energy mix
- Implementing the best available techniques (BATs) in future facilities
- Constructing new buildings to exceed the Estidama Pearl 1 ratings

The planning for achieving ADCOs vision is based on identifying, analyzing, and prioritizing 13 strategic initiatives to be delivered over a seven-year plan. Projects are implemented with defined six-stage gates across the project life cycle: from conception through to operations and maintenance. At each stage gate, there is a defined deliverable and project key performance indicators (KPIs) before it is progressed to the next stage.

ADCO's implementation of its *Strategy-to-Execution Premium* occurred over several phases. A pilot study was carried out in 2010 leading to two companies receiving ISO 50001 certification in 2013. This is further expanded by 16 certified operating companies in 2016. In 2017, ADCO had improved its energy efficiency by six percent—equivalent to 57 billion cubic feet of natural gas, U.S. $150 million cost savings, and an emissions reduction of 3.1 million tonnes of carbon dioxide. Further efforts are in progress to expand the initiatives to the rest of the ADNOC group of companies.

Case Study: Jaguar Land Rover

Jaguar Land Rover is a UK-based automotive manufacturing company built around two iconic brands: Jaguar and Land Rover accounting for nearly 33 percent of UK car manufacturing. Jaguar Land Rover defines its corporation's purpose as to deliver "experiences our customers love for life." It achieved its purpose by working on two strategic themes.

The first strategic theme is to "develop long-term, responsible, and sustainable business growth." The company achieves this by committing to and working toward reducing its environmental impact by (1) reducing its water consumption by 30 percent; (2) reducing energy consumption by 30 percent compared to 2007; (3) carbon offsetting for the remaining 70 percent of energy consumption; (4) sending zero waste to landfill; and (5) limiting it supply chain CO_2 emissions at 0.39 tonne per vehicle [91].

Jaguar Land Rover measures its performance through several KPIs on its balanced scorecard, both at corporate and functional levels. The company also actively consults its employees on its progress toward delivering its vision.

The second strategic theme is to "create products that lead in strengthening changing societal expectations and environment over generations". The company achieves this by committing to and working to become the industry leader for tailpipe CO_2 emissions, fuel economy, and cost of ownership [91].

In 2010, Jaguar Land Rover started to use aluminum in the vehicle body. As aluminum has a higher energy intensity and is more expensive than steel, it was targeted as an area to optimize. They collaborated with Novelis, Innovate UK, Stadco, Norton Aluminum, Innoval, Zyomax, Brunel University, and the Cambridge Institute for Sustainability Leadership to develop a closed-loop, low-cost, and low energy-intensity aluminum supply [92].

Together, they have identified several grades of aluminum made up of differing aluminum recycling processes and ran laboratory and production trials to determine the best aluminum grade for the car production, before launching the Recycled Aluminum Car (REALCAR) project in 2007. The project recycles aluminum from car manufacturing scraps, end-of-life aluminum car bodies, and postconsumer aluminum waste to manufacture the new car—a truly closed-loop process.

By 2015, 50 percent of the cars were manufactured using 50 percent recycled aluminum, saving over 40,000 tonnes of press shop waste. Using recycled aluminum is also 95 percent less energy-intensive than virgin aluminum, giving an additional savings of 400,000 tonnes of CO_2 emissions. The REALCAR project is progressing with a vision to increase the level of recycled aluminum [91].

4. *Use the aforementioned information to define and/or update your company's strategic intent.* The external and internal issues do not restrict or form additional barriers to the business. It is an analytical basis to analyze the issues (external and internal) and use it to define the strategic direction of the business that also satisfies the collective needs and expectations of various interested parties. Following the PESTLE and SW analysis, the next task is to have an honest look at the data and draw out an agreed future that senior managers want to achieve (or being tasked to create) and a balanced set of goals that the business must address to be successful over the long term.

While the PESTLE and SW analysis is complete, the work to gain collective agreement among the leadership team on its strategic intent may be the hardest to achieve. According to John Kotter, more than 50 percent of businesses fail in this [93]. A survey of 1,000 U.S. companies showed only 42 percent reported their company's strategic direction had any effect [72]. McKinsey & Company credit the low number to the difficulty for the boardroom to integrate nonprofit goals.

Leadership teams tend to gravitate instantly toward the customers and shareholders and pay cursory glances toward other issues. While this is understandable, it indicates the values to which a person wants to be in the leadership team in the first place. It is the main roadblock [94].

Suffice to say, some leaders are in the role due to being born with a silver spoon. Many more become leaders due to the prestige and lifestyles it affords, many of whom are motivated to maintain the status quo and continue enjoying the benefits with minimal efforts [95]. To maintain an easy life, some may also choose to copy (or adapt) other companies (or template) rather than doing the analysis and defining meaningful goals and targets.

As U.S. Senator Margaret Chase Smith once said, "The right way is not always the popular and easy way. Standing for right when it is unpopular is a true test of moral character." [96] A responsible leader has to have a solid belief and a burning desire to see past short-term profits—whether it is about resource productivity, health, safety, climate change, and so on; have difficult conversations with the customers, owners, management, and employees; and do the right things for the long-term success of the business.

The body of knowledge gathered so far indicates that being healthy, safe, using resources productively, and being environmentally conscious can bring about success and profits. It just comes about via different means than what a leader may be accustomed to. Without this personal commitment, no amount of resources and investment will bring about lasting results.

Another leadership team tendency is wanting to address every single issue identified in the analysis. From a strategy perspective, addressing everything would stretch existing resources. If money and resources are limitless, companies can address all of the external issues. In reality, real companies do not have unlimited resources and some trade-offs are required. A better "strategy" would be to sort out the *urgent but not important, important but not urgent*, and *nice to have*—focus on the important and the urgent, and to consider what issues are best done in-house and outsource or seek partnerships for the rest.

Unfortunately, there is no guidance on how the leadership team can have difficult conversations about profits and wider context or how to trade-off and seek an agreement on the goals and targets. It all depends on how the leadership team collectively values each of the goals and targets selected and how it fits into the strategic direction of the business.

While there is no guidance on how to "do" purpose, vision, mission, and values, it is clear what they must "be": (1) leaders must genuinely own the wider purpose and take an effective stand for making it happen; (2) the strategic intent must connect with the customer's and employee's personal and emotional values; and (3) the strategic intent must be aligned with one another and with the objectives and targets. This is where copying other company's statements or filling in a template will not work.

As mentioned earlier, for resource productivity initiatives to be successful, they have to have a home within the purpose, vision, mission, and values. How the alignment is made varies from business to business. This could be expressed in terms of creating a future work environment covering health and wellbeing of employees and addressing own environmental impacts such as climate change or water pollution. This can also be expressed in terms of creating a product (or service) that addresses the overall environmental impact from the end-to-end supply chain. Others may choose to take on additional initiatives to improve specific environmental and/or community goals.

If there is no link between energy, water, raw material, and waste with the strategic intent, then resource productivity initiative is doomed from the get-go. The business case will not gain the interest of the leadership team.

Case Study: How Do Purpose-Driven CEOs Take Action?

Ray Anderson, the former CEO of carpet manufacturer Interface, began to champion sustainability when a customer asked, in 1994, what the company was doing for the environment. A task force was set up to analyze this specific question and led him and the company to discover that the majority of carpets made were based on petroleum products, and they are doing more harm to the environment than good. Interface identified and committed to seven "Mission Zero" targets, including waste to landfill, fossil fuel energy consumption, process water consumption, and GHG emissions [97].

In 2000, Interface began to offer its customers end-of-life carpet collection and recycle the nylon fibers and vinyl backing layer. The company later introduced renewable and recyclable materials in its carpets and glue-free installation system—making its product less dependent on petroleum products. Over the years, Interface evolved its thinking and approach to include social impacts and new business models. The company began to pay fishermen for their end-of-life nylon fishing nets for use in its carpet, proving that a circular economy is an attainable goal [97].

In 2016, Interface set a higher goal, Climate Take Back which includes commitments to (1) reverse climate change; (2) create supply chains that benefit all life; (3) make factories that are like forests; and (4) transform dispersed materials into products and goodness [98].

Paul Polman, the former CEO of Unilever, concerned for his children's future well-being was the driving force behind his desire to tackle climate change and inequality urgently. For him, leadership is not only about driving a company forward but also about making it do the right thing, and it extends beyond the boundaries of the company [95].

In 2010, Unilever set out its Unilever Sustainable Living Plan (USLP) to become the world's most sustainable business by focusing on three strategic themes: sustainable growth, reducing its environmental impact by 50 percent, and improving health and well-being for more than one billion people. The key difference to USLP is that many companies see the goal as a separate and discrete activity. To Unilever, it is the same—inseparable. Unilever took action on these issues and has a long track record for working on these issues [99].

Laurence Fink, founder, chair, and CEO of BlackRock asset management took a stand in 2018 by writing a personal letter—and continues to do so every year—to more than 370 companies it invests in. Among other topical issues, the letter informs CEOs that companies must demonstrate a purpose beyond financial performance as the driving force behind creating an enduring contribution to their stakeholders, environment, and society.

The company launched a $60 billion fund dedicated to sustainable investment solutions and circular economy. In addition, BlackRock actively engages with the companies it invests in and votes against agenda items in their boardroom when their activities do not protect its stakeholders on environmental and social issues [100]. BlackRock is also involved with organizations such as the Sustainability Accounting Standards Board (SASB) and the Financial Stability Board's Task Force on Climate-Related Financial Disclosures (TCFD) [101].

Dan Price, cofounder and CEO of Gravity Payments—a Seattle-based credit card processing company for independently owned small- and medium-sized businesses, had an informal chance encounter with a shy and quiet employee in 2011. At first, the conversation was very difficult to accept; however, the industry average wage was less than what is needed to work and live in Seattle. This didn't bode well with the $1 million a year CEO while many of his employees fork out 40 percent of the salary for rent and could barely afford the cost of living in Seattle. It sowed the seed to introduce a "minimum living wage" in 2015.

Gravity Payments implemented a 20 percent pay rise every year for the next three years. In April 2015, having consulted with the board and several financial forecasts, Dan announced to all employees that starting that day, each employee would earn a minimum of $50,000 rising to $70,000 in three years—doubling the annual salary for most of its employees. In addition, Dan announced that he would reduce his salary to $70,000 to help fund the initial wage increases. The rest of the money will come from increased productivity and in new clients.

Some in the industry suggested that Dan was an arrogant fool and a misguided socialist, that it wouldn't be long before the novelty wore off, and that it would be irresponsible diversion of cash from other business needs such as research and development [102]. Six years later, in 2020, the company's customer base doubled, revenue tripled, and the head-count grew by 70 percent. Staff turnover dropped by half, 70 percent of employees paid down their debt, and the number of employees buying their own home and starting their family grew by 10 times [103].

Toward the middle and end of 2020, the Covid-19 pandemic led to a more than 50 percent drop in revenue, and Gravity Payments was facing bankruptcy in months. Dan met with all of his employees in small groups and made sure that they understood the financial situation [104]. To his amazement, his team volunteered nearly half a million dollars a month from their salaries. Some offered their entire fortnight salary, while others offered between five and 50 percent of their salary [105].

Case Study: BA Better World [104]

Created on March 31, 1974, British Airways (BA) is the second-largest and the flag carrier airline of the United Kingdom. It is headquartered in London with its main hub at Heathrow Airport and secondary hub at Gatwick Airport. BA is also a founding member of the OneWorld airline alliance which has grown to become the third-largest airline alliance program.

On September 07, 2021, British Airways announced their Triple Bottom Line commitment: BA Better World. The commitment contains three distinct strands of objectives and targets aimed at creating a great place for people to work: contributing to the communities BA operates, reducing their emissions and waste, and building a thriving, resilient, and responsible business.

BA's people strand commits the company to create and celebrate diversity, equable pay, race equality, and proportional representation of the UK populations across the company, particularly in leadership and management roles. BA is also establishing a network of 150 well-being and inclusion champions, working closely with external services, to offer support for employees' mental, physical, and emotional health.

On the societal front, the commitment includes creating a BA Better World Community Fund to deliver community projects that benefit the climate, community-based health and education services, its employees, and nature. BA is also committing to deploy its people and resources to save, protect, and rebuild lives in vulnerable communities that are impacted by major disasters and the shipments of lifesaving supplies.

BA's planet strand commits the company to achieve net-zero by 2050 by investing in modern airplanes, making changes to their flight operations, and forming partnerships for the development of sustainable aviation fuel, zero-emissions hydrogen-powered aircraft, and carbon capture technology. Through the same techniques, BA will also be reducing its noise pollution. The company is also eliminating single-use plastic where sustainable alternatives exist and reducing food waste. BA is also committing to develop an information and intelligence system with customs and law enforcement agencies about the illegal wildlife transportation and refuse cargo suspected of containing illegal wildlife products.

BA's profit strand commits the company to embed BA Better World into the core corporate strategy and business model. However, BA Better World did not make commitments for their business performance and financial forecasts. It is assumed that business performance will follow the existing strategy. BA believes that they have a robust governance framework that extends from the parent company board through to BA's Management Committee and into delivery functions.

Many of the commitments in BA Better World complement existing BA programs, but it is the first time BA is pulling them together into one umbrella and integrating them into its purpose, business strategy, and operations. Time will tell if BA's commitment will turn into reality, remain a hot air, watered down in the future, or be replaced and/or sidelined.

5. *Agree on a series of high-level objectives, performance targets, and major milestones for each of the goals to be addressed.* Finally, a balanced set of goals and performance targets can be defined. These goals and targets will also be aligned with the company's strategic intent. Call a meeting to review the outputs so far and to identify a set of activities that directly deliver the objectives and those that enable the objectives and targets to be achieved. Often, several objectives can be grouped into themes that can be worked on by different groups of people in the company.

The high-level objectives must also be backed up by major milestones and deliverable initiatives or projects for each milestone. Leaving those lower down to define the major milestones, come up with a list of projects, and/or hoping for some "future" technologies to emerge is not a responsible thing to do. The level of detail for capital and revenue growth plans, even at a high level, tends to be better thought out. The details for resource productivity initiatives need to be as detailed as capital and revenue plans.

Yes, the goals and targets need to be Specific, Measurable, Achievable, Realistic, and Time-bound (SMART). If the SMART objectives and targets are arbitrarily assigned based on past results or guesstimates or are determined without a concrete plan, there is a danger that the objective and targets are unachievable or too easy to achieve. Both are equally demotivating and slow progress. A good practice is to use baselines (see Chapter 5) when setting targets. This way, targets can be scaled up or down relative to the productivity levels.

A good goal and target also need to be based on known opportunities (not hedging against some future opportunities or technologies to emerge), stacked up to optimize the whole business (rather than individual departments), appropriately resources, managed, and delivered. An agreement at this strategic level commits top management and compels a concerted companywide effort that moves the business toward achieving that desired outcome.

The work up to this point is to use analysis to assess the business environment, identify the themes that will drive the future of the business, appraise its strength and weakness, and identify additional resourcing, competence, communication, and documentation needs. The output of the exercise is a strategic direction of the business (purpose, vision, mission, and values) and a balanced goal, performance measurement, targets, and milestones. This balanced set of strategic direction, goals, and targets is commonly known as a *balanced scorecard.*

The context of your company will not be a one-off analysis. Depending on the type of business, the context may change more frequently than others. For example, companies in the fast-moving consumer goods (FMCGs) and fashion retail will have a context that changes over the weeks or months. Commodity goods manufacturing or commodity services like medical services will have a context that spans several years. So, the context of a business will need to be revisited as appropriate to ensure that it remains relevant and up-to-date.

The Price of Going at It Alone

One interesting phenomenon, or human behavior, is that there is a tendency to go at it alone—wanting to do everything on his or her own. When he or she is successful, he or she takes all of the credit for one or two of the key contributions and ignores (or forgets the contributions of others). While this is admirable, success in this manner is few and far between.

History tells us that when we cooperate and work together, there is a leap in advancement (methods and technologies), and take a step closer toward a goal. Take a look at the Hanging Gardens and Towers of Babylon, the Mayan and Egyptian pyramids, and the Great Walls in China and India. Putting aside the megalomania and brute force, people were working together to achieve a specific goal. There were divisions of labor; they coordinate and collaborate to achieve the mega construction projects.

History also tells us, when there is division and discrimination, everyone loses. Wars and battles were waged because of differing opinions and beliefs. People suffer. In the capitalist environment, more competition didn't result in long-term lower prices; it resulted in suppliers cavorting with each other and fixing their prices—consumers lose out. Politics that prioritizes divide and conquer and discrimination sow the seeds for future public discord.

In the modern world, the miracles of airplanes, space shuttles, and space stations—technologies that seemingly defy gravity—are the result of cooperation and coordination. And the result? It brought us another leap toward the sky and space. Teamwork and collaboration are not only vital; it was the keystone enabling people to travel between Europe and Australasia in slightly over one day instead of the seven-day journey on the Kangaroo Route in the 1950s and 28 to 40 days on a ship.

As the saying goes, no one can be an expert in everything, but someone somewhere knows something relevant. When it comes to resource productivity, as intimated in the previous section, the existence of a collective of people, cooperating and coordinating with others, especially others within the same company, speed up progress.

It reduces the need for each individual to learn a large number of disparate knowledge (technical, managerial, and leadership), put that knowledge into practice, learn from mistakes, and build a large network of relationships. It allows us to operate within our strengths and focus on delivering tasks that we are good at while entrusting others to do what they are proficient at. A large community of interested people allows a collectively wider perspective compared to that of an individual, thus identifying and resolving issues faster, organizing and taking action expediently, and enabling faster progress.

It allows us to think outside the box—in this case, outside the perimeter of the company. As the saying goes, one man's waste is another man's food. Similarly, there are many instances where other industry or company can (re)use their waste as raw materials. Some fantastic cases in point are Land Rover which uses recycled aluminum, ReNewCell which recycles jeans and denim to make new fabrics, Herman Miller who recycles/repurpose end-of-life chairs, and Dell which recycles exotic metals such as gold from electronic components.

In terms of energy, very frequently, excess heat or waste heat could be used by a neighboring factory or domestic customers. Often, a more centralized approach, thus large combined loads, can benefit from more efficient generation, both in terms of costs and in the energy efficiency of machines.

It also allows us to club together and benefit from a larger collective and shared experiences. By clubbing together, the collective group can share their experiences, learn together, and challenge each other while working on a common problem. A good example is the works of Sustainable Ireland's Large Industrial Energy Network and many similar networks and groupings. The grouping can also be inside a business, as observed in Bourne Leisure, where the energy team is a loose collection of subject matter experts making up the full competency to optimize the whole company's sustainability performance.

Working collaboratively and cooperatively enables companies to focus on their core competence. For Tesco, their strength is their large buying power. Tesco's buying club facilitates its suppliers by buying and implementing low carbon technologies in bulk, thus taking advantage of pooling quantities to lower prices for products and services. The Knowledge Exchange offers their knowledge of multiple industries and thus facilitates discussions around reusing and repurposing specific types of waste materials.

Working cooperatively and collaboratively also enables large companies to work through their supply chain and optimize the whole rather than optimizing individual companies independently from one another. An efficient supply chain does not mean that each component within the supply chain must operate at its peak efficiency. On the contrary, trade-offs and compromises are frequently required to optimize the whole system. Sometimes, some parts of the supply chain had to be made less efficient.

PepsiCo's Walkers Crisps and GSKs inhaler supply chain initiatives are success stories where for the whole supply chain to be optimized, analyzing and accepting trade-offs at specific components in the supply chain is necessary. Another good example is Unilever's low water and low-temperature soap powders. The optimization does nothing to Unilever's operating costs as the benefit occurs when the customers use Unilever's soap powder following the recommended washing machine settings, thus consuming less energy and water.

For these reasons, everyone should resist the urge to think and work on resource productivity alone, but seek to create a community, focusing on working together as a team to get initiatives and projects off the ground.

Policy as an Output of the Strategic Direction

The strategic intent and high-level objectives, targets, and decisions are often cascaded through the whole business via a series of policy statements.

There is a lot of confusion as to what is a "policy" as there seems to be an overuse of the word. For some, a policy is a regulatory instrument, an act of parliament, or a national/regional strategy. For others, it is a way of working, action plan, procedure, and so on. The Oxford Advanced Learner's Dictionary defines policy as "a plan of action agreed or chosen by a political party, a business, etc.; a formal principle that you believe in that influences how you behave; a way in which you usually behave."

A policy is a deliberate guideline (or directive) made by the leadership team to drive the business toward its strategic direction and to achieve its goals. When it is coherent with other goals and plans, written well, and communicated consistently, Michael Porter and Claas van der Linde found that a policy statement serves six functions: [104]

1. Focuses a company's attention where improvements are required
2. Builds companywide awareness based on data gathering and information analysis
3. Reduces the uncertainty that investment to address the deficiencies are valuable
4. Creates pressure to overcome in-company inertia and drive self-sustaining progress
5. Sets the minimum expectations for performance
6. Sets the pace at which improvements are to be achieved

So, a resource productivity policy is, first and foremost, a communique to the business that sets out its goals and priorities established by the leadership team. This should form the basis for which detailed activities are driven and measured.

A constant and consistent interpretation of policy and evaluation of projects against the policy reinforces the message that the business is serious about resource productivity and directs employees to focus on the issue. When this is followed up with a continued and consistent action, regularly monitored, and where necessary, corrective, and preventive actions applied, a culture for valuing resource productivity surfaces. An absence of such practice demeans the policy and makes it an "all talk no action" communication.

A good test to see if a resource productivity policy is sufficiently concise, motivating, and engaging is to do the five-minute *elevator pitch* test. According to John Kotter, "If you cannot communicate the vision and the plan to someone you don't know (or your grandparent or your grandchildren) in five minutes or less and get a reaction that signifies both understanding and interest, you are not yet done!" [93]

Another test, although not as good as the first test, is to replace the name of your company with a name from a different industry. Let's say you are a supermarket, replace your name on the policy with, say, a petroleum refining company. Then, see if the policy statement is equally applicable to that "fictitious" company. If it does, then, as John Kotter says, "you are not yet done!"

CHAPTER 2

Gain and Keep Leadership Commitment

... Strategy is 10% vision and 90% execution. ...
—Percy Barnevik, 1998 [107]

A good definition of a company's strategic direction and balanced scorecard, and achieving a collective agreement by the leadership team, is just the tip of the iceberg. Whether this remains a corporate slogan (also known as feel-good statements, fluff, greenwash, or hot air) or turns into reality lies in its execution—launching the new initiatives, communicating the strategy throughout the company, providing the relevant resources, making strategic choices and trade-offs, aligning the capabilities to take action, implementing projects, monitoring the actions, and applying corrections to achieve the intended outcome.

Whatever is the chosen initiative and projects, be it improving quality performance, improving health and safety performance, improving resource productivity, or reducing environmental impact, two things are certain. Firstly, that initiative is in addition to the day-to-day operations of the business—if the business stops its production or service, it ceases to exist. Secondly, it will involve changing or disrupting the existing business practices, learning and executing a new skill, and embedding it into existing operations.

If resource productivity is a top-down driven initiative, it's easy. The decision has been made. The directive comes with authority, allocated resources, and a defined objective, target, and performance measurement. You only need to fill in the detailed plans, get them implemented, and direct uncooperative people to the said directive. What if you have to convince individual members of the leadership team or senior management to implement resource productivity?

For those who are unfamiliar with business management, this can appear to be an insurmountable task. For some reason, employees and external providers want to target the leadership team directly and get frustrated when they do not have access to the top team. If they do have access to them, many present their business cases with so many technical details, they confuse and lose the interest and focus of the top team. This risks getting a "no" answer. They may also inadvertently "open a can of worms" and be drawn into political turf wars among the top or worst still, lumbered with a lot of additional tasks in addition to delivering resource productivity.

A lack of management knowledge, and perhaps being "burnt" on several occasions, can cement a person's experience and thoughts on engaging with the leadership team. IBM [108], Pfizer, and MTV [109] have demonstrated that engaging with and getting a commitment from the top does not have to begin at the top, it can begin from the opposite end or in the middle.

The Role of Middle Management

A good place to start is to enroll the middle management—the focal point where all operational data, customer data, and relationships with other stakeholders are funneled up to the leadership team or down to the shop floor. They are sufficiently close to the top to understand strategic issues and economic pressures faced. They are also closer to customers, employees, and other stakeholders to understand their needs and issues [110].

This places middle management in a unique and tactically strong position—having an ability to bridge the strategic-operational divide—to (1) identify, define, and propose resource productivity to the leadership team, (2) leverage the right and meaningful issues when communicating with them, and (3) mobilize teams and implement the initiative.

1. *Enroll middle managers and persuade them to take part in your initiative.* Every company needs to make sure that any resource productivity projects they propose have a high certainty of success. This means the proposal must have appropriately defined details with corresponding key performance indicators (KPIs) as a measure of

progress. Share your ideas with trusted middle managers, collectively improve on the idea, and make it a success within your areas of work. The availability of financial and human resources is always tight, but experienced middle managers will know where and how to find them—be it human resources, specialized skills, finance, time, information, authority, space, and tools—and carry out trials in a small and controlled manner.

Middle management could also help supply relevant organizational information, do some PR work, and identify members on the leadership team to engage and actively smooth over company silos and politics. Having implemented some of the ideas on a small scale and showing success, the next step would be to persuade the other middle managers to try the same technique in their areas of work.

You'll also be able to gather more supporters to push the proposal ahead. Early wins (although small) and supporters giving your ideas a thumbs-up help to engage with the leadership team. It gives them some assurance that the initiative will be a success.

2. *Choose the right time to engage with the top.* In many companies, there are designated quality, energy, environmental, sustainability, and social responsibility meetings. This would be a good time to talk about resource productivity. Another great time is when the leadership team reviews and signs off resource consumption bills (or invoices), financial and nonfinancial reports, and so on [111]. While choosing and waiting for the correct moment to reveal to the top, use the time to refine the concepts, collect evidence for the proposal, and grow grassroots support of the initiative.

3. *Ask leaders who are known to "talk the talk, and walk the walk" to champion resource productivity.* Leaders who deliver on what he/she says is an indicator that they are doers. This is an indication that if they support your idea, they mean business and will want to and take an active part in delivering the work—an indicator for avoiding the smart-talk or all-talk no-action syndrome that plagues many businesses.

According to McKinsey & Company, only 17 percent of leaders are completely disengaged and up to 13 percent would immerse themselves in their commitments. Those sandwiched between the two extremes have a varying degree of engagement [112]. Each member of the leadership team also has different ways to understand information and data. As such, identifying leaders who will be engaged and interested in resource productivity and understanding how they like their information and data presented is vital to ensure buy-in. Then, use this information to craft a resource productivity business case that ticks their boxes. If they are open and agreeable to the business case, ask if they would champion the business case at the leadership team.

4. *Discuss with your leadership team, not talk to them.* As a general rule, prepare resource productivity proposals and/or presentations as if you are having a two-way discussion with the board. Then, envisage the questions that may arise and have the additional details in hand. Simple as it may sound, many proposals and business cases suffer from one similar drawback—there is too much scientific and technical information and it is presented in "passive" and "third person" forms of words. While this style of writing is perfect for the scientific community, it removes personality, hinders communication, and is not suitable for communicating with nontechnical folks.

When leadership teams do not understand the communication and/or do not feel that the communication is targeted at them, they switch off and focus on other things. The advantage of having a conversation is that you are drawing them in and bringing them into the proposal. What is your proposal? What are the benefits? How does it fit into the business strategy? What is the competition doing? Give them the insights and information to assess its impact. Share case studies from similar applications, especially from the competitors, are fantastic social and competitive pressure [111] for top management to pay attention to.

It does not mean that all of the technical details should be deleted. Put the additional and technical details in the appendixes. Use them to support the business case, rather than being the business case itself. If someone else, say your champion, is presenting it on your behalf, also give them the additional information, and tell them what is in it. This is so that they can answer questions that may come up during the meeting. It is much better to overprepare rather than come up short during the board meeting.

There is a need to simplify the words used in a report and presentation. Technical folks tend to associate resource productivity initiatives with big words like "high efficiency," "premium," "eco," "low carbon," "green," "smart," and many more. Using these words means something to the technical folks. It makes them feel knowledgeable and important. However, this creates friction in the communication process.

Firstly, not all on the leadership team are engineers and can understand these big words. Using technical lingos is akin to the Chinese saying, "chicken and duck talk"—no one understands what the other says. Secondly, these big words can be interpreted differently by different people thus creating a perfect environment for confusion. It neither helps the top team assess its risk and rewards nor does it facilitate the board to make informed decisions. Therefore, nothing gets done.

Words are not created equal. Some words elicit joy. Others evoke hatred and polarize beliefs. Choose your words and phrases that align with the leadership team and the strategic intent of the business. Communicate with them using words that they understand and prioritize the essential messages and place them at the front for maximum effect.

Resource productivity is frequently raised to top management either as compliance or a cost control issue. While many think it is a sure way to spur disinterest and disengagement by leaders of a company, it works for leaders that are more conservative by nature [113]. Conservative leaders are energized and engaged by maintaining the status quo—compliance and tax, along with naming and shaming, are synonymous with a business risk that needs to be managed at minimum cost.

However, leaders who are more liberal are open to long-term business benefits, environment, and social responsibilities. They will not be interested in compliance and see these as beneath them, something that middle managers do. Studies have found that messages of hope have a positive correlation with prosocial investment, happiness, and engagement [114]. They are more likely to engage when resource productivity is presented in-line with its strategic direction and investment analysis.

Understanding the values, motivation, and drivers of each top management and then using them to communicate your proposal helps to obtain and maintain their interest and engagement. It allows top management to see strategic and tactical fit between resource productivity and the company's purpose, vision, mission, and values.

In boardrooms where there is a split between conservative-liberal ideologies, it may be prudent to present the business case three times: Once for the liberal-oriented, once for the more conservative-oriented, and finally bringing all together for the stamp of approval.

Case Study: Novozymes and Royal DSM

In Novozymes, a Danish biotechnology company, all Vice Presidents from the company's whole value chain are mandated to sit in a Sustainability Development Board. Meeting five times a year, each VP has to identify challenges from their functional area and propose the sustainability targets and strategies for achieving them.

Where Novozymes does differently are (1) as the board is made up of senior and busy people in the company, they take a no-nonsense view to results achieved and the proposal for the next planning cycle, often challenging each other, and collective amending and approving the targets for each VP; and (2) instead of delegating the accountability and responsibilities to lower-level teams, the VPs are accountable to the board and their performance is partly appraised based on achieved results.

In the case of Royal DSM, 50 percent of each board member's bonus is based on meeting sustainability targets.

Case Study: Diversey

Diversey, an industrial and commercial cleaning and sanitization company, now part of Sealed Air, has been implementing a variety of ad hoc energy reduction projects. In 2008, Diversey pledged to reduce its energy consumption by eight percent below that of 2008 (as a base year) by 2013. Initially, the team at Diversey identified 120 improvement opportunities, of which 30 met the standard hurdle rate, to achieve a total energy reduction of eight percent.

Top management at Diversey began to examine these 120 opportunities and found that, due to a mismatch of priorities, resources, and incentives, their managers lacked the capabilities and motivation to maximize energy reduction and select the minimum resources required to meet the corporate target.

The active involvement of top management in managing energy, assessing projects, realigning priorities and incentives, and ring-fencing corporate finance allowed Diversey to implement 90 opportunities, achieving a 25 percent energy reduction with $5 million less capital [115].

Case Study: Johnson & Johnson [116]

Johnson & Johnson is a global consumer health care, medical devices and diagnostics, and pharmaceuticals company. With approximately 250 independent operating companies employing 117,000 employees in 57 countries, it was ranked 103 on the Fortune Global 500 list in 2008.

In 2000, it set a corporate objective to reduce its greenhouse gas (GHG) emissions from its global operations by seven percent below 1990 levels by 2010. Pilot studies indicate that capital spend of $200 million is required.

In April 2003, Johnson & Johnson issued a worldwide Climate-Friendly Energy Policy mandating each operating company and each business unit to meet the emissions reduction target. It sets out a five-pronged plan for energy efficiency improvements; use of cogeneration plants; on-site renewable energy generation; purchase of renewably sourced electricity; and carbon trading and sequestration projects.

Even with a clear mandate and strategy in place, strong buy-in from its top management, and an approximately $200 million capital budget allocated for projects, Johnson & Johnson faced significant challenges in executing this policy at the required scale and speed.

As a decentralized company, decisions are made at a local level within each company or business unit. Each Johnson & Johnson company has its capital plans and budgets. In the first years after the pilot study, the identified projects had not taken off at the predicted scale and speed. Investigations at the corporate level indicated that capital budgets are the principal source of delay—budgeting capital for GHG reduction projects meant that the local units had to divert capital away from other essential expenses such as sales and marketing and local R&D. Local-level managers were prioritizing their financial profits and losses—hence slowed down the corporation's overall GHG emissions initiative.

The groups' environmental steering committee, chaired by the Group Chief Financial Officer, put in place a $40 million per year capital relief funding for GHG reduction projects. To qualify for the capital relief, projects had to meet two criteria: it had to achieve (1) a GHG reduction of $1,000 per tonne of CO_2 avoided; and (2) a minimum internal rate of return at 15 percent or more.

By 2009, the capital relief funding had approved a total of 80 projects worth $187 million and saved 129,000 tonnes of CO_2 saving per year with an average rate of return of 18.6 percent.

Case Study: Siemens [117]

Siemens has a global target to half its CO_2 footprint by 2020 and be CO_2 neutral by 2030 against the reference year of 2014. To facilitate and accelerate the progress of CO_2 emissions reduction, Siemens has launched two internal carbon pricing pilot projects in the United Kingdom, called the Carbon Reduction Investment Fund.

Siemens levies £13 per tonne of CO_2 emissions from natural gas and electricity consumption from its UK business units. In 2019, this is equivalent to £240,000. More than 60 innovative ideas were submitted by employees over six weeks to rapidly reduce carbon emissions in the Siemens UK operations. The six most compelling ideas were implemented through the Investment Fund.

Lock in the Commitment With a
Strategy-to-Execution Premium

The previously mentioned ideas help to increase interest, focus, and attention of the boardroom by providing a framework where better communication can be crafted, targeted, and upsold. McKinsey & Company and Wharton Business School found a 10-fold increase in environmental, societal, and governance investment between 2004 and 2019 [118], and 83 percent of C-suite would spend 10 percent of its value to achieve a positive record [119]. The initial commitment will mostly be based on the initial feel-good generated from the productive use of resources, coupled with the altruistic concern for the welfare of its people and planet. Soon, when their focus moves away, normalizes back to the day-to-day concerns, the initial commitment disintegrates and fades back to memory.

As with all new initiatives, it is introducing a change—an unknown and perhaps unstable element—into the existing work routine. Employees and managers alike will think and feel the new initiative draws additional requirements and resources away from the productive use of their time to generate saleable products and/or services. Until the business fully embeds resource productivity into its culture, it is easy for the business to lose its focus from the new initiative and back to old ways of working.

Many studies, such as those by Michael Mankins and Richard Steele [121], John Kotter [93], McKinsey & Company [122], and Harvard Business Review Analytical Services [120], show a large proportion (50%–83%) of change efforts fail to achieve its strategic intent. When it comes to initiatives that are not the core purpose of the business, the success rate is merely two percent [123]. Figure 2.1 shows the common reason why this is so and serves as a useful reminder on the type of issues found and that need to be resolved.

Those that do succeed, again, as mentioned in the Introduction, depending on which anecdotal evidence and published data you use, can achieve between two to three times better resource productivity (and other business performances) compared to business-as-usual or your competition. Another research finding from successful companies is that after four years, 80 percent of them still show continuing progress and improvements [122].

Too many strategic and/or change initiatives			
Poor communication and information sharing			
Insufficient resources			
Senior leaders not in agreement			
Purpose of initiatives is not well understood			
Inability to make timely decisions			
Insufficient talent / skills			
Insufficient project management			
Lack of engagement with senior leaders			
Unrealistic timelines			
Lack of employee buy-in			
Other obstacles			

0%   5%   10%   15%

Figure 2.1 Top reasons companies lose steam during implementation

Source: Data adapted from [120]

As can be seen from the success and failure rates, only a small number of companies are naturally proficient in designing great strategies, translating that strategy into action, and achieving sustained and long-term improvements on their own. Paul Leinwand and Cesare Mainardi's study [56] suggests that only eight percent are naturally capable to do so unaidedly. For the remaining 92 percent of the companies, developing leadership and management capability will rely on using some form of management system models, or as this book calls it, a *Strategy-to-Execution Premium*.

However, when companies think about management systems, many immediately think about the International Organization for Standardization (ISO) certification schemes like ISO 9001 (quality), ISO 14001 (environmental), ISO 50001 (energy), and the likes—a certificate or a "permission to trade" with certain customers. ISO indeed has many discipline-specific management systems standards. However, equating a management system to an ISO certification limits the power for your business to develop its competitive strategy, align the delivery process, and excel from its competition.

To explain the true nature of a management system, let us imagine a fully functional human body. The body has 11 bodily systems: circulatory, digestive, endocrine, excretory, integumentary, lymphatic, muscular, nervous (receives and sends messages), reproductive, respiratory, and skeletal systems. Within each system are several organs, which itself consists of specialist cells. To function in perfect unison, each organ and system sends information from the individual organs through the nervous system up to the brain for processing. The brain sends its decisions through the nervous system to constituent systems and organs for execution.

In a business, the equivalent of a nervous system is a management system. Robert Kaplan and David Norton define it as "an integrated set of processes and tools that an organization uses to develop its strategy, translate it into operational actions, and monitor and improve the effectiveness of both" [66].

To put it in other words, it is the collective, purposeful, and deliberate actions to direct and deliver a successful strategy that is, not *ad hoc* or *by accident.* It does so by: (1) planning its course of action, (2) allocating the appropriate resources, (3) each constituent part drives the plan forward, (4) each part send information upward on its progress to plan, and (5) the leadership team reviews the progress against its strategy and applies course corrections, and the cycle repeats itself, each iteration driving it closer to its vision.

As introduced in the Introduction, a fully functional *Strategy-to-Execution Premium* contains 10 elements (or leverage points) and addresses 10 common issues or barriers faced in companies. This was shown in Figure I.5 and is summarized as follows:

1. *Embed resource productivity into the company strategy.* Resource productivity and all of the technical analysis and management effort need to have a home in your company's strategic intent. In Chapter 1, top management needs to evaluate and identify how resource productivity fits in with its purpose, vision, mission, and values. When there is a strategic fit and is well articulated and understood, management and technical elements of the initiative have a True North. It will also make it easier for top management to evaluate, appraise, and trade off the risks and opportunities, and in allocating the all-important resources for execution.

2. *Form a cross-functional coalition for action.* In Chapter 2, we explored some ideas to get an initial "yes" from top management for the resource

productivity initiative. When implementing the initiative, obstacles and difficulties will emerge along the way necessitating some form of changes—be it in the form of normal routines and ways of working or diverting time and resources away from the business process. These changes will also generate friction and conflicts between various job functions that need to be resolved. To overcome this, top management needs to be fully committed to the initiative, lead by example, create a psychologically safe work environment, take action that is consistent with its policy, and actively seek out and disarm the conflicts that can derail the resource productivity initiative. For most businesses, using a *Strategy-to-Execution Premium* to lock in the whole top management's commitment and a cross-functional steering team is a simple and effective way to look at the big picture; spend time, money, and effort on resource productivity; look out for potential issues; cut across organizational barriers; and "steer" the whole company forward.

3. *Define appropriate scope and boundaries.* When initiatives are left unsupervised, many end up optimizing areas that are statistically insignificant or made improvements in one area at the expense of the whole. A good understanding of the core process and support processes in your company, and their impact on resource productivity, is necessary to optimize the whole rather than individual parts. If your company has a large or complex supply chain, sustainability risks can also originate from your supply chain. In this instance, extending the boundaries to include your supply chains can result in an optimized supply chain. A conscious definition of scope and boundaries for resource productivity will focus the business on identifying and improving the overall performance.

4. *Measure and benchmark resource productivity.* When it comes to improvement projects, companies typically face one or more of the four technical problems. The first problem is to implement projects without first obtaining the relevant measurements and data, assessing the overall resource productivity improvements, and evaluating it against the company's overall performance. If the assumptions used to develop the proposals are different from the actual operations, the calculations will not be representative. It is important to use appropriate measurements that build a picture of which resource

your core process consumes: raw materials, energy, water, and waste generation. A good, accurate, and repeatable measurement allows you to set relevant performance indicators that drive improvements. It also allows you to compare your performance with similar industries, best-in-class, or even just your competitors' performance. That comparison shows how effective you are using resources, and if there is a gap, the economic value of the gap.

5. *Make resource consumption visible.* The second problem many companies face is that many resources consumed are not visible to the human eye and people forget about them. A good example is energy consumption in an office. Many will immediately identify with the lighting and IT equipment. However, many will forget about the fresh air supply, heating, and cooling even though they typically account for up to 70 percent of a building's energy consumption. Good measurements allow you to determine how much resource each user consumes, thus enabling the identification of statistically significant resources and where it is consumed. This, in turn, allows you to target the areas where resource productivity should be controlled, prioritized, and improved.

6. *Set science-led improvement targets.* The first two technical problems give rise to the third—unknowingly set arbitrary improvement targets that are either too easy or impossible to reach. Another great technical element is to use improvement baselines that are science-based—the relationship between your company's resource consumption and the productivity of the business, for example, sales, production throughout, and customers served. The analysis shows the average, minimum, and maximum resource productivity levels based on your company's current operational setup. Using this as a baselining tool ensures that the resource productivity targets are achievable. It is also an excellent engagement with top management by communicating the fact that resource consumption is not a fixed cost, but one that is variable and controllable.

7. *Identify improvement opportunities.* The fourth technical problem stems from rushing through the identification, assessment, and implementation of resource productivity projects. As such, the technical details are poorly conceived, not fully appraising the technical fit, benefits, or knock-on effects on existing operations, or are rushed

to completion. Issues begin to surface during operations, or worst still, left unresolved. The final technical analysis involves identifying and fully appraising the benefits of a range of improvement opportunities, not just a selection of superficial opportunities, that are cost-effective for your business. The business cases for the opportunities also need to be presented in line with your company's strategy and using terms that are used in your company. This ensures that the risks associated with the opportunities are understood, fully quantified, and prioritized. For example, water-saving projects should be evaluated on water benefits plus other applicable benefits, such as energy savings, brand enhancement, long-term customer loyalty, and so on.

8. *Involve people from all job levels.* When implementing resource productivity projects, apart from top management commitment and engagement, you will also need to bring a large number of people with you to get the projects off the ground and into fruition. This includes people working in design, procurement, operations, maintenance, research, development, and so on because they know more about what is going on as they see them every day. Apart from needing to engage them, you will need to figure out the details of the engagement plan, that is, the how, when, why, what, and where. Everyone in your company needs to be consulted, provided with adequate competence, information, and appropriate resources such as time, notices, and so on so that they can do what is needed of them.

9. *Manage the implementation program.* Traditionally, businesses pay little attention to the delivery or project management process. The engagement and cooperation of different departments and job functions mentioned previously perform their duties and responsibilities at different speeds; thus, for a project to be delivered on time, in full, and on budget, everyone needs to carry out their respective roles at the required time, to get all parts of the jigsaw to be delivered and completed. This means that there is a need for you to (1) identify and plan every activity and milestone and (2) implement and manage the plan to ensure that everything happens according to the plan when it is required, in the right quality and quantity, and at the right cost.

10. *Celebrate, learn, and repeat.* Regardless of whether the resource productivity project is immediately successful, can be further improved

or not, there is a need to celebrate the success and thank all stakeholders for their cooperation and support. Studies from social science indicate that celebration leads to more, better, and faster improvement in the future. There is also a need to consciously learn from previous mistakes, find new areas for improvement, and renew the resource productivity initiative or risk it becoming a one-off initiative. Then, the cycle can restart because all companies operate in a dynamic environment, customer preferences change, legal requirements change, new technology emerges, and even your knowledge will improve over time. You may find that some unviable opportunities can become viable in the future or new opportunities arise.

A *Strategy-to-Execution Premium* does not even have to be called that. Over 80 percent of companies call their aligned strategy and execution by different names ranging from a management system, operational excellence, process excellence, performance excellence, business process management, strategy-to-execution, lean, lean six sigma, process improvements, business transformation, or change management [124]. Regardless of what it is called in your company, for it to work effectively, efficiently,

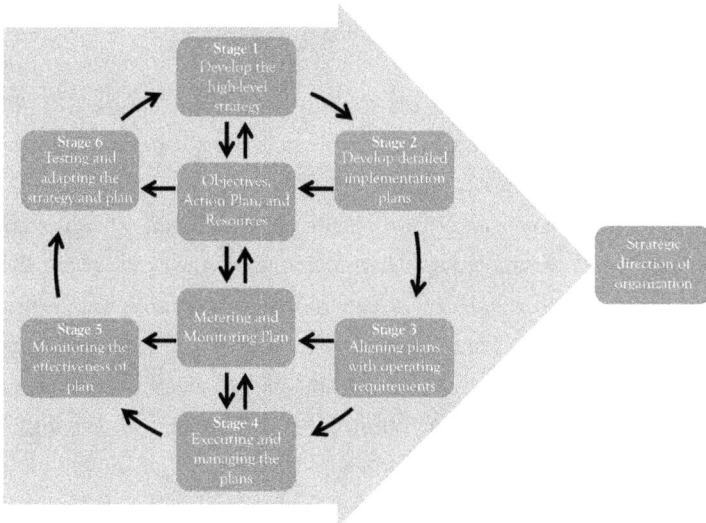

Figure 2.2 Closed-loop management system

Source: Adapted from [66]

Case Study: Arcelor Mittal

ArcelorMittal Saldanha Works, located on the west coast of South Africa, manufactures Hot Rolled Coil Steel products for the sub-Saharan markets. Energy costs are approximately 44 percent of the site's total operating costs [125]. In 2008, due to rising energy prices, rolling blackouts, and the global economic downturn, ArcelorMittal needed to significantly reduce its energy costs to compete with its competitors.

Before implementing an energy management system and systems-based energy audits, the site implemented multiple energy-saving projects, many of which have been implemented on an ad hoc and departmental silo basis.

In 2012, the site formed an energy team to implement a management infrastructure (ArcelorMittal's energy management system) covering three of the most significant energy uses, accounting for 70 percent of the site's energy consumption. The site's top management allocated 25 percent of the site's budget toward improving its energy performance.

According to Reinet van Zyl, ArcelorMittal's energy manager, "The risk, with the focus on energy, was that it could have been just another initiative and as a new priority could have been dropped as a result of too few people being dedicated to the cause. … Implementing an energy management system is the only way to ensure that the knowledge and practices are captured and institutionalized within the corporate culture and not reliant on any specific individual" [126].

Using a systems-based energy audit approach, the energy team identified 12 energy reduction projects involving staff awareness, opportunities not requiring any capital cost and without any impact on production and productivity levels. Within the same year, the site saved 80 GWh/year or 5.3 percent of its energy consumption, including a 26 percent reduction in LPG. The value of the savings is calculated to be worth R90 million with a capital cost of R0.5 million. These projects have a payback of four days.

By April 2013, three additional projects were completed, giving a total energy savings of 6.6 percent and a reduction of its specific energy consumption from 25.1 to 23.7 GJ/tonne.

and in a self-sustaining manner, it must contain all the 10 elements of a *Strategy-to-Execution Premium* (Figure 2.2).

Forming a Cross-Functional Coalition for Action

Typically, companies appoint one person and task him or her with the responsibility for resource productivity. This is a bad course of action. Why? In a small company, the area covered by one person is small, and he or she can be nearly everywhere and at all times. The core and support processed are simpler (compared to large companies), and the opportunities for improvements are also correspondingly simpler. Getting things done while keeping the production or service operational is doable.

However, as the size of the company grows, or the business process becomes more complex, companies organize themselves into hierarchies with people working in specialized departments and functions, the core and support process(es) may also spread over a large area and could span multiple sites, and also multiple geographies. When only one person or a small team is responsible, the ability for the person or the small team to be present in all areas and at all times, coordinating over a large area or a large number of people diminishes.

Hierarchical organizations are also designed to ensure efficiency and consistency in the core process. The structure itself resists change as it is changing the design of the work organization. So, while one person or small team may be committed, the significant majority have no ownership and buy-in. As such, the person or the small team will not be able to push resource productivity initiatives forward as they are effectively "fighting" against the momentum of the business to produce its products and/or services.

John Kotter, the change management guru, recommends forming a "guiding coalition"—a diverse, cross-functional, multilevel group with different skills and strengths who are excited about the change and are tasked with specific roles making up the *Strategy-to-Execution Premium* [127]. Specifically, they will be tasked with promoting resource productivity, implementing projects, leading by example by doing and living the initiative, actively seeking and resolving conflicts and competing objectives, removing policies that don't fit the vision, recognizing employees' efforts, and so on. Essentially, guiding the whole company along with all elements of the *Strategy-to-Execution Premium*.

They should, when carrying out the guiding coalition roles, operate with no existing bureaucratic hierarchy to allow creativity to plan, identify, break down, and overcome existing organizational issues that hinder progress. Ideally, the guiding coalition should have a transferrable skillset ranging from leadership skills, credibility, relationships, authority, analytical skills, and a sense of urgency for action [128].

Individually, they do not have to be competent in all aspects of resource productivity, but the team as a whole should have sufficient competence on the core process, basic knowledge of resource productivity to assess the applicability of opportunities and to ensure its fit-for-purpose, and know how the business functions and has sufficient authority to develop detailed plans, to lead and direct the initiatives, and to hold each other to account and support each other in achieving the overall objectives.

When identifying the ideal candidates for the guiding coalition, and assessing their availability, the use of *Responsible, Accountable, Consulted, and Informed (RACI)* or *Responsible, Accountable, Support, Consulted, and Informed (RASCI)* chart or matrix alongside their existing job demands are beneficial.

There is little point in appointing someone to take on additional tasks when there is no time or no capability for the candidate to do so. When this happens, again, the leadership team is setting up for the initiatives to fail. If additional resources are required, they can come from new hires, internal promotions, contracting external support, and many other avenues. Enthusiastic and capable university student placements are also good sources of temporary support.

CHAPTER 3

Define an Appropriate Scope and Boundaries

... The literature on re-engineering employs the term processes. Sometimes it is a synonym for activities. Sometimes it refers to activities or sets of activities that cut across organizational units. In any case, however, the essential notion is the same—both strategic and operational issues are best understood at the activity level. ...

—Michael Porter [129]

Except for capacity expansion and quality improvement projects, almost all other improvement projects be it energy reduction, waste packaging reduction, water reduction, or environmental projects are implemented by optimizing the support processes, ... the so-called utilities, environmental pollution control plants, waste recycling plants, or building services. The core process(es)—manufacturing or service provision processes—is rarely touched. Even when companies apply resource productivity to their core process, they are typically about buying the most efficient equipment and/or retrofitting the existing with efficient add-ons such as variable speed drives and better controls.

It is easy to understand the attractiveness of implementing resource productivity the way companies do: there are no risks of affecting the profit-making core process and no need to review equipment capability or fit-for-use parameters. Thus, it provides improvements without the "perceived" sacrifice and worrying about the "just in case" situations. For some regulated industries, such as health care, food manufacturing, and pharmaceutical processes, there is also no need for revalidating their processes.

Such an approach to resource productivity is an outdated belief where the core process is 100 percent efficient or we cannot or will not touch the core process. As a consequence, the management of resource consumption and resource productivity is consigned to the inputs and outputs of the core process, that is, the quality of raw materials, water quality, the efficiency of energy plants—boilers, chillers, compressors, and so on—and dealing with the consequence of the core process—waste, pollution, and so on.

Improving resource productivity by adding more efficient equipment and machinery will result in small improvements over and above the true potential in the business. The experience of UNIDO [130], U.S. DOE [131], and IEA [132] shows an average of two to five percent energy savings based on equipment efficiency improvements. A "whole" system, process, or building energy optimization can give savings of between 10 and 20 percent with an ultimate energy savings of over 60 percent [24] [133].

To get at the big improvement opportunities, there is a need to look at the core process, see how it consumes resources, and determine what can be done to make it productive.

What Is a Core Process? How Is It Related to Resource Productivity?

There are many types of processes in a business. Some examples of processes are the strategy development process, governance process, sales process, manufacturing process, energy generation process, maintenance process, documentation process, HR process, finance and payments process, procurement process, and so on.

To a large extent, it may be easier to group the various processes described earlier into three categories: core processes, support processes, and leadership processes. A core process is a process that generates revenue for your company. That would be the process that makes the product, services, or both that your company sells and generates revenue.

A company may also have multiple core processes in series or parallel. A good example is a hotel. The core processes relate to accommodation, food and beverage, and events or meetings. Other good examples are as follows: (1) a hospital with multiple departments such as emergency, surgery, cardiology, radiology, primary care, outpatients, and so on—each having a unique way of working and has different equipment; and (2) a manufacturing plant manufacturing several different products.

In addition, the inputs and outputs for each of the core processes can be independent of the other processes or are derived from other parts of the core processes. For example, in a hospital, triage is used to determine the severity of a patients' condition and prioritize where the patient goes within the hospital. In a manufacturing plant, the reprocessing plant may take the graded products and products with quality defects, that is, the outputs of the manufacturing plant, postprocess it, and send it back to the manufacturing plant as part of its inputs.

Support processes, as the name implies, are the processes that support the core process to do its work and to generate revenue. This includes human resources, finance, sales, raw materials, energy supply, water supply, waste management, maintenance, engineering, and so on. In some multibusiness units and multigeography companies, some of the support processes are common to all business units or geography, and these are sometimes called common processes or shared services.

The leadership process is the process that occurs in the leadership team where a decision can impact the whole business, that is, strategic planning, overall performance review, and emergency/crisis response.

The concept of measuring the efficiency of a company and its activities is not new. It has been in the study of engineering for a very long time. There is no definitive date when companies began to pursue efficiencies in companies. The earliest records (I could find) date back to William Stanley Jevons in 1865 [134] and Henry Ford in 1922 [135]. William Jevons questioned the sustainability of industry due to the then thought to be imminent peak coal. Henry Ford was talking about the need to eliminate all types of waste in his manufacturing process.

Political and economic commentators accredited the explosion of a "spend-to-save mentality" by using and retrofitting efficient technologies to a time when Ronald Reagan unseated and succeeded incumbent President Jimmy Carter as the President of the United States.

Specifically, one of the key manifestos in that Presidential election campaign centered on energy: that is, Jimmy Carter's "must consume energy responsibly and conserve" manifesto lost out to Ronald Reagan's "we'll roll out energy-efficient equipment to reduce energy consumption." The political implication, rightly or wrongly, leads to a global change away from using energy responsibly to let technology do it so we "don't have to" [136].

Suffice to say, as businesses pursue revenue and profits, the element relevant to resource productivity is cost. The higher the revenue and the lower the cost, the more profit is available. This is why leaders and managers always talk about "reducing cost" when it comes to resource consumption. The disconnect between a business process and resource productivity is this, when businesses want to reduce their resource consumption, say energy or water, many focus their attention on the energy plants and the water plants.

Unfortunately, it is the core process that consumes resources in the business, and support processes merely supply whatever the core needs plus some losses. Activities to optimize support processes would make it very efficient. However, if the core process is ineffective or inefficient, the overall resource productivity is still low. Figure 3.1 shows a generic relationship between processes and the consumption of resources.

A process view of the company also has quality, health and safety, and environmental implications. Quality issues are generally created by the core process due to raw material imperfection and the imprecisions of process technologies, machines, and people operating them. Health and safety issues are, again, created due to people operating the processes. Environmental pollution—air emissions, liquid effluent, particulates, groundwater, heat, odor, waste, and so on—is also created by the processes. The impact of the pollution can sometimes be local to where the pollution is generated and related health and safety issues. Often, the impact of environmental pollution and environmental harm is experienced at some distance away from the site, and sometimes, it can only be quantified over a long time.

To break away from the mental image of resource productivity to mean "increasing the efficiency of resources delivery to core process," there is a need to make a distinction between the different ways to improve resource productivity, thus directing the attention to the core process(es) of a company.

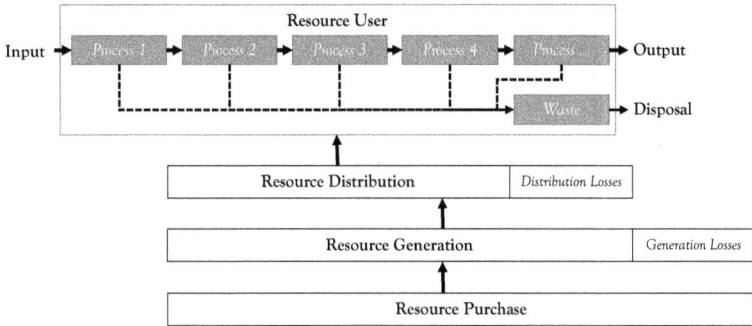

Figure 3.1 Process view of a company

Background: Different Ways to View Resource Productivity

User

Process, activity, or equipment that requires raw material, energy, and water to function and/or generate waste

Example: Specific equipment in a production line, service provision, transportation, ventilation, lighting, heating, and cooling.

Consumption

The quantity applied to the user

Example: "X" liters of water, "Y" kg of raw materials, and "Z" kWh of electricity.

(Energy) efficiency

The ratio of an energy equivalent output of performance to an input of energy

Note: The equivalent for raw material is called yield. There is no equivalence for water. When water is part of a product, it is calculated as yield. When water is consumed as a service, for example, washing, the input of water must equal the output of water. Otherwise, something is wrong with the process and should be investigated.

Example: Conversion efficiency, the energy required/energy used, theoretical energy used to operate/energy used to operate [137].

(Energy or water) effectiveness

The relative ability for a resource to produce the desired output for a user

Note: This is sometimes referred to as efficacy. The equivalent for raw material and waste is called yield.

Example: Quantity of water consumed per unit of cleaning achieved, the quantity of energy consumed for a unit of production.

(Raw material) yield

The ratio of a raw material equivalent output of goods to an input of raw material

Note: The equivalent for energy is called efficiency. There is no equivalence for water. The portion of raw material that does not create the product is waste.

Example: Conversion efficiency

Waste

Any material or object which is (or will be) discarded

Note: Waste can exist in gaseous, liquid, and/or solid forms.

Example: Production waste, by-products, graded products, packaging waste, air emissions, effluent.

As alluded to by the aforementioned terms and definitions, it is possible to save resources by playing with several variables. In the context of energy, it is possible to reduce the number of energy users thus reducing energy consumption, reducing energy consumption without changing the number of users, increasing energy efficiency, and increasing the effectiveness of the user in consuming energy. Let's use fresh air ventilation (user) for an office or in a manufacturing environment to illustrate:

- *Reducing user:* You could decide that certain rooms or places are irregularly occupied and do not need constant ventilation. This could, for example, be a storeroom for stationary or a records room where people only go in and out within a few minutes. Therefore, such places do not need a constant supply of fresh air from the ventilation system and existing ventilation for that area can be removed.

- *Reducing consumption:* You could find that the occupancy in an area varies significantly and is never at the designed maximum capacity. In such instances, it is possible to vary the speed of the fan to match occupancy rather than operating it at a maximum. You may also decide that if the windows are open, the air conditioning unit should be off. Therefore, giving rise to savings without changing the users.

- *Improving efficiency:* You could replace the fan and motor of the ventilation system with the highest efficiency variant, thus consuming less electricity and giving rise to energy savings.

- *Improving effectiveness:* You could be sitting in front of a large pile of boxes that blocks the air movement from reaching you, thus making you feel hot and stuffy. So, you could either remove the large pile of boxes or relocate your desk so that fresh air can reach you.

Let us use another example, water for cleaning (user) in a kitchen:

- *Reducing use:* You could decide that a different food preparation technique negates a need for additional washing. In this instance, a requirement for water has been removed and water is saved.

- *Reducing consumption:* You found several taps that are constantly dripping or kitchen staff keeps the water flowing even though they are not cleaning. You elect to repair the leaking tap or issue a communication not to leave the tap running when there is no washing required, thus saving water. In this case, the number of water users remains the same, but the time it is left flowing is reduced.

- *Improving efficiency:* You found that using water spray for cleaning is more efficient in dislodging food from pots and pans compared to soaking in a water bath, thus less water is needed for the same amount of cleaning duty.
- *Improving effectiveness:* You may find that the last water rinse for the pots and pans is relatively clean, and draining the relatively clean water is a waste. You opt to retain that water and use it as the first wash cycle in the next cleaning batch. As such, you are reusing the water, and therefore consuming less freshwater.

As can be seen, there are at least four ways resources can be saved: reducing use and consumption and increasing yield or efficiency and effectiveness. *Resource efficiency*, as it is used in the common language, is not the correct term as it implies implementing "efficiency improvement" only. Savings from reducing use, consumption, and effectiveness tend to be simpler actions with lower costs, whereas increasing efficiency would require some form of capital investment. In addition, the equipment can be the most efficient in the market, but there is no need for it to be there or to be "ON"—no improvement opportunity can offer more savings than not needing to use it at all.

One last concept needs to be introduced before we move on: the systems effect. Sometimes, all equipment that is coupled together may individually be efficient, but when they are operating together as a system, the system is inefficient and/or ineffective! A centralized heating, cooling, and ventilation system inside a building (Figure 3.2) is a good example of multiple equipment that are interconnected.

The overall efficiency of the ventilation system is dependent on the interaction between all of the equipment. The individual pump, fan, boiler, or chiller can be the most efficient or can be retrofitted with energy-efficient variants in the market. However, when there is no need for ventilation at night, or if there is a big hole in the wall, the ventilation, heating, and cooling are effectively treating outside air for no productive purpose. Alternatively, both the heating system and cooling system are operating simultaneously due either to: the heating and cooling valve not closing tightly, or the instruments are not calibrated. In this instance, without addressing the system issues, the individually efficient pump, fan, boiler, or chiller will be of no use.

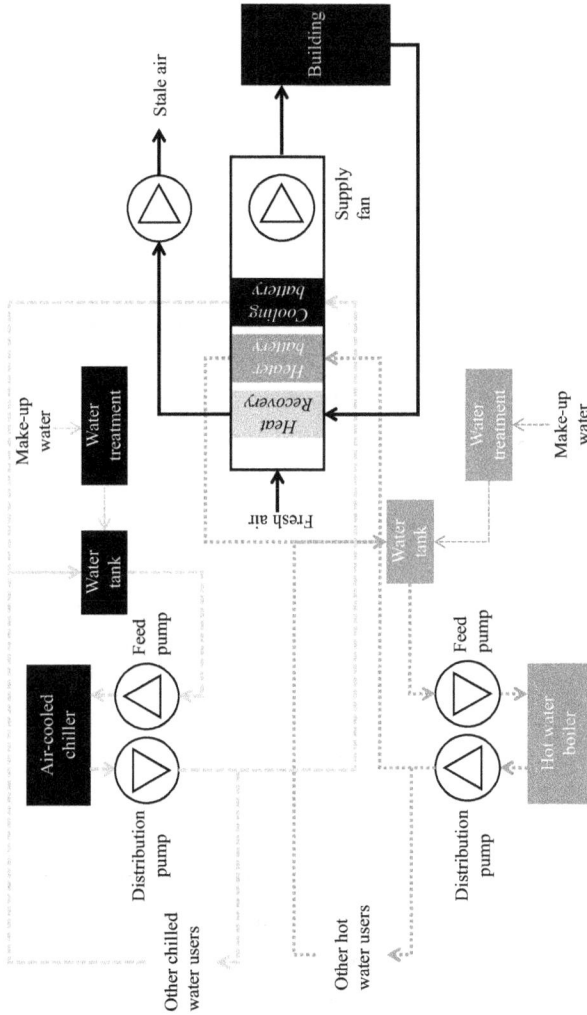

Figure 3.2 The relationship between the ventilation, heating, and cooling system in a building

Ways to Connect Resource Productivity and the End Users

As discussed in the previous section, large resource productivity gains come from analyzing and understanding the resource needs from the core process within the company. To tap into the large resource productivity gains, it is essential to construct a map of the core process and to understand where and how much each of the individual users is consuming resources and how efficient and effective are the resources consumed.

Start by looking at your company's core process. Identify and map the necessary steps that deliver this process. In manufacturing plants, this would be the main manufacturing process from raw material input to the final product output. In service-oriented companies, these would be the touchpoints between the potential customer and a happy customer. In some companies, there may be multiple core processes. Figure 3.1 gives a generic concept of energy users from inputs to outputs.

Then, identify the raw material, energy, and water required by each process or equipment, and map out how the resource gets to them. The same exercise goes for waste generation from the processes. Initially, you may find using arrows and labels sufficient. The support functions, such as the energy plants, maintenance, engineering, and offices, may also consume resources, such as energy and water, and generate wastes.

The true power of the process view lies in quantifying the resource consumption for each process or equipment. This can be accomplished by measurements, calculations (e.g., mass and energy balances, yield and efficiency calculations), and identifying any losses and opportunities for improvement.

Sometimes, you may find that several processes require the same resource, but the resource is of different quality. For example, a tomato juice plant requires hot water. However, the temperature for pasteurization is 60°C and for cleaning at 80°C. A hospital may require water of three different qualities: potable (city) water, purified water, and water for injection. In these instances, it is important to treat them as separate resources, especially if they are generated and distributed separately.

You may also find that several processes have the same resource requirement and at the same quality, for example, a single-ventilation unit supplying all floors in the same building. In such a case, the resource productivity of the ventilation unit can be optimized as a system.

For each process, identify if every constituent part adds any value to the final product and/or service. All of the constituent parts should be "adding value," and the resource consumption is more or less as per design. If you find some process or equipment is installed but do not know what it does or its contribution to the core process, it is a good time to find out.

Finally, identify the parameter(s) that drive (or cause) the quantity of resource consumption. For example, the production speed or throughput may be the primary driver in a manufacturing plant. If in doubt, the use of *Success Maps* or *5-Whys questioning techniques* helps by getting to the root of the driver. Some of these may be uncontrollable (e.g., weather), process characteristics (e.g., preprogrammed action by the controller), or require a person to take actions.

Understanding resource use and consumption from this perspective enable you to identify users that add value and the parameters that change resource consumption. It enables you to embed the right operational controls and behaviors at the right place. It also allows you to communicate relevant and meaningful information and to use the right performance indicators for the various job roles.

Lenses to View Core Process and Resource Productivity

The process shown in Figure 3.1 (reproduced in Figure 3.3a) is an in-company linear core process flow, and there is a defined input and output with all resources utilized discreetly and all wastes handled by others. A good approximation of this process is a simple manufacturing facility or a leased office space. Each component (sometimes called a unit operation or subprocess) in the process has an input specification and an output specification. Except for the first and the last components, all other components in the series are "customers" of the previous component and "suppliers" to the subsequent component.

A business managing its core process typically has "owners" or managers for each component within the process—each managing within the confines of their own imaginary "boundary" but no one manages

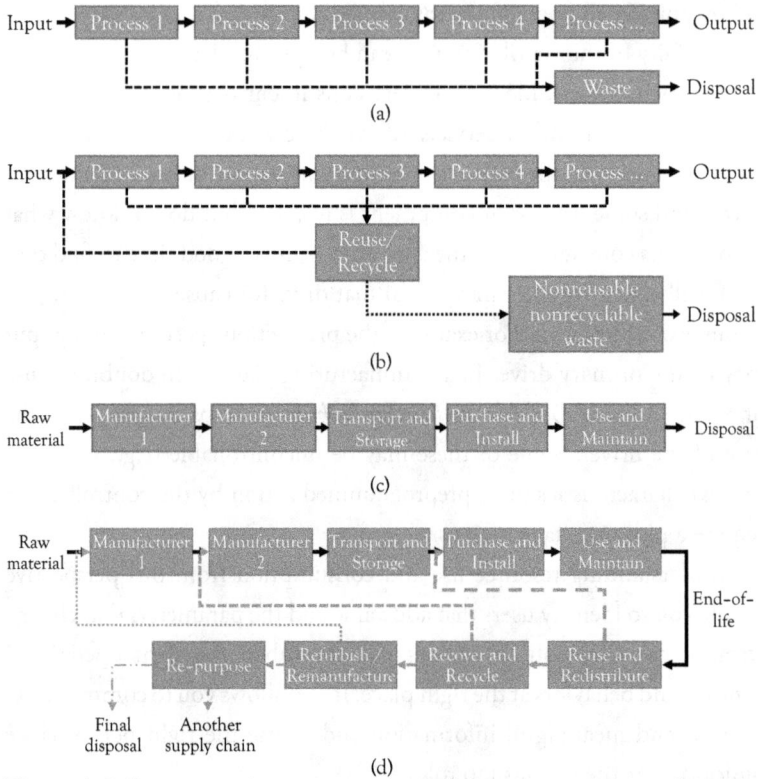

Figure 3.3 Lenses to view core process(es) from a resource productivity perspective: (a) in-company single resource, (b) in-company multiple resources, (c) cradle-to-grave, and (d) cradle-to-cradle

the interface between the components (called white spaces) or the whole process. This form of management introduces an opportunity for each component to be very efficient, but it may come at the expense of other components and drags down the performance of the whole.

A mismatch in specifications from the output of one component would result in poor resource productivity in downstream components, thus giving rise to an opportunity to optimize and improve the core processes as a whole. A good office-based example is to optimize a centralized ventilation system with heating and cooling described earlier.

Most of the companies who view their core process in this manner also appraise their resource productivity from a single resource perspective, that is, energy only, water only, or raw material only. As all the equipment are interlinked, changes to the quality of one resource may have a corresponding change in other resource consumption or other parameters of the core process. Collating and appraising the total benefit of a given opportunity allows for the project to be "paid back" through multiple avenues, giving a higher overall return on investment.

This simplified core process analysis is a good place to start your resource productivity journey as it is a smaller scope and carries smaller risks as compared to the other ways to define the core process. Also discussed earlier, many companies have multiple core processes, some of which are in parallel. The parallel core processes can be studied individually, thus simplifying the analysis. Once you become proficient in linear core-process optimization and gained new insight and value from it, you will be ready to take the next steps in gaining more improvements. Each step-up (or maturity) sees an increase in complexity but has its rewards.

The first step-up is to apply the principles of 4Rs: reduce, reuse (in situ), recycle (reuse elsewhere in the process), and recover (as another form of resource, e.g., recover heat from wastewater) and is typified by Figure 3.3b.

Take water, for example, a component manufacturer might consume water, for cleaning components at different stages of its manufacturing process. It may be just as good to complete the manufacturing process and clean it once. You may also decide that using a water bath allows the same water to be used a few times before needing a water change. After this, you may also decide to recover heat from the hot washing to preheat the cold freshwater.

Case Study: Dawn Meats

Dawn Meats is a supplier of beef and lamb for food retail and food services markets throughout Europe. They consume natural gas to generate steam. Their steam boiler has a typical efficiency of 80 percent. This means that 20 percent of the energy is emitted into the environment via the stack (or chimney) in the form of 150°C hot exhaust gas. Some of the steam is used to generate hot water for cleaning and sanitization purposes. By applying horizontal thinking across departments, Dawn Meats installed a state-of-the-art heat exchanger to condense the hot exhaust gas to preheat water used for cleaning and sanitization, thus reducing natural gas consumption by 18 percent [138].

Case Study: Coca-Cola Hellenic Bottling Company

Coca-Cola Hellenic Bottling Company emits nearly 900,000 tonnes of CO_2 per year as a result of consuming energy during manufacturing and running its transport fleet. The bottling of Coca-Cola also consumes food-grade CO_2 purchased from external suppliers. Apart from the various initiatives to improve plant energy efficiency by 23 percent, one of the key initiatives is to reduce its emissions by generating energy efficiently using a tri-generation (heating, cooling, and power) plant and to recover CO_2 generated from the tri-generation plant for reuse in its bottling plant.

A tri-generation plant with CO_2 recovery is known in the industry as "quad-generation." With an investment of nearly €200 million, quad-generation plants were installed in Hungary, Romania, Northern Ireland, Italy, Nigeria, Poland, and Ukraine. Coca-Cola HBC estimates that this initiative will reduce 40 percent of its direct emissions from energy generation and recover approximately 40 percent of food-grade CO_2 for use in its bottling plant [139].

While this approach offers high overall benefits to the company, it is inherently riskier as it makes changes to multiple resources and affects the whole process. Projects involving reuse, recycling, and recovery could potentially introduce contamination issues that may not exist if new resources are utilized. As such, exploiting these types of opportunities requires better knowledge and understanding of your core process and their interactions between each of its constituent components.

Similar to managing whitespaces within a company, a mismatch of requirements and specifications can also occur between companies in a supply or value chain (also known as a business ecosystem). From an energy and greenhouse emissions perspective, this is important because 50 to 60 percent of the world's CO_2 emissions appear in the supply chain of just 500 companies [140] [141] within eight sectors: food, construction fashion, FMCG, electronics, automotive, professional services, and freight [142]. Making the whole supply or value chain or business ecosystem resource productive, typified by Figure 3.3c, is the next logical step-up.

According to an analysis by Boston Consulting Group, the price mark-up for products with a net-zero supply chain will only increase the end-user price between one and four percent [142].

Opportunities typically arise as a result of one of two scenarios as follows: (1) a mismatch of specifications between companies in the supply or value chain leading to overprocessing or underprocessing by upstream companies and subsequent rework in downstream companies; and (2) reimagining new ways of producing the same products and/or services using fewer resources without sacrificing the needs of the customer.

Sometimes, this is called "green chemistry" by manufacturing its products from an entirely different production method that consumes significantly fewer resources. It is also referred to as "light-weighting" in applications that manufacture the same products but use lighter materials or different methods.

As we move the scope and boundary of resource productivity to include other companies in the supply or value chain, three terms tend to crop up: Scope 1 emissions, Scope 2 emissions, and Scope 3 emissions. Scope 1 refers to the emissions generated directly from the combustion of fuel in the company, for example, natural gas combustion in a boiler or a furnace. Scope 2 emissions refer to the energy consumed by the company but it is generated (hence combustion occurred) elsewhere, for example, electricity is produced in a powerplant. Scope 3 refers to emissions from the energy consumed and hence emissions from your supply chain or value chain.

Case Study: Walkers Crisps

Walkers Crisps, a subsidiary of PepsiCo, is one of the largest snack food manufacturers in the United Kingdom. In their energy assessment of their supply chain, they discovered that farmers were storing potatoes in humid rooms to keep the potatoes' skin soft, to avoid them drying out, and thus meeting Walkers Crisps' purchasing specification. When the potatoes arrived at their manufacturing site, the potatoes were dried and then fried, that is, to remove water from the potatoes.

With a simple change in its potato specification based on dry weight, plus other specifications, farmers are now able to reduce their energy and water costs and Walkers Crisps uses 10 percent less energy to make its crisps [143].

Following a trial in 2020, Walkers Crisps is implementing an anaerobic digester in Leicester, one of their manufacturing sites in the United Kingdom, where potato wastes will be diverted from landfill to produce methane gas to power 75 percent of the site's electricity demands, thus reducing the sites CO_2 emissions by an equivalent amount. The potato cake will then be converted into fertilizers and reused in the potato farms [144].

Case Study: GlaxoSmithKline

GSK has a long-term vision for its operations and for its supply chain to be carbon-neutral by 2050. An analysis of the CO_2 emissions of its products, from the raw materials to their final use by its customers, revealed that its business operations and manufacturing plants account for 11 percent of CO_2.

Detailed knowledge of GSK's supply chain showed GSK that 89 percent of the CO_2 arose not from its manufacturing processes but from elsewhere—38 percent came from raw materials manufacturing, 35 percent from the use of medicinal inhalers (where CO_2 is the propellant), seven percent by the end-use customers, three percent from logistics and business travel, and less than one percent from its disposal [145]. If GSK was to focus purely on its operations and become carbon-neutral, its products would still emit 13.4 million tonnes of CO_2 via its entire value chain.

It also showed GSK that a significant quantity of CO_2 emissions came from the supply chain of two products: inhalers and Horlicks. This allowed GSK to formulate strategies and prioritize R&D activities to maximize CO_2 reduction and minimize the impact of its products on the environment, for example, low-carbon inhalers, recycling of its inhalers, and working with its supply chain to minimize energy consumption while maximizing its operational efficiencies and energy reduction.

Case Study: Proctor & Gamble and Unilever

When Proctor & Gamble (P&G) began to assess its impact on the environment, it carried out a life cycle analysis of the whole supply chain. The findings showed that the largest energy consumption was from its laundry products by its customers, due to the need to heat water in the washing machine for washing.

According to Len Sauers, Vice President of P&G's global sustainability initiative, "This surprised me. I thought our highest energy impact was going to be somewhere in the manufacturing process." P&G set off working on creating a product that enables its customers to wash in cold water without compromising the performance of the laundry detergent in hot wash cycles [146].

P&G's competitor, Unilever, took the concept further and included water savings. An assessment of Unilever's laundry products showed that around 38 percent of all domestic water is used to clean clothes. In water-scarce places, water is an expensive resource. Unilever's solution is called "Comfort One Rinse"—saving up to 50 percent of domestic water consumption and the corresponding energy reduction [147].

Like the previous step-up, opportunities to improve resource productivity also carry higher risks where changes in one company can affect the whole supply or value chain: from the raw materials down to the end consumer. The level of knowledge and expertise extends beyond the individual company into all processes in the supply or value chains. The ability to initiate a supply chain optimization will be limited to the companies with the biggest purchasing power and is usually one of the 500 big corporations mentioned earlier.

The highest form of resource productivity, typified by Figure 3.3d, was first popularized by Michael Braungart and William McDonough as *cradle-to-cradle* in 2002 [148] as a call to action for designing products that reduce, reuse, and recycle the material at its end-of-life versus the normal practice of cradle-to-grave—manufacture, consume, and dispose mentality. This concept has evolved to include a closed-loop economy, circular economy, planetary boundaries, doughnut economics, and

UN's Sustainable Development Goals (SDGs) where multiple resources, their impact on the environment, and social aspects are optimized simultaneously. In a simplistic form, this form of resource productivity applies 4Rs plus another R (repurpose) or sometimes also called upcycling to the entire supply or value chain.

Here, the supply chain manufactures products that are capable of being reused (with or without refurbishing) at the end of their life cycle. This may also be achieved by repurposing the components for use in another supply chain, recycling and recovering the resources before disposing of any remaining wastes, and thus eliminating the need to consume new (also called virgin) raw materials.

Examples for repurposing resources include converting waste carbon fiber in B787 Dreamliner production into protective equipment used in athletics [149], converting waste blood from meat processing into bio-based plastics [150], converting coffee waste into biofuel [151], mixing waste plastics or waste tires into asphalt mix for road construction [152], and converting waste bread into ales [153], spent grains from malting process into malted flour.

Case Study: Renault [149]

Renault, the car manufacturer, implements resource productivity in four areas:

1. Designing cars that are easy to dismantle and contain recyclable or recoverable materials.
2. Through its wholly owned subsidiary, Renault Environment, it maintains technical and economic control over the flow of its vehicles' waste materials and parts.
3. For interested customers, uses reconditioned or remanufactured parts coming from its end-of-life vehicles collected from its sales network, plants, or suppliers.
4. Forming partnerships with other interested parties for the recycling of recovered copper, aluminum, plastics, platinoids, and textiles recovered from its end-of-life cars.

Case Study: ReNewCell [156]

Cotton and viscose in clothing cannot be recycled with satisfactory quality, and the vast majority of worn-out or no longer wanted garments end up in landfills or are incinerated. ReNewCell pioneered a process of converting cotton and viscose garments into new biodegradable pulp, new fibers, new yarn, and new fabrics to be fed back into the clothing industry.

ReNewCell's plant in Kristinehamn receives used garments with high cellulose content (cotton and viscose). The textiles are shredded, de-buttoned, de-zipped, de-colored, and dissolved into a slurry; any contaminants and noncellulose content are removed and dried to produce pulp, which is packaged into bales and fed into the textile production cycle. Tests compared ReNewCell fibers with textile fibers made from dissolving wood. They report that ReNewCell fibers have higher quality in several areas and meet industry textile specifications.

The plant is capable of producing 7,000 tonnes of biodegradable ReNewCell pulp per year. They estimate that for every kilo of clothing recycled instead of being produced from virgin sources, it saves thousands of liters of water and decreases emissions of both CO_2 and chemicals.

Repurposing is not limited to the manufacturing industry. It can and is also applied in the service industry. Airlines such as KLM (uniforms), Finnair (seat covers, seat belts, curtains), Delta (seat covers), Air France (life jackets), Southwest (seat covers), and Virgin Atlantic (seat covers) repurpose their wastes into stylish bags, luxury branded shoes, and sports equipment [150], [156]. Emirates, on the other hand, purchases blankets that are made from repurposed plastics for use in economy cabins [157].

Optimization at this level, while giving the biggest resource savings, requires multiple stakeholders to work together openly and transparently. Experience from Sustainability Consortium's Material Pooling [158] [159], Tesco's buying club [160], and University of Ghent's EPOS [161] indicates that sharing information with external stakeholders is more difficult than it seems, but it is not an impossible feat.

The work by the University of Ghent's EPOS and UNIDO [162] also suggests that the companies wanting to take advantage of a closed-loop economy will benefit if the various parties are close to one another or ideally within the same geography, such as a purposed built and integrated site or park. Otherwise, there is a transportation element and its associated costs.

Case Study: Herman Miller [163]

Herman Miller offers a suite of office furniture to many S&P 1000 companies many of whom are multilocation and multinational companies. The company has adopted and practices a triple bottom line philosophy (financial, environmental, and social responsibility performance) since 1989.

In 2001, the company began working with McDonough Braungart Design Chemistry to operationalize the cradle-to-cradle design protocols and have used the protocol to design and develop a new product—the Mirra Chair—a mid-level office chair that is fully recyclable at the end-of-life. The process to bring the chair from concept to production consists of four stages: exploration, development, launch, and maintenance.

- *Exploration:* The Design for Environment team was involved early on to incorporate cradle-to-cradle principles before a high-level specification is developed.
- *Development:* The high-level specifications were split into modules where teams are assigned to develop prototypes. The prototypes were assessed according to the cradle-to-cradle protocols for material chemistry, disassembly, recyclability, and recycled content. The output of the assessment was returned to the team in the form of a scorecard where the design and prototypes were further improved.
- *Launch:* The design and development were finalized and the product was manufactured.
- *Maintenance:* Considerations for replacement materials and parts were developed.

For Herman Miller, not all of the changes were positive. Some design decisions increased costs. Other negatives include working with materials that are not familiar, working with different (sometimes terminating existing) suppliers, and working with various parties to compile material information for Herman Millers' Green-Yellow-Orange-Red list of materials—some of which are confidential or trade secrets.

However, the changes were in line with the company's values and triple bottom line culture. Some of the benefits include replacing a Y-spine of the chair from a single piece of metal with plastic over-molding with two-piece recyclable nylon, replacing foam materials used in seat and back support with co-polyester elastomer, and replacing the Polyvinyl chloride (PVC) used in the arm pads with thermoplastic urethane, all of which are more environmentally friendly and recyclable.

The final product, the Mirra chair, was launched in 2003 and is made from 42 percent of recycled materials, and at the end of its useful life, 96 percent of the chair is recyclable. The Mirra chair was also easier to assemble with a shorter assembly line compared to other chairs manufactured by Herman Miller and won the Ergonomics Excellence Award (2004), a silver Industrial Design Excellence Award (2004), and a silver cradle-to-cradle certification by *Business Week* magazine [164].

Working with the same designer, Studio 7.5 a decade later, the Mirra chair was redesigned from the castors up. The most noticeable change between the Mirra and Mirra 2 is the overall reduction in size. All improvements together reduce the chair's weight by 25 percent, improving the sitting posture, decreasing materials consumption, and enabling lower fuel consumption during shipping [165].

Case Study: Dubai's Fat, Oil, and Grease (FOG) Waste

Founded in 1954, Dubai's sewerage network and sewerage treatment plants serve the population of the emirate of Dubai and the needs of local businesses and industry. Dubai has witnessed significant economic growth in the last 20 years, along with it, a growth of restaurants and hotels. There are approximately 17,000 restaurants and hotels preparing food in large quantities in Dubai, and large quantities of FOG waste go down the drains. FOG congeals into large fatbergs, blocking the sewerage pipes. Over a typical year, 12 million U.S. gallons of FOG are produced resulting in more than 2,000 FOG-related blockages, costing the Dubai Municipality AED 2.1 million to dislodge.

To overcome this issue, a waste edible oil recycling facility was designed, installed, and commissioned at Al Awir to treat FOG. FOG from restaurants and hotels are transported to the plant where it is filtered before going through a thermal polymerization process to produce clean oil, wastewater, and sediments. The oil collected in storage tanks is sold to the cosmetic industries, and the wastewater is sent to the Dubai Municipality's sewage treatment plant for further processing in a downstream wastewater treatment plant.

Case Study: Bristol Waste Water Treatment Plant (WWTP)

Originally built in the 1960s, the Bristol Waste Water Treatment Plant treats sewage sludge from over one million people and approximately 300 industrial effluents in the Bristol region, United Kingdom. In 2012, GENeco built and operated the UK's only food waste recycling facility to be colocated on a WWTP. The food waste recycling facility utilizes two anaerobic digesters to produce a compliant digestate (bio-fertilizer) without the need for any secondary storage. The food waste recycling facility processes 40,000 tonnes of food waste per year, converting this waste into usable resources, biogas, and biofertilizer.

The plant produces more biogas than its heat and electricity requirements. The company decided that the excess biogas would be better utilized if converted to biomethane (efficiency = 98 percent) than if used as fuel for a combined heat (efficiency = 38 percent) and power (efficiency = 33 percent) plant.

In 2014, the plant installed a biomethane generation plant, which uses high-pressure water to strip CO_2 and other contaminants from the biogas to produce biomethane. This biomethane generation plant converts enough biogas into biomethane to power 7,000 homes every year, 10,000 MWh of green energy for five Unilever sites in the United Kingdom, and injects around 1,000 m³/hour of natural gas into the national gas grid.

In 2014, GENeco also introduced the first biomethane-powered Bio-Bus with a range of over 300 km on a full tank of gas. 150 biomethane-powered buses have become operational in the city of Bristol and the surrounding areas.

In 2015, the plant installed a real-time monitoring system to help them further optimize biogas production and to reduce the consumption of chemicals and raw materials. The real-time monitoring system enhances the process-monitoring capabilities of the plant by combining raw data signals and lab analysis results into usable performance parameters. Visualization of these parameters has been configured into supervisory dashboards to achieve efficient process operation and increased the input of food waste into the recycling facility by 38 percent.

GENeco estimates that for every tonne of food waste diverted from landfills, 0.6 tonne of CO_2 will be displaced from the atmosphere, reducing the environmental impacts associated with landfills. The increased food waste recycling rates also increase the amount of nutrient-rich biofertilizers where farmers can reduce their reliance on inorganic fertilizers, which often pollute waterways.

The combined plant fulfills the strategic intent of the company to use its resources to their fullest potential and contributes toward a closed-loop economy. To further its vision to create a sustainable circular economy within Bristol, GENeco plans to launch the UK's first food waste collection vehicle (the "Bio-Bee") which will be powered by biomethane produced from food waste and sewage. The Bio-Bee will be used to collect the food waste that feeds the anaerobic digesters.

While there are many lenses to view your company's processes, it is not a requirement, nor is it necessary to choose the most advanced form of process view to begin your resource productivity journey.

An easy way, and most convenient starting point, is to choose a process view that is closest to your company's process and start from there. As mentioned in the Introduction, the scope can be expanded in the subsequent planning cycles.

Once the scope has been selected, the rest of the work can begin. But, before we move on, it is important to know your company may or may not have operational controls for all of the scopes selected. While having operational control over the selected scope is ideal, there are other ways to influence those outside your control. Using design and procurement specifications and contractual agreements is a good example. Forming joint ventures, partnerships, and similar-interest groups are further good examples.

CHAPTER 4

Measure and Benchmark Resource Productivity

… We are being ruined by best efforts, doing the wrong thing, with hard work, putting forth best efforts, with hard work, putting forth the best effort, everybody putting forth best efforts. I've inquired of 50,000 people (as a rough estimate) at my seminars: "Who here is not putting forth his best effort? Let him stand." No one has stood up yet!
—W Edwards Deming [166]

Once you have identified the appropriate core process for analysis and have overlayed the resource supply and distribution to each user described in Chapter 3, the next step is to identify the relevant resource productivity measurements that will allow you to proactively and predictively monitor resource consumption, analyze and compare performance, and benchmark it with others.

The need for resource consumption, yield, and efficiency information does not necessarily mean that you should buy and install meters and automated data logging systems everywhere. The result of such a "big data" approach can be costly, swamps and overwhelms the business with an ocean of information that is not meaningful, and contributes toward what Michael Hammer calls the "seven deadly sins of performance measurement" [167]:

1. *Vanity:* The availability of numerous resource measurements and data can lead managers and employees to select indicators that they can explain and make their resource productivity numbers look good.
2. *Narcissism:* It allows them to think that their indicator is the best indicator without consulting and discussing with others and without looking at the big picture.

3. *Provincialism:* As such, functions or departments optimize their resource productivity and yet, have poor resource productivity performance as a whole.

4. *Laziness:* Over time, the set of functional or departmental measurements is reduced to the few key indicators that make the department look good without giving any thought as to what the measurement means to the other function or department, or the necessary trade-offs for the whole business to succeed.

5. *Pettiness:* Continual use and defense of the department's choosing create silos and halos that encourage office politics and turf wars within the business.

6. *Inanity:* The arbitrary choice of performance indicators without giving thought to or how it relates to activities carried out, the action required from employees, and/or the consequence of the measurement to human behavior.

7. *Frivolity:* Measuring performance for measurement's sake without taking any action to the information, finding superficial root causes, finding excuses for poor performance, and/or passing the blame.

The ocean of data creates an eighth deadly sin, what I call "burnout":

8. *Burnout:* The presence of a very large quantity of seemingly meaningless and senseless performance indicators is overwhelming, especially if their use and meaning are not explained and understood. Over time, everyone stops looking at it and tunes them out, and thus the measurements and data become a white elephant.

Connecting Business Processes and Resource Consumption

To overcome the eight sins of resource productivity measurements, a good place to start is to overlay your resource use and consumption measurements to your core process to identify the reasoned and meaningful measurement and performance indicators.

1. *Your starting information is your monthly invoice for raw material, energy, water, waste, and other resources.* All businesses will have

regular (monthly and sometimes bimonthly) bills. So, the first step is to check that the main meters and measurements are accurate. From an energy and water perspective, the main meters may be under the authority of the energy or water supplier. Sometimes, it is easier to leave the existing incoming meters alone and install a second meter immediately after the incoming meter. This second meter is within the boundary of your company and can be subject to routine calibration checks. If the incoming meters are reading higher than your meters, it is possible to seek repayment from the supplier.

2. *You may already have the necessary consumption information in your existing equipment manual or have a way to calculate it.* Raw material, waste, and water consumption can be measured by weights, volume, and flows—things that are related to your process(es), for example, mass, volume, length or height, flow, temperature, pressure, time "on" or time "off" status, and the number of pushbuttons. In a well-controlled business, most of the measurements are available in local gauges, building management systems (BMS), human-machine interfaces (HMIs), distributed control systems (DCS), and energy information management systems (EIMS). If they are not, a simple spot measurement of the said parameter can be done. The background boxes explain how these parameters relate to thermal and electrical power.

Background: Thermal Measurement

All measurements of heat: heating (something that is heating up) or cooling (something that is cooling down) follows two forms of thermal energy: sensible heat and latent heat.

Sensible heat does not change the state of the material, that is, if it is solid, it remains solid, liquid–liquid, and gas–gas. To calculate sensible heats, we use the concept of heat capacity—the energy required to heat or cool the material by 1°C—and follows the formula:

$$\text{Power} = \frac{\text{Mass} \times \text{Heat capacity} \times \text{Change in temperature}}{\text{Change in time}}$$

Where the material changes state, for example, solid to liquid, liquid to vapor, and vice versa, we use the concept of enthalpy and follows the formula:

$$Power = \frac{Mass \times Change\,in\,enthalpy}{Change\,in\,time}$$

The units for the various terms are power in kW, mass in kg, heat capacity in kJ/kg°C, temperature in °C, enthalpy in kJ/kg, and time in s.

Heat capacity and enthalpy information for common materials are widely available on the Internet. Enthalpy information requires two pieces of information to obtain the enthalpy values: pressure and temperature. So, in terms of calculating thermal energy, all you will need is the measurements for each element required, and power can be calculated.

Background: Electrical Measurement

Depending on what is installed for your site, electricity is available for use at several voltages and ranges from 10 to 110 V (the United States and Canada) and 240 V (Europe) for domestic and light commercial uses, and up to 132,000 V (or 132 kV) for heavy industrial use. A domestic and light commercial use tends to be supplied with single-phase electricity while industrial users can have a mix of single- or three-phase electricity supply.

The formula to calculate electrical power depends on whether the supply is single-phase or three-phase as follows:

For single-phase, $Power = \frac{Volts \times Amps \times Power\,factor}{1,000}$

For three-phase, $Power = \frac{\sqrt{3} \times Volts \times Amps \times Power\,factor}{1,000}$

The units for the various terms are power in kW, volts in V, amps in A, and the power factor does not have any units. So, you only need volts, amps, and the power factor to calculate power—something that any good power meter or good electrician can measure.

3. *Work out which formula to use, measure, and plug in the right numbers to get consumption numbers.* As all of the resource consumption is related to your core processes, collating this information, together with information from the equipment manuals, equipment nameplate data, and spot measures, you will be able to calculate resource consumption information using the established formulas. The so-called smart meters will still be measuring the same parameters (which you already have) and using preprogrammed formulas to calculate the consumption information.

Background: Converting Power (kW) Into Energy (kWh)

To convert power into energy consumption, additional information is needed—the time in which the power is expended. A common unit of energy consumption measurement is kWh, which is a product of power and time (in hours):

$$\text{Energy consumption} = kW \times hour$$

4. *Active management of your core process should also manage your resource consumption.* The next step is to uncover, as complete as you can, the drivers that can affect the quantum of resource consumed by your core process. Sometimes, these drivers are called factors or variables that cause consumption. This step identifies the parameters that change consumption and distinguishes parameters that you can and cannot control. If you are familiar with your process, you should be able to identify a large majority of the drivers. However, there may be drivers that escape your thoughts. A more systematic and thorough way is to develop this by using a *Success Map* or Five-Why technique. The following background box illustrates how to do this using energy as an example. The same methodology can also be applied to the support processes within the business.

Background: Using Success Maps to Identify the Variables That Determine Energy Consumption

Let us use a building's heating system as an example. To develop a success map for the heating system, ask "What can cause the natural gas consumption of the boiler to change?"

- The room temperature is too high.
- The heating system has become inefficient.
- The cooling water valve is not fully closing.
- The ambient temperature is low.

For each answer, drill down the likely causes until some form of human action is required. Using the "heating system has become inefficient," for example, ask "What can cause the heating system to become inefficient?"

- The temperature probe is faulty.
- There is missing or faulty insulation.
- There is scaling on hot surfaces.

An example of a completed success map is shown in Figure 4.1. This success mapping technique is equally applicable in the manufacturing environment. Figure 4.2 shows an example of an air dryer in a manufacturing plant. A series of these maps can be developed for the whole company to give an overall picture of resource use and consumption.

5. *Overlay existing controls used on to the Success Map and check if additional measurements are needed.* The *Success Map* creates visibility of the key control measures for day-to-day operations. It also shows you how controlling the individual variables can minimize resource consumption in a repeatable manner. Once you have a complete *Success Map*, the next step would be to identify which parameters you can control and which you cannot, which parameters you monitor and measure, and if there are any things that you should control and monitor but currently do not. These, if any, would be the additional control measures required for resource productivity.

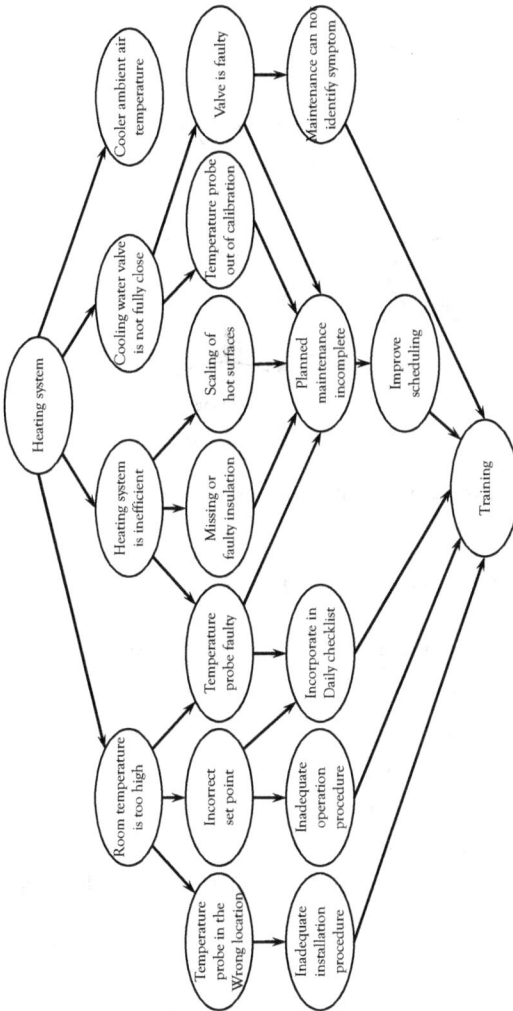

Figure 4.1 Success map in a building

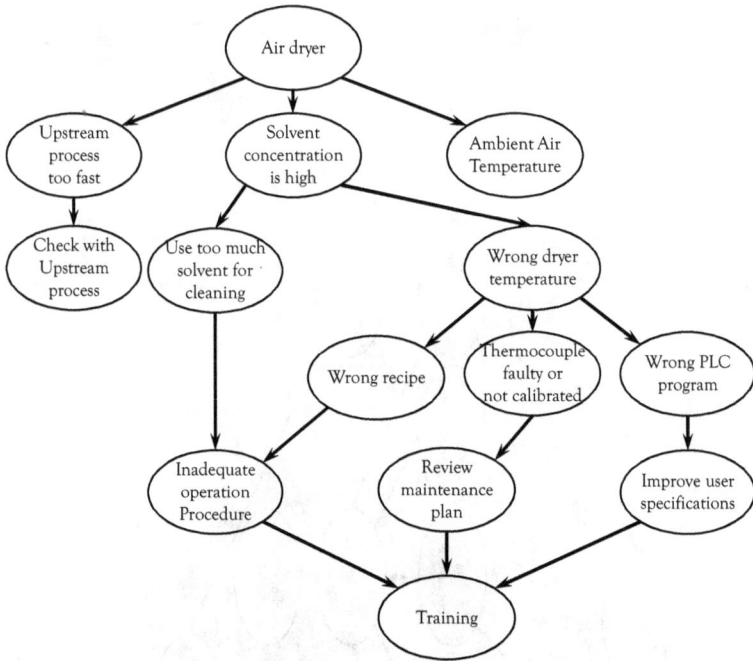

Figure 4.2 Success map in a manufacturing environment

Metering and Monitoring Plan

As mentioned earlier, the need for managing and improving resource productivity does not mean a "license to install" meters everywhere in the business. It is not about "big data"—the availability of granular pieces of information—or "Internet of Things"—having the data on the Internet—but the information and knowledge derived from the data that enables the business to make timely decisions and, if any, course corrections.

Overlaying the existing metering in the business with the *Success Map* helps to visually establish how the various resources are distributed to each user. It helps to identify the existing metering layout, to define any missing meters, or where additional submetering is beneficial. This forms the basis of a metering and monitoring plan.

At a basic level, a metering plan can be a simple table or a simple chart describing: (1) the main meters, (2) how the resources are distributed to the various users, (3) if there are any submeters (it's location, type, etc.), (4) virtual meters (formulas to calculate the meter reading, background data, records of assumptions, etc.), (5) means to extract and analyze the data, and (6) means to ensure accuracy and repeatability.

Graphical examples for a small office and an office block are shown in Figures 4.3 and 4.4. A metering map for large buildings and manufacturing plants would be more complex.

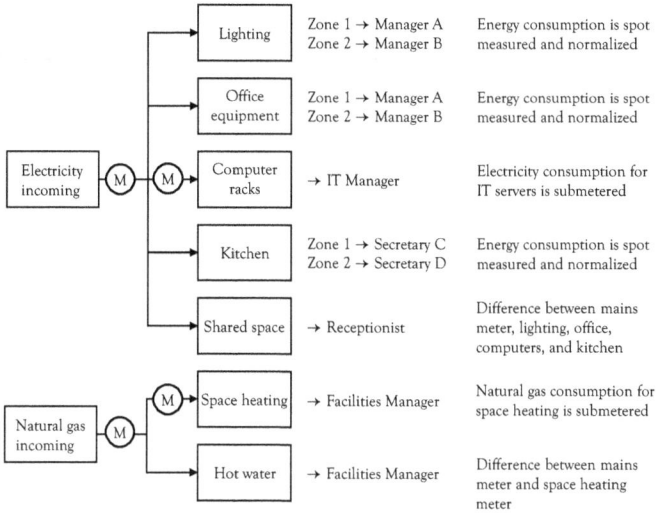

Figure 4.3 Simple metering map for a small office

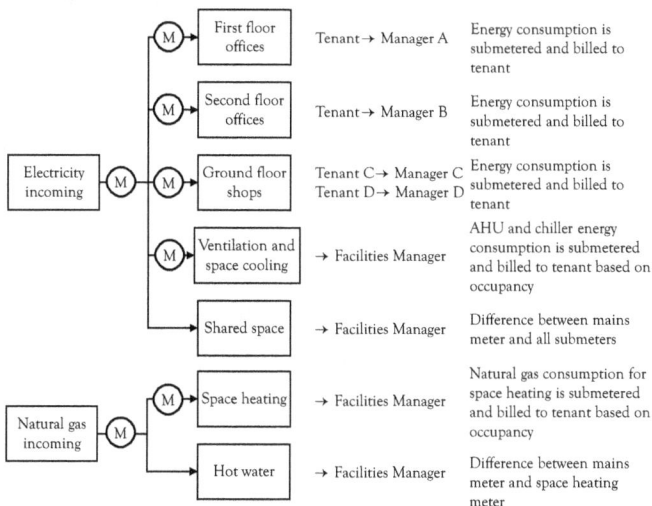

Figure 4.4 Simple metering map for a small office block

On the off chance that key measurements identified in the *Success Map* is not available, or perhaps, you'd like to submeter different sections of your core processes, the decision to install new meters should be based on economics, that is, what is the economic value of the resource consumption information or what is the economic benefit of catching a deviation in resource consumption by a set value, say 10 percent, 20 percent, or even 30 percent.

That value serves as a guide as to how much money could be invested in the submetering system. For example, in application A, a five percent deviation might be worth $10,000, whereas, in application B, the same deviation might be worth $100. For a meter that costs $2,000, it is economical for application A but not for B.

Performance Indicators for Resource Productivity

Once the existing and any new metering information is installed and calibrated, the next step is to define performance indicators for the business as a whole, and various functions and processes.

Very frequently, when it comes to performance indicators for any corporate initiatives such as energy, quality, or health and safety, attention is focused on a few high-level indicators that represent the overall results. In the context of resource productivity, this would typically be "right first time" or percentage of waste, absolute energy consumption or specific energy consumption, absolute water consumption or specific water consumption, and so on.

These types of high-level indicators are, while simple to use and easy to benchmark against other companies are a lagging indicator, that is, there is no way to affect and change the performance indicators once it has been reported. Take specific energy consumption (e.g., kWh/unit output) or specific water consumption (e.g., m³/unit output), for example, it is computed by measuring the whole month's consumption and dividing it with the whole month's production or service provision. Once the indicator is calculated, it is too late to make improvements or changes that can affect the performance for that month.

To actively manage resource productivity and to manage the process on a day-to-day or week-to-week basis, businesses use leading indicators—indicators that, when monitored, can physically allow employees to take action, correction, and corrective actions to positively affect resource productivity before the month-end data are set in stone.

This is where the *Success Map* comes in handy as it also highlights how different functions within the business use different information for their day-to-day work, thus the different types of indicators for resource productivity purposes. A *Success Map* is also useful in identifying the type of information and communication that is specific to the people performing their tasks and job roles.

Operators and technicians in a manufacturing environment readily relate to information such as flows, temperatures, pressures, idle time, and mean time to failure. Occupants in an office and/or build environment staff need a different set of indicators to those of manufacturing operations. Some examples are office temperature and lighting hours.

For managers within the same business, their activities and responsibilities vary depending on their job roles. A performance indicator relevant to one manager isn't the same as the other managers in the business or indicators for his/her subordinates. It is most probably a composite of indicators or indicators based on their job function within the company. For example, a production manager will relate to production throughput, right first time, the idle time during a changeover, and so on; a maintenance manager will relate to mean time between failure, frequency, and duration of downtime, and so on; a utilities/facilities manager will relate to boiler or chiller efficiency, leaks, and so on; a sales manager will relate to sales volume to capacity ratio, and so on.

While the above indicators have an indirect effect on resource consumption, they are indicators that affect day-to-day operations, thus when monitored and controlled, affect resource productivity. They are meaningful only to those at the right job roles and levels and can be measured and/or qualified.

The energy manager, water manager, environment manager, or other roles responsible for resource productivity will relate to the overall resource use, consumption, and efficiency, number of identified projects, and so on. These lower-level (but leading) indicators aggregate up to through the company where the leadership team looks only at the overall (but lagging) indicator.

To communicate effectively with different groups of people, it is important to tailor different sets of information to the needs of the people. Using one or two resource indicators for everyone in the company means that many employees cannot relate to the information and are less able to participate in the company's efforts to reduce consumption.

Similarly, the overall resource productivity initiatives or projects also need a performance measurement against their overall objectives and targets. This includes items such as the status of initiative against the planned result and may be measured in multiple ways including financial budgets, project timelines, number of improvement projects identified/in progress, the status of the project, and so on making up the whole initiative.

When performance indicators are organized and planned using a mix of leading and lagging indicators and strategic and tactical indicators, employees understand how their job roles contribute toward resource productivity, how this is measured, and everyone can come together and put in a concerted effort to make it happen.

Benchmarking

The primary purpose of measuring resource consumption and calculating performance is not about having the data for filing purposes or reporting to the shareholders, stakeholders, and/or interested parties. The primary purpose is about knowing how much raw materials, energy, and water you are consuming and how much waste you are generating, compare that against where you want your company to be, and make a decision on the gap to close and how fast you want to close it compared to your competitor.

There are two major categories of benchmarks available in the industry. The first type of benchmark is a measure of overall resource productivity, that is, an overall measure of resource consumption per unit of output, for example, manufacturing energy benchmarks (kWh/unit product and kWh/m^2); and water consumption benchmarks (L/room and m^3/kg), and so on. These benchmarks are generally published by NGOs, professional bodies, and/or trade bodies. They may also be published as minimum efficiency standards or regulations.

The second type of benchmark is in the form of equipment-specific resource productivity, for example, boiler efficiency and chiller COP. These benchmarks are more widely available and come from sources such as design specification of your existing equipment, manufacturer specification for new equipment, similar equipment from other companies, facilities, and/or installation. These types of benchmarks may also be compiled in testing standards, equipment ratings, and technology lists.

As mentioned earlier, the key is in measuring and calculating your resource productivity, comparing it with the relevant benchmarks, determining if there is a gap, and using the information to generate business cases and prioritize actions and speed for improvements.

CHAPTER 5

Make Resource Consumption Visible and Set Science-Led Improvement Baselines

... I often say that when you can measure what you are speaking about, and express it in numbers, you know something about it; but when you cannot measure it, when you cannot express it in numbers, your knowledge is of a meager and unsatisfactory kind ...

—Lord William Thomson Kelvin [168]

To a large extent, resource use and consumption are invisible to many people: they don't see the resource (e.g., air flow inside ducts and electricity in cables); if they do, they see it for a fraction of time (e.g., water flow from taps in washrooms); and they also don't pay for it. As such, many people do not think much of resources.

To get the leadership team, your peers, and colleagues interested in resource productivity, you will need to make it visible. There are four technical tools to bring into light knowledge of how much resources they consume, and what improvement opportunities are applicable and economical—these are benchmarks, profiles, baselines, and auditing.

In Chapter 4, we looked at measurements, performance indicators, and benchmarks. This chapter looks at the role of profiles and baselines as a tool to make resource productivity visible, thus allowing you to view it as a variable cost (as opposed to a fixed cost), and how it could be managed and controlled. In Chapter 6, we will look at audit as a tool to identify relevant and cost-effective opportunities for improvement.

Profiles

In simple terms, a profile is a graphical representation of the users of a specific resource (say energy or water) and the proportion of consumption compared to other users at a specific moment in time. Figure 5.1 shows two types of profiles: a pie chart and a Sankey diagram.

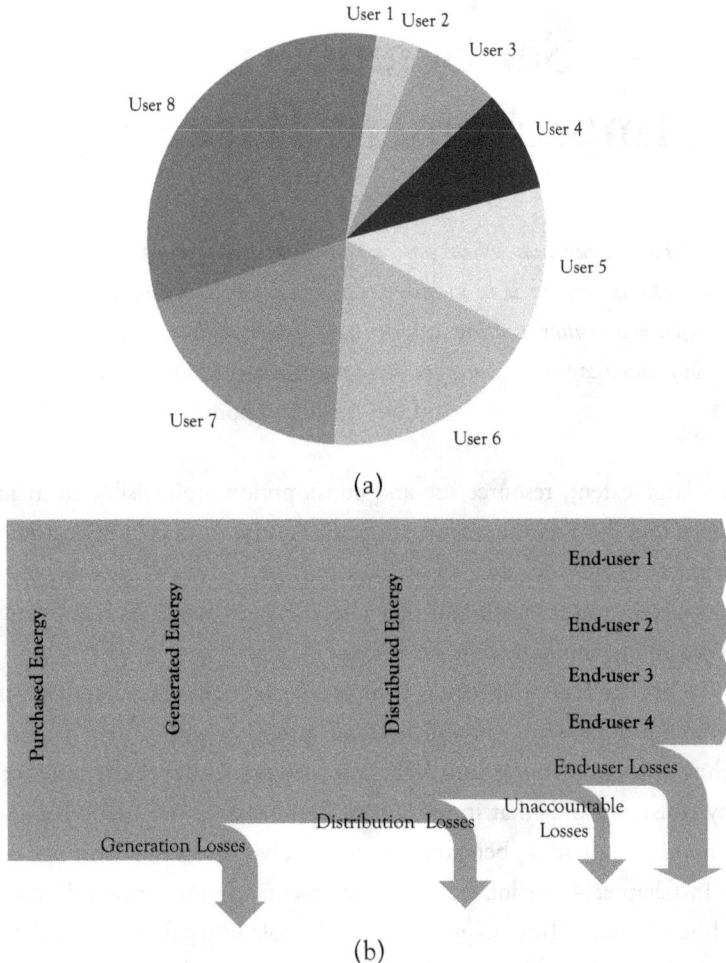

(a)

(b)

Figure 5.1 Two different types of profile: (a) pie chart and (b) Sankey diagram

As can be seen, a profile indicates where a particular resource is used and its relative quantities. A profile, thus, becomes beneficial in highlighting and communicating with nontechnical folks about resource use and consumption which are hidden from view.

A good example is energy use and consumption in an office-based business. An office worker would think that his or her energy consumption is limited to lighting and IT equipment. Energy consumption in an office is more than lighting and IT. Figure 5.2 shows the typical energy users in an average office and their typical proportion. Energy consumed by ventilation, heating, cooling, and hot water is significantly larger, yet it is frequently unseen by office employees.

Without the knowledge of a profile, many building operators focus their improvement efforts on lighting and computers. As ventilation,

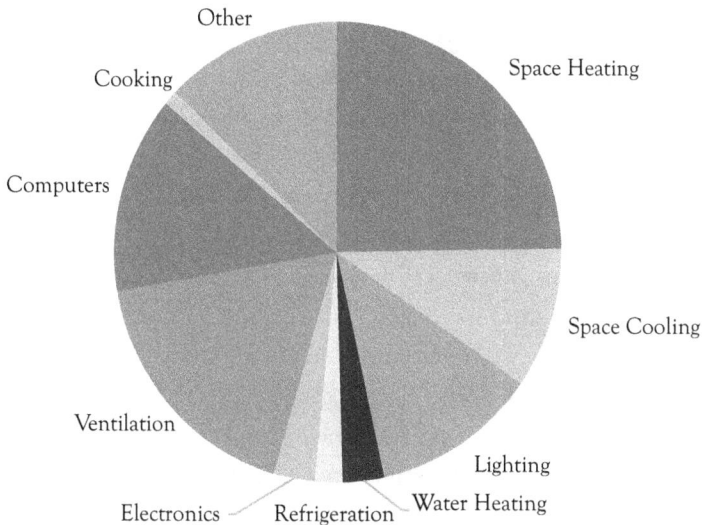

Figure 5.2 Energy profile of an average office in the United States

Source: [169]

heating, and cooling are not seen, no initiatives are carried out in these "invincible" energy users. With the aid of a profile, these hidden users can become visible, and reduction efforts are targeted and managed based on statistical significance.

Another good example is purified water consumption in, say, a hospital or a food manufacturing plant. Often, the people who operate, maintain, and routinely test the water quality are different people, departments, or even from a different company who do not know how purified water is consumed or if the application warrants it.

On the other side of the coin, the users of purified water seldom know what processes were involved in making the purified water, in maintaining the water system, or that it costs at least 2.5 times more to generate and dispose of them compared to potable water. Purified water can sometimes be found dripping from many taps thinking that they are "just" small drips and of no significant matter, or they are used for applications where potable water would suffice.

To prepare a profile is relatively straightforward, but it has to be done by an individual resource, that is, energy only, water only, and so on. This is because, energy, water, raw material, and waste are measured using different methods and in different units. As such, comparing different resources using the same pie chart will be like comparing apples, oranges, strawberries, and pineapples. An initial pie chart can be prepared by summing up the total quantity of resources consumed. This could be based on the monthly invoice, average month, or the sum of 12 months' data.

Then, split the consumption by various users. Take energy (natural gas) for a start, we can spot measure the boiler efficiency and calculate the losses due to boiler inefficiency. The ventilation system might be a fixed airflow system with known ON and OFF times. It is, therefore, possible to calculate the heating duty and natural gas consumption due to heating. The same can be done for other natural gas/heating users.

Then, we can use the same technique to break down electricity users. For all fixed speed pumps and fans, such as the ventilation system mentioned, we can spot measure the electricity consumption and calculate the electricity consumption. The same can be done for other fixed consumption users with known ON–OFF timings, such as lighting, PCs, and IT equipment. If you are using an air conditioning unit for cooling, it is possible to analyze the electricity consumption and cooling degree-day data to derive the electricity due to cooling. (See baselines) For other electricity users, spot measurements over a representative period would be a good start.

Once all of the known users are calculated, an "energy" profile can be prepared. Apart from a representation of various energy users and their proportion, it can also be used to ensure the sum of calculated consumption is the same as invoice, and that identified opportunities do not save more than its actual consumption!

Baselines

Baselines are the graphical relationship between resource consumption and business activity. Using a simplistic diagram to illustrate, when a company plots its resource consumption versus its key business activity, for example, production output and service provision, they may be able to draw a best-fit line depicted in Figure 5.3.

The formula that describes the best-fit-line is the baseline. Figure 5.3 shows this as a straight-line relationship, $Y = mX + C$. Three types of information can be gleaned from the baselines.

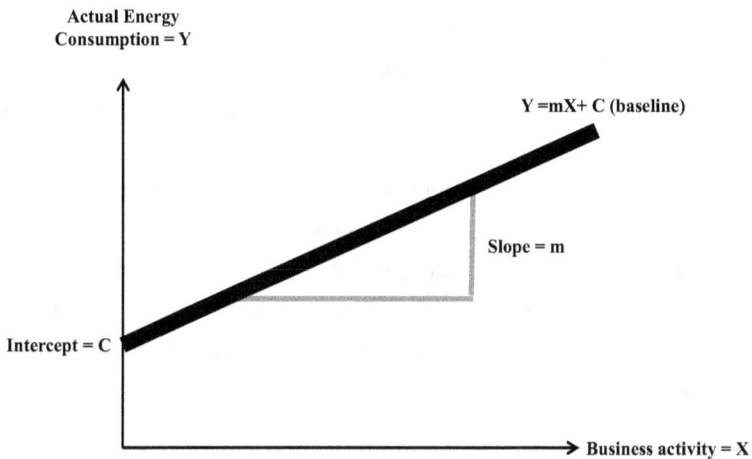

Actual Energy Consumption = Y

$Y = mX + C$ (baseline)

Slope = m

Intercept = C

Business activity = X

Figure 5.3 Energy baseline of a fictitious industrial company

Source: Adapted from [174]

1. The relationship contains an intercept, C, known as fixed consumption, or baseload. This would be the energy consumption regardless of whether the process is in operation or not.
2. The relationship contains a slope, m, known as the marginal consumption, specific consumption, or energy per unit production or sales. This would be the energy consumed to create a saleable product or service.

The same can be developed for other resources consumed in any business. Often, for energy and water consumption, the energy consumption and water consumption are rarely zero when the business isn't producing or selling its products or services. The electricity or heating or cooling stills need to run, and the kitchen and toilet still need to be flushed. Recalling the types of benchmarking information in Chapter 4, the overall resource productivity benchmark is a measure of "m" only. For raw materials and waste, C can often become zero. In the course of preparing the baselines, if you expect C to be zero but it isn't, then an investigation is required to understand where the raw material leakage is/are.

A business can use its baselines to forecast and budget resource consumption: with known or forecast production levels or service levels (X), the baseline predicts, based on historical data, the expected resource consumption (Y). Baselines, therefore, graphically demonstrate to top management that resource consumption varies with business activity—a variable cost.

By comparing baselines from two different periods, a business also can confirm if they have achieved improvements. For example, a comparison of a company's water baselines before and after implementing improvement projects (comparing the m's and C's) can determine if the business has made an overall improvement or merely moved the consumption from fixed to variable or vice versa.

3. A closer examination of baseline information informs the business where they should target their resource productivity efforts by looking at the marginal consumption and the fixed consumption.

A business may find it has a big fixed consumption and a small marginal consumption (Figure 5.4 left). The priority for this business would be to look for opportunities to reduce its baseload (C). This would be to look for equipment and machinery that are running when there is no production or business activity. Some of this may be machines being left idle for significant periods, resource wastage, and so on. Some fixed loads such as data centers, server rooms, and uninterruptible power supply rooms may be business-critical and/or cannot be turned off or turned down.

While rare in real life, a business may have a small fixed consumption and a large marginal consumption (Figure 5.4 right). These companies should prioritize by looking for opportunities to reduce their marginal

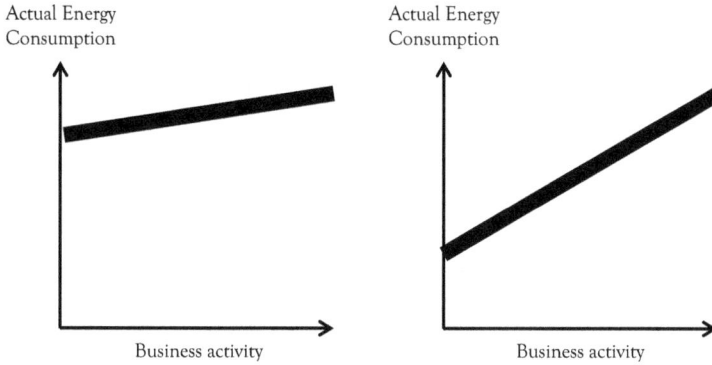

Figure 5.4 Two different energy baselines

Source: Adapted from [174]

consumption (m), that is, opportunities associated with the production process or service provision. These opportunities are normally associated with using efficient equipment and machines such as high-efficiency pumps, variable speed fans, or modern control systems.

A business may also find that its resource consumption does not vary with its business activity, this is, no baseline relationship can be drawn. In this case, resource consumption has not resulted in any productive use. Priority should, therefore, be in identifying the root causes and plugging these losses.

In the manufacturing environment, product mix (or formulation), machine choice, and weather may exert a statistically significant contribution to resource consumption. In the built environment, weather and occupancy tend to be the dominant variables. These components could be established independently using techniques described earlier and brought together into a multivariable (sometimes known as multivariate) analysis.

Even identical manufacturing plants or service providers located in different geographic locations will use resources, particularly energy and water, differently. Take a water treatment plant generating softened water. A location with higher calcium content in water would require higher salt consumption compared to one with a lower calcium content.

Therefore, in real companies, not many baseline relationships conform to a straight line. This means that other relationships or multivariable relationships are possible and that each business will need to determine its baseline and decipher the information contained in the baseline.

Case Study: DerGrundhofer Vollkornbäcker— Peter Thaysen [170]

DerGrundhofer Vollkornbäcker—Peter Thaysen is one of over 20,000 small craftsman bakeries in Germany. It bakes loaves of bread, buns, rolls, cakes, and pastries daily from its 950 m² production facility. A detailed material and energy balance was developed to account for all of the raw material, waste, and energy consumption.

The bakery utilizes electricity and furnace oil as sources of energy for which 85 percent of the energy is in the form of heating with lighting, mechanical systems, and cooling contributing five percent each in the form of electricity. Of the heating users, 73 percent is due to baking the bread, six percent in fermenting the dough, five percent in mixing, six percent used in cleaning processes, and two percent in office and shop heating. The remaining seven percent are utilized in various locations.

Energy performance of the bakery, as is common in the baking industries, is through kWh/kg of flour processed, works out to be 1.37 kWh/kg, and compares better than industry averages ranging between 1.47 and 1.56 kWh/kg. Only electric ovens have better energy performance at 1.27. At the time of analysis, DerGrundhofer Vollkornbäcker—Peter Thaysen had three oil-fired ovens and five electric ovens and had a program to replace the oil-fired ovens with electric variants.

The use of a methodological energy audit process and life cycle costing showed that the electric ovens are more expensive to run as electricity is nearly twice more expensive than oil. The audit also identified 11 opportunities to further improve its energy performance, including the following:

- Scheduling the production runs to operate the baking at full loads rather than partial loads.
- Scheduling the production runs to enable the ovens to bake loaves of bread with the highest temperature followed by lower

temperature bakes, thus minimizing product changeover and the need to reheat ovens to higher temperatures.

- Recovering heat from the hot ovens to preheat hot water used in the manufacturing process.
- Reusing adjacent oil-fired oven exhaust to preheat cooler ovens.
- Halting the replacement of oil-fired ovens with electric variants.
- Insulating heated pipes.
- Periodic cleaning of light bulbs to prevent dust build-up, necessitating more light fittings over time.
- Routinely check the calibration of the heating thermostat, thus avoiding excess heating.

The management approved and implemented all of the identified projects to enable the production facilities to measure and report on their energy performance, to use a science-based targeting for future energy consumptions, and to keep track of the budgeted improvement projects. The identified projects gave an energy performance of 1.28 kg/kWh or an equivalent of six percent energy savings.

Case Study: Lodge at Winchelsea [171]

Lodge at Winchelsea is a small-to-medium-sized hotel in Sussex, England. The hotel consists of 28 guest rooms of various sizes and capacities, a reception, bar and restaurant, kitchen, one function room, guest and staff toilet facilities, laundry, staff accommodation, and potted plants and hedges.

Water consumption by paying hotel guests, by and large, is hard to monitor and control while maintaining customers' positive experience and without impacting or diminishing guest comfort. Analysis of the water consumption weighted to the occupancy ranges between 270 and 310 m^3/occupied bed. The hotel's water performance is comparable to the industry benchmark with the best at 227 m^3/occupied bed and the worst at 435 m^3/occupied bed.

All water consumed by the hotel incurs two separate charges: water consumption charge and eventual wastewater disposal charge. Any water saved would also save on wastewater disposal. In an initiative to reduce wastage, improve competitive pricing positions, and improve its environmental impact, the hotel assessed, identified, and implemented several water reduction projects.

Analyses of the water consumption indicate that 80 percent of the water consumption is in the guest rooms. With showers accounting for over 50 percent, toilets, taps, and housekeeping account for the remaining guest room consumption in roughly equal proportions. Kitchen, restaurant, laundry, and staff accommodation account for the remaining 20 percent.

An audit of the water consumption showed several options for reducing water consumption. Among others:

- Replacing the pressurized showers with aerated showers reduces the water consumption by nine L/minute.
- Using behavior change messaging to reduce the average shower times from eight minutes to four or five minutes would give an additional 20 percent water savings per shower.
- Reducing the average flow rate of cold water of 20 L/minute and hot water of eight L/minute to five L/minute through the use of mixer taps with flow regulators.
- Replacing the standard 13 L/toilet cisterns with a dual flush (13 L/6.5 L), thus giving an average of 9.5 L/flush.
- The retrofits above would also provide water savings in the same proportion for the housekeeping activities.

Postretrofitting, the water performance figures were reported to be averaging at 242 L/occupied bed with a range of between 210 and 267 L/occupied bed. This represents a savings of between 20 and 24 percent water savings. With a capital cost for the retrofits at £2,500, it has a simple payback of 1.25 years. Factoring in a scheduled tariff increase for water and wastewater, the payback reduces to one year.

Case Study: Ginsters [172]

In 1968, dairy farmer Geoffery Ginster began baking Cornish pasties in an almost derelict egg packing barn in Callington, United Kingdom. With a 30-strong staff, he set out to bake 20,000 hand-crimped Cornish pasties in a week. Now, Ginsters manufactures 3,000,000 pastry products per week at its factory, including deep-fill sandwiches, tortilla wraps, buffet bars, sausage rolls, a deep-fill savory slice range, and Cornish pasties. It employs over 900 people. The Cornish pasty is Ginsters' best-selling product.

The bakery process includes (1) delivering, unpacking, and chilling ingredients; (2) preparation for mix and pastry; (3) rolling and cutting the pastry and removing scraps for reworking; (4) adding the fill ingredients, sealing with pastry, cutting and glazing; (5) cooking, followed by cooling and chilling; and (6) quality assurance, wrapping, and boxing before warehousing and dispatch.

In 2003, following site visits from Envirowise (a former UK Government initiative), Ginsters realized it knew little about its resource use, waste streams, and that there was a potential to realize significant cost and environmental benefits. A monitoring system was established to identify the true costs of waste and to calculate the cost savings.

Originally, Ginsters believed its waste costs five to 10 p/kg of waste—the disposal costs it paid. Taking into consideration energy, water, raw materials, labor, and transport, the true cost was closer to £1/kg—10 to 20 times higher than the disposal costs.

Ginsters established a range of key performance indicators (KPIs) and managers were allocated consumption quotas. Performance against the KPIs were discussed at daily meetings and then reported to management using a "traffic light" system to highlight anomalies and pinpoints problem locations.

Armed with the monitoring system, regular environmental best practice training, and awareness on the cost of poor practices sessions were organized. There were regular communications on environmental performance in all factory areas. Improvement projects were implemented in part fulfillment of its ISO 14001 environmental management system certification, and in part due to cost savings.

The monitoring system revealed a significant amount of water was being consumed for cleaning in the bakery and production areas. To reduce this consumption, Ginsters introduced a low-volume high-pressure hose nozzle system with trigger controls. During 2006/2007, total water consumption (hot and cold) in the production area fell by around 50 percent.

Pastry waste was another big improvement made at Ginsters. In the past, it used 22 different pastry specifications for different customers. This meant that scraps from different lines could not be mixed and reworked together, leading to the generation of significant food waste. Ginsters minimized this by standardizing the pastry recipe, in consultation with its customers. The production line creates six rows of products in one go with trims on the sides. With a minor retooling and the purchase of extra cutters, seven rows of product could be achieved through no major additional investment. This reduced pastry wastage and increased productivity.

Other food-saving initiatives include installing new meat mincers that are more effective at removing gristle. This has halved the original four percent meat loss to two percent, and there are plans to introduce more sophisticated machinery to reduce meat loss to 0.5 percent.

Despite a 16 percent increase in production between 2003 and 2006, total food waste has fallen by 47 percent, with a corresponding 38 percent reduction in disposal costs. All food waste is now sent to an anaerobic digestion plant in North Devon where it adds to the fuel stock for renewable electricity generation and fertilizer manufacture.

In addition to food waste reduction, Ginsters worked with its suppliers and customers to reduce the packaging associated with incoming and outgoing goods. For example, it changed from receiving margarine in small, individually wrapped blocks to bulk reusable containers with a one-tonne capacity, and to receiving meat in returnable, reusable plastic trays and bins instead of cardboard boxes.

The introduction of robotics to the packing stage further reduces damage to boxes and speeds up the processing. Collectively, a 30 percent reduction in cardboard waste per tonne of product in 2006 compared with 2003. All cardboard waste is now returned to Ginster's cardboard supplier, which provides a compactor on-site, collects the cardboard free of charge, arranges for its recycling, and supplies new cardboard at a discount.

CHAPTER 6

Identify Improvement Opportunities

... You can waste time, you can waste labor, and you can waste material—and that is about all. You cannot waste money. You can misuse money, but you cannot waste it; it is still somewhere. ... Time, energy, and material are worth more than money because they cannot be purchased by money. Not one hour of yesterday, nor one hour of today can be bought back. Not one ounce of energy can be bought back. Material wasted, is wasted beyond recovery. These things are in the front of values. They are the precious elements out of which all wealth is made. ...

—Henry Ford [135]

As introduced in Chapter 5, the fourth tool to make resource productivity visible is through a resource audit. The primary function of an audit is to use a systematic and methodological approach in identifying the relevant, practical, and cost-effective opportunities to consume less and/or fewer resources in the business as a whole. If you recall from various chapters, making every component of a core process efficient does not mean that it, as a whole, is efficient.

When it comes to identifying ways to use less energy, water, and raw materials or generate less waste, most businesses are aware of the opportunities available to save and reduce wastes in their workplace. Many people can instinctively identify typical opportunities for improvements, such as fixing leaks, turning lights off, using LED light bulbs, fitting variable speed drives, using high-efficiency motors, and using aerated water taps.

The gut-feel approach to resource productivity is a great start. It is said that if you can see an opportunity, the opportunity can be quantified and turned into reality. If you cannot see the opportunity, the opportunity does not exist. An audit de-biases the gut feeling by putting real numbers to it. It achieves this by applying *systematic and methodological* processes to identify opportunities that are *relevant* to your company, are *practicable,* and are *cost-effective.*

For many, the gut-feel approach is also based purely on the efficiency principle without looking at the reducing use and consumption principle, which would require a good look at the core process needs. If done right, the audit looks at the core process to identify its needs, find ways to reduce use and consumption, and increase effectiveness, before finding the most efficient means to deliver the needs.

In industry, many people and companies provide audit services. Some called their service using different names. When I use the term *audit*, I specifically mean a resource productivity audit of your core and support process. It has defined steps (or stages) in the audit process, a description of tasks to be carried out in each step, and a defined outcome.

The audit process generally starts by collecting evidence, analyzing data, developing options for improvement, quantifying the costs and benefits, and planning its implementation. The audit process facilitates planning and serves as a checklist to study all resource productivity elements required by the core and support process and to ensure all possible benefits and costs are analyzed.

The recommendations have to be relevant to the context of the business (Chapter 1). Imagine a tenant of a leased office space receiving an energy audit report to improve the building fabric. Those recommendations, while valid, are relevant to the building owner but not to the tenant.

The audit findings and recommendations have to be practicable. For example, retrofitting a ventilation system with a heat pump may look good paper and is a commonly found recommendation. If there is no space to install a heat pump and/or the working area is inaccessible, it makes the recommendation not practicable and useless.

The recommendations also need to be cost-effective. In this case, it points to a prerequisite: the audit is based on real and measured data. Some of the data may be available from existing processes; others may need additional measurements according to the formulas established in Chapter 4. The resource productivity opportunities are quantified, costs are established, and the return on investment is calculated and compared to the company's investment threshold.

Technical Audits

As mentioned earlier, a resource productivity audit has many names in the commercial and industrial world. Audits, assessments, analysis, diagnostic, studies, surveys, scan, opportunity finding, treasure hunt, and kaizen are some of the variants commonly found. For energy audits, companies prefix the word with *energy*; others may choose *energy efficiency*, *low carbon, opportunity days, ESCO proposal development*, and so on. The same can be said for water, waste, and other resources.

Variations can also be found in terms of the scope of works, approaches, and work methods that are specified by the service provider. Some service providers use the term "audit" to mean a cocktail of tools and techniques with varying levels of applicability, detail, thoroughness, and degree of confidence in the findings.

A source of consistency between the available resource audit offerings is in a generic ISO 14015 environment due diligence assessment, and specifically for energy, ISO 50002 energy audit. Both standards specify the key steps and the specific tasks in the various steps, the roles and responsibilities of the auditors and business, and the required reporting output. Between the two standards, ISO 50002 closely resembles and can be applied with little changes to resource productivity.

With the steps and requirements defined, businesses can compare audit offerings on an apple-to-apple basis and transparency in pricing audits. It also allows managers to follow the progress of an audit and to check if every task has been carried out. The process of an audit, as specified in ISO 50002, is shown in Figure 6.1.

The detailed requirements of the standard are beyond the scope of this book because the majority of companies will engage some form of external support to do the audit. Those interested in carrying out resource audits can look at ISO 50002 for the details of an energy audit process. Of relevance to resource productivity and this book, ISO 50002 shows the application of the standards to three different details and accuracy, from the high-level overview (Type 1) to the very detailed (Type 3).

```
┌─────────────────────────────┐
│  Plan overall energy audit work  │
└─────────────────────────────┘
              │
              ▼
┌─────────────────────────────┐
│     Kick-off meeting with        │◄──────┐
│          stakeholders            │       │
└─────────────────────────────┘       │
              │                            │
    ┌─────────┴─────────┐                 │
    ▼                   ▼                  │
┌──────────────────┐ ┌──────────────────┐ │
│ List of necessary │ │ Plan to measure  │ │
│ data and          │ │ and collect site-│ │
│ information        │ │ readings         │ │
└──────────────────┘ └──────────────────┘ │
         │                   │             │
         │      ┌────────────┘             │
         │      ▼                          │
         │ ┌─────────────────────────┐     │
         │ │ Site visit to identify   │─────┘
         │ │ opportunities            │
         │ └─────────────────────────┘
         │           │
         │           ▼
         │ ┌─────────────────────────┐
         └─│ Analyze data and         │
           │ opportunities            │
           └─────────────────────────┘
                     │
                     ▼
           ┌─────────────────────────┐
           │ Report energy saving     │
           │ recommendations          │
           └─────────────────────────┘
                     │
                     ▼
           ┌─────────────────────────┐
           │ Close-out meeting with   │
           │ stakeholders             │
           └─────────────────────────┘
```

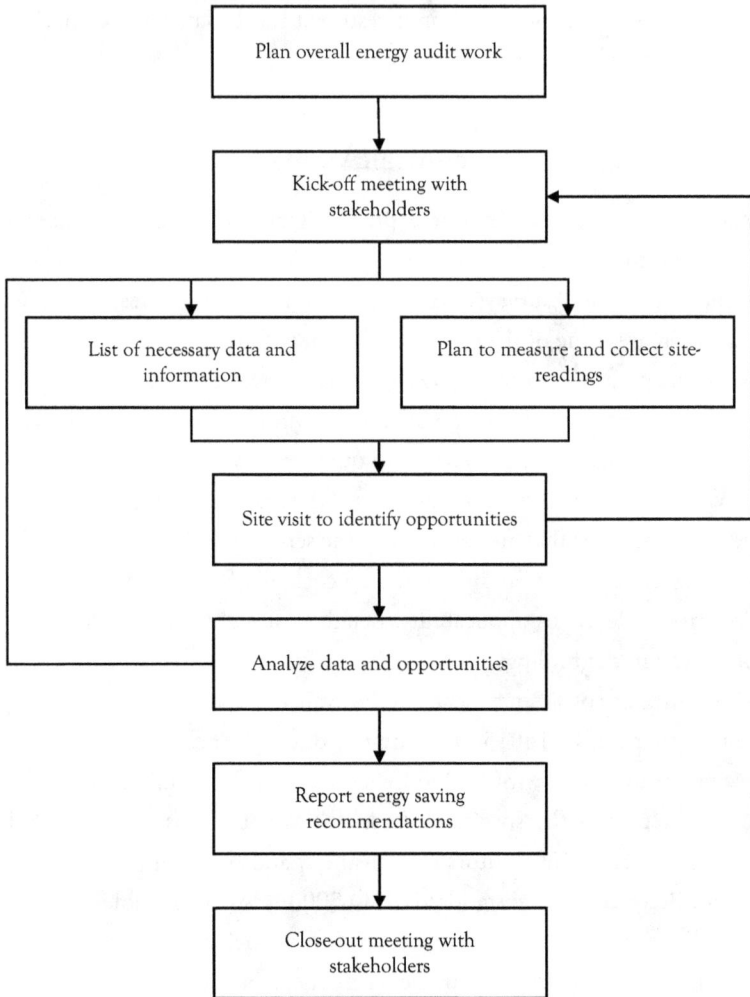

Figure 6.1 Typical flow of energy audit tasks

Source: Adapted from [173]

Type 1 audits are short and low cost, typically with one or two days on-site and several days off-site for analysis. They identify high-level key opportunities that are available in a business—a good starting point for a resource productivity initiative. Due to the short duration of the audit, opportunities identified may not contain all of the necessary information or fully represent the business processes in the company. For no-cost and low-cost opportunities, or in small- to medium-sized companies, this may be sufficient as the investments and risks are small.

Type 2 audits are more detailed than Type 1, typically lasting one to two weeks on-site, where more time is expended to understand the core process, collect data—via spot measurements or measurements over a representative period—and quantify opportunities with more accuracy. Type 2 is suited to interdependent systems of resource use, for example, manufacturing with multiple interrelated processes, ventilation with heating/cooling systems of a whole building, or opportunities identified in a Type 1 audit involving higher risks and/or capital investments.

Type 3 audit is the most detailed and uses detailed measurements over a long period. Due to the length and cost involved, it is not uncommon for Type 3 audits to be commissioned based on specific recommendations made in a Type 2 audit, especially when it will involve significant changes to the business such as major renovations, large-scale introduction of new technologies, and alternative or unfamiliar supplies of resources.

Regardless of which type of audit is done, resource productivity opportunities can come from a variety of sources. Figure 6.2 shows the proportion of improvement opportunities arising from poor design choices, poor installation and commissioning, poor planning, poor operational control, poor maintenance practices, and modification and retrofitting with more efficient equipment.

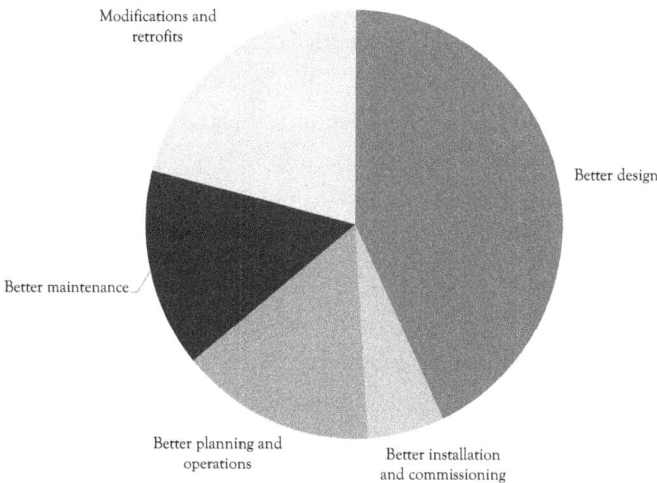

Figure 6.2 Typical sources of energy-saving opportunities

Source: Adapted from [174]

In the present market, as alluded to in the introduction and Chapter 3, there is an overreliance on retrofitting and replacing equipment with the most efficient variant. If you look at all of the types of opportunities in the previous paragraph, relying on efficiency is also one that involves capital costs. Opportunities like making better design choices, better commissioning, better planning, better operational, and maintenance controls do not involve capital costs.

Case Study: General Electric Treasure Hunt

General Electric's (GE's) "Energy Treasure Hunt"—originally developed by Toyota—is a hands-on employee engagement program. It begins with a site leadership team committing to implement identified improvement projects and putting together groups of cross-functional employees. These employees are trained to scrutinize energy use and identify inefficiencies [175].

The idea behind the treasure hunt is about applying small and incremental improvements. GE utilizes its internal knowledge about the manufacturing process, its operational and maintenance expertise, and newly gained skills to map energy flows, assess energy use, track down wastes, identify opportunities for improvement, and generate a list of projects and an action plan. If there are specific skills where in-house experts are not available, external expertise is sourced.

The treasure hunt starts on a Sunday, observing and quantifying opportunities when the manufacturing plant is not producing products. The treasure hunt continues on Monday and Tuesday when the manufacturing plant is ramping up to production speeds and into the production phase. At the end of the three-day treasure hunt, the energy treasure hunt teams would analyze and quantify at least 10 opportunities for which they would own the implementation of identified opportunities. If necessary, formal cost-benefit analyses are carried out by the same team after the event. The same team is also responsible for implementing the opportunities.

Even though there are no formal mandates for GE sites to carry out energy treasure hunts, more than 300 sites globally have carried out the hunt and have saved more than $150 million [176]. Each site typically saves 20 percent of its energy consumption. While the treasure hunt is primarily focused on energy, the most successful hunts were those that integrate operations, health and safety, energy, and other site-specific commodities [177].

The success of the treasure hunt had resulted in GE collaborating with the Environmental Defense Fund (EDF), under the Ecomagination Treasure Hunt branding, to apply the same processes to cities, universities, businesses, and other companies [178].

Case Study: GlaxoSmithKline Kaizen [179] [180]

Using a similar approach to GE's treasure hunt, GlaxoSmithKline (GSK), a pharmaceutical company based in the United Kingdom, utilizes a home-grown methodology called an *Energy Kaizen* to identify energy reduction opportunities.

Several months before the kaizen event, GSK utilizes teams of energy consultants to carry out energy audits of key energy use that are less familiar to GSK site employees. Their function is to collect energy use data, carry out preliminary data analysis of energy consumption, assess efficiency, and identify nonproduction-based improvement opportunities, such as boilers, electricity, ventilation systems, chillers, steam traps, and motors and drive systems.

Using a week-long, facilitated workshop approach, a cross-functional team—consisting of cross-functional GSK employees and the team of external experts—reviews the energy use pattern, understands the operating patterns, operational and maintenance controls, and carries out site walks during the daytime and at night-time, to identify and quantify opportunities for improvement. All opportunities for improvement are prioritized into an implementation plan.

At the end of the week, a draft implementation plan is presented to the site's management. The site's management may decide if additional work is necessary to develop the details of the plan or to approve it for implementation. Since their inception in 2009, Energy Kaizens have helped GSK sites reduce their energy consumption by 20 percent on average. A similar program for water has been developed and deployed.

Case Study: PrimePac

PrimePac is a continuous extrusion blow molding manufacturer for a range of plastic bottles, containers, and jars in North West Belfast, Northern Ireland. Due to age, only 63 percent of raw materials are turned into plastic bottles. In addition, the bottles produced had large size variations and a long tail, necessitating the use of a heated granulator to recycle the extruded "waste" back to the extruder. In addition, the time it takes to manufacture a bottle has increased by 20 percent to 12 seconds.

One of the improvement recommendations received was to replace the motors and drives. This option was tried and eventually implemented resulting in a 93 percent conversion of raw materials while consuming 60 percent less electricity at the extruder and five percent less at the granulator (due to waste reduction). In addition, the bottles and containers are consistently more uniform, much cooler to operate, released capacity for 30 percent more production from existing machines, and avoided the need to invest in another injection molding machine.

With purchase costs of £7,000, it had a payback of less than one year from the direct energy savings. When factoring in the indirect savings, the project had a payback in a matter of weeks [181], [182].

Please do take note that "behavior change" or something to that effect is not a valid improvement opportunity. As you will see in Chapter 7, many precursors need to happen or be established before the application of "behavioral change" can be made in a company. Furthermore, when technical auditors say behavior change, it means something else, like doing better planning, operating the equipment better, or carrying out maintenance, and so on. Chapter 7 also shows that without identifying the specific behavior that needs changing, it is not possible to change.

Maximizing the Value of Resource Productivity Opportunities

As can be seen from the many case studies in this book, improving the productivity of one resource can often lead to changes, sometimes positively and sometimes negatively on other resources within the business. There may also be other direct benefits from resource productivity opportunities. Some examples include quality improvements, capacity increases, maintenance reductions, greenhouse gas (GHG) emissions, other atmospheric pollutants, liquid effluents, groundwater pollution, availability of supply, price fluctuations, health and safety, employee wellbeing, capital avoidance, and so on.

Apart from the direct benefit, there may also be some indirect benefits that can increase value for the business: increasing business growth, reducing legal interventions, increasing employee productivity, and enhancing returns on investments [118].

Due to the many and varied benefits from resource productivity opportunities, it is important to identify all of the direct and indirect benefits, detractors from each opportunity, and quantify as many of them as possible. This information can then be used to generate a "holistic" business case using your company's prescribed financial evaluation tool.

From Chapter 4, you will have noted that there are many different units of measurement for energy, water, raw material, and wastes. When computing the benefits of improvement opportunities, it is important to note that a common unit is necessary to add the benefits from saving different resources.

Financial figures—cost savings or avoided capital is one such unit—but is not the only way, especially when some benefits cannot be quantified by monetary values. Some examples are reduction in environmental pollution (atmosphere, effluent, etc.), improvement in health and safety, improvement in welfare, and "intangible" benefits, such as green credentials.

Costa Coffee, for example, values three things: the benefit for the company (financial), the benefit for the employees (healthy and safety, welfare, etc.), and the benefit for the customer and local communities. Costa Coffee called this "Our Planet, Our People, and Our Communities" [183]. Other companies include additional elements such as penalties (from regulators, etc.) and media coverage into the valuation.

If multiple financial evaluation models are used in your company, preference should be on choosing a tool that is proportionate to the payback and complexity of the opportunity. For opportunities with a fast return on investment, a simple payback calculation would suffice. For opportunities with large capital costs and/or high business risks, evaluating the opportunity over its planned life considers its full benefits and costs before it is disposed of. One of the commonly used financial models for evaluating projects over their planned life is the life cycle cost analysis.

Case Study: Aviation Fuel Efficiency

Aviation is an industry where airlines traditionally look toward the next and new plane to reduce their fuel burn. Among the latest airplanes available to purchase at the moment is Airbus's A350 and Boeing's B787 series of planes.

B787 was designed for 20 percent less fuel burn than B767, and A350 burns 10 percent less than A330 through a combination of carbon fiber reinforced fuselage, improved wings, propulsion, auxiliary power, and other minor improvements.

While using the latest and fuel-efficient aircraft is a sure way of improving efficiency, there are also other operational and behavioral methods to gain efficiency. The following are some of the published examples.

In the aviation industry, airline captains maintain a considerable amount of autonomy when it comes to fuel and flight decisions during preflight, in-flight, and postflight. Virgin Atlantic experimented on 335 captains, across 40,000 flights over 27 months. They have found that providing regular feedback on their fuel burn and providing everyone a target significantly encourages fuel-efficient behaviors during preflight, in-flight, and postflight. They estimate a savings of more than $6 million over the study period [184].

The outer paint of the aircraft is normally painted in multiple coats. Up to six coats were reported in the media. Iberia found a paint formulation that would give it the wet look characteristics in just two coats: the basecoat and a clear high-gloss varnish which also protect the fuselage against the effects of weather and erosion. The net benefit is a 30 percent savings in paint and spending less time in the hangar. The paints are more durable and hydrophobic—they repel water and also discourage the buildup of dust, thus requiring less cleaning and repainting [185].

Lufthansa Technik and BASF jointly developed and successfully reduce the frictional resistance of an aircraft in the air, thus lowering the fuel consumption by mimicking nature—the structure of a shark's skin. In 2019, Lufthansa validated AeroSHARK on one of Lufthansa's Boeing 747-400 fuselage, the fuel burn and emissions reduced by 0.8 percent. By 2022, Lufthansa plans to install AeroSHARK on all of its Boeing 777 freighters which are estimated to reduce drag by more than one percent, translating to an annual savings of 3,700 tonnes of kerosene and 11,700 tonnes of CO_2 [186].

Due to noise restrictions at Heathrow Airport, wide-body aircraft take off from the airport using the "TOGA" procedure (maximum power) originally developed for the Boeing 747-400 [187]. Airbus, Singapore Airlines, Heathrow Airport, and NATS have analyzed 10 to 12 months of operating data and flight path data to implement the fuel-efficient "Flex" take-off procedure utilized at other airports. This procedure involves the A380s departing Heathrow using less power. Once the aircraft reaches a height of 1,500 ft., it uses flexible acceleration up to 4,000 ft., before continuing on its journey. This new procedure gives a fuel saving of 300 kg of fuel during every take-off [188].

Traditionally, airlines fly from preflight planned routes. On the routes are beacons and waypoints where pilots fly from one to another to get to the final destination. Emirates (in Australia) can use a "flex track" approach where airlines and ground personnel can track tailwinds and favorable weather conditions. The approach allows pilots to choose a route that is more fuel-efficient. According to Emirates, this approach saves the airline two million liters of fuel and 150 hours of flight time per year [189].

Like takeoffs, airlines traditionally land a plane by descending and leveling off multiple times before making the final approach to the runway. In some airports, particularly in modern airports, All Nippon Airways uses a "continuous descent approach" where it is more fuel-efficient and has a lower noise footprint [190].

When an aircraft is running, dust collects on the fuselage and inside the engine components. All Nippon Airways (ANA) regularly cleans their aircraft's fuselage and engines. It makes them visually appealing to customers and saves up to one percent of fuel [191].

Minimizing the Capital Cost of Resource Productivity Opportunities

Most companies will not have the opportunity or luxury to ditch the current business process and/or buildings. As such, improving its resource productivity will be based on the existing site and the existing business process. But, for businesses who have an opportunity to design from scratch or are planning to undertake major modification or refurbishment, getting the design right from the start would give the biggest resource productivity gains. This will be covered in Chapter 8.

For those with an existing business process and site, how opportunities are implemented can affect the total (or overall) resource productivity benefits and the capital costs. To illustrate this, let's consider the natural variation of energy or water consumption over time in Figure 6.3 (left). The figure shows a lot of "noise" in the measurements.

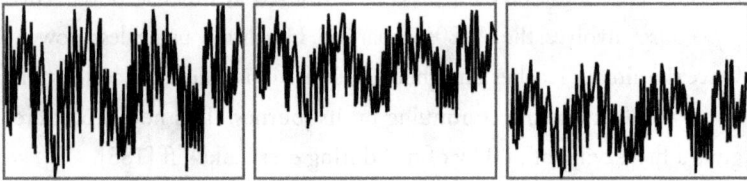

Figure 6.3 Consumption variation over time

Source: Adapted from [174]

Better planning, operations, and maintenance will "quiet down" the variation of resource consumption, that is, have a smaller spread of data points. The resource consumption spread may center on the original mean. It could settle at a higher (middle) or lower (right) mean than its original mean. This is particularly true for manufacturing plants with many different types of machines and processes that interact with one another.

For cases where the variation centers on its original mean or lower, the resource consumption no longer peaks at the original mean, thus enabling the use of smaller machines during retrofits, refurbishments, and equipment replacement. The smaller equipment will also be cheaper to buy, install, and operate, making the economics even better. As such, to maximize the benefit of resource productivity and minimize investment cost, how opportunities are prioritized for implementation should follow a simple five categories as shown in Figure 6.4.

The first category is to identify and implement housekeeping opportunities. Using a simple yet common sense "turn it off; turn it down" thought process, these opportunities can be identified with relative ease, especially when the business is not producing any products or providing any services. Companies familiar with lean manufacturing may find the 5S methodology or Defects-Overproduction-Transportation-Waiting-Inventory-Motion-Processing (DOTWIMP) methodology familiar and applicable.

An example of this thought process in a build environment or a small- and medium-sized manufacturing process comes from operating according to manufacturer's guidelines and best practices, implementing good maintenance, turning things off when they are not needed, reinstating and improving insulation, reducing waste, leaks, idle time, production rate losses, and policy for not opening taps and hoses when it is unattended.

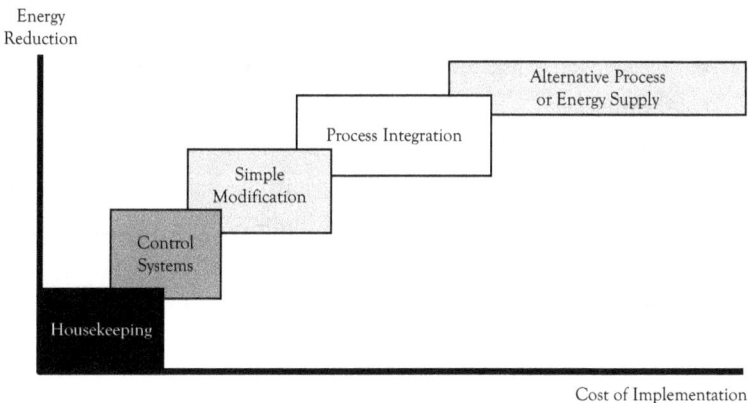

Figure 6.4 Energy maturity model

Source: Adapted from [174]

In larger manufacturing plants and industrial processes, the same thought process can be targeted through eight focus areas:

1. Ensuring that all equipment is sized to match actual demand with minimal excess capacity. Some of the areas to consider are ensuring the minimum, normal, and maximum operating requirements are known and/or established; and ensuring that equipment specification meets the operating requirement without excessive excess capacity.

2. Ensuring all equipment is installed correctly as described in the user manual and design drawings. Some of the areas to consider are requesting installation information from the supplier before purchasing the equipment; reviewing the design to ensure that the recommended design requirements are met; reviewing the actual installation to make sure it is as per design; allowing time during installation for these reviews; and ensuring all issues are satisfactorily addressed before handover.

3. As far as practicable, ensure that all equipment can be turned off safely when they are not required. Some of the areas to consider are ensuring there are isolation valves, ensuring there are arrangements to make safe the plant and machinery, and ensuring the plant and machinery can be reinstated on short notice.

4. If there is a choice of machines, choose to operate one that meets the demand and at the highest efficiency point. This tie-in handily with the knowledge of the minimum, normal, and maximum operations conditions.

5. As far as possible, minimizing idle time. Some of the areas to consider are stopping the machines as soon as possible; starting the machine as late as possible; and finding opportunities to minimize product change over time and/or production handover times.

6. Ensuring that all insulation is in good condition. Establishing a routine inspection to check the state of insulation is a good way to ensure insulation is always kept in shape.

7. Ensuring ample time for good-quality maintenance to be carried out and completed. Some of the areas to consider are maintenance according to guidelines, implementing a maintenance schedule based on the recommended schedule, using the correct part, allowing sufficient time for maintenance, and ensuring maintenance is carried out by competent personnel. Where a machine uses heating and cooling, making sure that the heating and cooling valves can be tightly shut off to avoid situations of heating and cooling at the same time.

8. For recurring plant failures, ensuring that the root causes are identified and/or the issue designed out. Some of the common areas

to consider are ensuring that everyone is committed to uncover the root cause instead of a superficial analysis; using available data and information when analyzing for root causes; it may be necessary to carry out experiments and tests to arrive at a valid root cause or causes; and ensuring that the root cause or causes are addressed effectively without introducing another issue elsewhere.

In transportation, this may involve making sure the tires are inflated as instructed, ensuring the annual maintenance is completed, and increasing the vehicle's capacity utilization, for example, driving one car with four people to the same location rather than driving four separate cars.

As can be seen, it is easy to find many of these opportunities—thus the sum of these opportunities, while individually are small, can become a big saving. For example, a water leak of one drop per second is equivalent to 0.5 L/min—a tiny opportunity. However, if you have 500 of them, it becomes 250 L/min. Furthermore, the effort, cost, and business risk for addressing these opportunities are also small.

Most of the housekeeping opportunities are frequently missed, ignored, or not prioritized. In some companies, these opportunities are unknowingly side-lined in preference for larger resource productivity opportunities. In other companies, these are side-lined as a way to avoid addressing organizational politics and/or covering up previous mistakes.

However, the benefits from steadfast and zero tolerance in good housekeeping can quiet down the consumption fluctuations observed by the meter and can result in reducing the sizing, thus capital investment of latter resource productivity opportunities.

The second category requires you to tighten the control systems of existing processes. It further dampens consumption fluctuations observed and allows the process to operate closer to its mean. Some small investment may be necessary to repair, reinstate, replace, and/or introduce new control parameters into the control philosophy. A shortlist of examples in this category is as follows:

• Introducing temperature dead bands in air conditioning
  systems

- Using preventive maintenance and condition monitoring to predict and prevent equipment failures
- Improving the consistency of water quality
- Reducing excess flows, excess pressures, and excess temperatures
- Increasing cycles of concentration
- Reducing blowdown
- Utilizing control tuning
- Monitoring the efficiency of key plants or machinery

The next categories involve looking at opportunities from simple retrofits and system integration perspectives. These opportunities involve fitting (or replacing existing) with a more efficient variant or option. Examples include aerated water taps; compact heat exchangers; utilizing closed-loop systems; material and/or heat recovery—ideally locally without the need for tanks such as a closed-loop condensate system, pipework, and pumps; heat recovery for applications local to the sources of heat; and the use of variable speed drives to match supply with demand.

In large buildings and large manufacturing plants, several pieces of equipment may operate as a system, that is, several users are connected via pipes and/or electric cables and function as one whole system—each is dependent on the other, and changes in any parameter affect the whole.

For example, a motor is connected to a pump that pumps water around a distribution system (series of connected pipes) to various locations inside a building or manufacturing plant. This distribution loop may contain other pumps. Simply fitting a variable speed drive on one pump may not result in any savings as a reduction in speed may result in other pumps speeding up.

As another example, a centralized ventilation system for a large building may have heating, cooling, and humidification systems connected to it. Reducing the ventilation rate also reduces heating, cooling, and humidification. In this case, the overall savings are more than the individual savings when considered individually.

The same is also true for manufacturing plants. Say there are five processes (A, B, C, D, and E) to make a product. Reducing the resource consumption in B might also reduce the quality, and C, D, and E compensate for lower quality with more "processing" and may end up consuming more energy, water, and waste.

For these interrelated systems, assessing the resource savings for the system as a whole is necessary to quantify the overall benefit. Systems thinking is also key to unlocking larger savings quoted by the University of Cambridge [24] and Fraunhofer Institute [133]. Table 6.1 shows the key recommendations for reducing energy consumption in buildings, processes, and transport.

Table 6.1 Recommendations to achieve large-scale energy reduction

Sector	System	Recommendation
Building	Heated or cooled spaces	Wall, roof, and floor ≤ 0.15 W/m²K Windows and doors ≤ 0.8 W/m²K Thermal bridging ≤ 0.01 W/m²K Air infiltration to ≤ 0.6 Air Change Rate (ACH) Recover heat from extract air to preheat fresh air
	Hot water systems	Eliminate hot water tanks Reduce set point to 50°C Drain-water heat recovery
	Stove-top cooking	Use lids Add 30-mm-thick insulation to pots
	Ovens	Add 100-mm insulation Avoid steel casing Seal oven throughout the cooking time
	Fridge-freezer	Defrost frozen food in the fridge Mount compressor at top of the fridge Add 200-mm insulation
	Washing machines, dishwashers, and dryers	Reduce temperature set-point Recover heat from wastewater Heat recovery from dryers
Industry	Fired system	Increase insulation thickness by 150 mm Improved heat recovery from exhaust flue Recover heat from discharged heated products
	Steam system	Point of use generation Increase insulation Reduced thermal conductivity
	Driven system	Increase pipe diameter by 25% Reduce corners in pumped systems, and similar increases for conveyor and other handling systems Match flow demand with pumped supply

(Continued)

Table 6.1 Continued

Sector	System	Recommendation
Transport	Car	Reduce drag coefficient CD to 0.1 Reduce frontal area to 1.5 m^2 Reduce loaded car mass to 300 kg Reduce tire rolling resistance to 0.001
	Truck	Reduce tire rolling resistance to 0.005 and drag coefficient to 0.31
	Plane	Laminar fixed wing aircraft Unducted fan engine design
	Ship	Improve propeller and hull design Reduce fleet speed by 10%
	Train	Adapt train to tilting train designs Limit average speed to 100 km/hour for freight and 150 km/hour for passengers

Source: Adapted from [24].

The highest category, giving the biggest resource savings, comes from a step-change either in manufacturing or building design, energy and water demands, waste reduction, or all at the same time. This would be the costliest and carries the highest business risks compared to other categories described so far.

A good example comes from the pharmaceutical industry where active ingredients are traditionally manufactured in continuously stirred vats (also known as continuous stirred-tank reactors, CSTRs). The active ingredient is later extracted, and depending on the product, is crystallized, or mixed with Water-for-Injection quality water (very pure water) into vials. A new method of manufacturing involves the use of a plug flow reactor (PFRs) where the active ingredient is formed as it flows through the pipe. For the pharmaceutical industry, this is a huge change with very large resource productivity benefits but also carries very large risks.

Other examples are introducing an alternative source of energy, say, combined heat and power plant or heat pumps, changing the source of water from city water to borehole water, refitting the process with the latest designs and improvements, applying dynamic simulation and predictive controls, and extending the energy or waste heat into a district heating and/or cooling.

Case Study: Pfizer's Energy and Resource Conservation Master Plan

Pfizer, a U.S. pharmaceutical company with manufacturing and research and development (R&D) facilities across five continents, has ambitious energy and climate change program. The company, having achieved a 43 percent reduction in energy consumption relative to its sales in 2007 from a baseline of 2000, announced that it was going to reduce its energy consumption by a further 20 percent by 2012 [191].

The site in Freiburg, Germany, achieved its reduction by designing and fastidiously following an energy and resource conservation master plan. The plan identified and assessed a portfolio of about 200 projects according to their cash flow implications for the site, in terms of energy, engineering, maintenance, profit, risks, and the company's future investment plans.

The project ranged from no-brainers with low, upfront investment and relatively low risk, such as insulation, turning off and turning down air conditioning systems, heat recovery, adiabatic cooling, and automatic power shutdown procedures to high-end building renovations to improve building fabrics and utilizing renewable energy sources such as CHP plants, biomass boilers, and photovoltaic systems.

By 2011, the site implemented five major projects and 200 small projects giving 30 percent energy savings and enabling the site to operate 91 percent of the site's energy demand from renewable sources with an ultimate aim to become carbon neutral. The site was awarded the Facility of the Year 2011 by the International Society for Pharmaceutical Engineering (ISPE) [192].

Case Study: Ingersoll Rand

Ingersoll Rand is a $12 billion global corporation with brands such as Club Car, Hussmann, Ingersoll Rand, Schlage, Thermo King, and Trane. In 2014, the company made a global climate commitment to reduce its energy consumption and GHG emissions of its operations by 2020.

With 100 manufacturing sites globally, it uses three-tier energy audits (treasure hunts, expanded energy audits, and systems-specific audits) across its sites to identify opportunities for improvement by applying a sound discipline of generating business cases with the right level of detail for each of the opportunities. This has helped the company to overcome three of its biggest barriers:

1. Creating visibility in energy consumption among employees and management
2. Providing adequate information tied to each type of improvement
3. Engaging management buy-in for resources to minimize energy consumption

The energy auditing events also serve as a training opportunity for employees and managers to learn how the organization uses energy. The program has saved Ingersoll Rand more than $5 million since its inception in 2005 [193]. Ingersoll Rand achieved its target two years ahead of schedule and is working on new goals on energy consumption [194].

Case Study: Empire State Building

One of the best-known examples of an energy audit in the built environment is the iconic Empire State Building, New York. Opened in 1931, the Empire State Building draws in almost four million visitors every year to its observation tower. The building is also home to 2.8 million square feet of leasable space. At its prime, it was an exemplar of the mechanical age, with the tallest elevators and broadcasting masts atop the building.

In 2006, after 75 years of continuous use, the Malkin family and the Leona Helmsley Estate (both are the owners of the building) decided to embark on a $500 million top to bottom renovation, upgrading the aging infrastructure, and making it an exemplar energy-efficient building. The motivation was to [195]:

1. Prove the cost-productivity of energy efficiency retrofits
2. Reduce GHG emissions
3. Address other aspects of sustainability, namely water, recycling, and reuse of building materials
4. Examine the economics of capital improvement based on cash flow from reduced energy costs

In 2008, Anthony Malkin assembled a team of experts consisting of Clinton Climate Initiative as the facilitator and convenor of the project, Johnson Controls, Inc. (JCI) as the performance contracting company, Jones Lang LaSalle as the program manager and Malkin's representative, and Rocky Mountain Institute as a not-for-profit, independent peer review. Four criteria were discussed and agreed upon between the four parties [196]:

1. If the energy savings did not pay back the capital investment, JCI would pay the difference.
2. All of the team were to forgo the payment for developing the program of work, opting to be paid in its implementation.
3. Anyone should be able to copy the energy reduction process of the Empire State Building and reap similar benefits.
4. The retrofit had to emphasize energy reduction and energy efficiency to keep the cash flow and jobs in the United States.

The Empire State Building had an electrical maximum demand of 9.6 MW and emitted an equivalent of 25,000 tonnes CO_2 every year. This equated to an energy cost of $11 million per year and an energy performance indicator of 3.8 W/sq. ft.—considered to be average in Manhattan. The energy audit took seven months to complete and was executed in four distinct phases.

Phase 1 (identify opportunities) took almost one and a half months to survey the building's mechanical and electrical systems, calculate energy usage, and develop a theoretical minimum energy consumption model based on the existing tenants. The team also carried out a gap analysis using Leadership in Energy and

Environmental Design (LEED) and Green Globes criteria. More than 60 opportunities were identified.

By this time, major capital projects were underway to refurbish the building. The team also took an active part in modifying the existing capital project strategies. Of the 23 capital projects, four were put on hold, six were modified to achieve higher energy reduction, and six benefited from a capital cost reduction. The findings at this stage indicated an energy reduction of between 15 and 25 percent, with a payback (including capital cost savings) of five years.

Phase 2 (evaluate opportunities) took one and a half months where the team took detailed measurements to create an insight into how the building's tenants used energy, understand the consumption patterns, and refined the energy model developed during Phase 1. Conventional thinking regarding heating, cooling, and ventilation strategies, interior wall designs, and lighting strategies were challenged. This phase also saw the introduction of life cycle costing and tenant agreements to reduce energy consumption. The quantified opportunities for the same projects increased to between 40 and 50 percent.

Phase 3 (create packages) focuses on tenant engagement by (1) installing tenant submetering; (2) working with tenant energy champions to reduce their energy consumption; (3) providing tenants with online energy reduction education material, and (4) providing real-time energy consumption feedback.

Phase 4 (model iteration). By utilizing portfolio analysis and sensitivity analysis, the team's primary task was to minimize capital expenditure and maximize returns on investment from all available opportunities. Reasonable cost escalation factors, such as fuel, construction, inflation, discount rates, and rent premiums, were incorporated into the 15-year life cycle costing. The original 60-plus opportunities were narrowed down to a portfolio of 17 projects, reducing the maximum demand by 3.5 MW and giving a 37 percent reduction in energy.

The energy savings projects include using digital demand control (nine percent), redesigning the layout to maximize tenant exposure to daylight (six percent), removing electrically powered ventilation fans and using mechanical dampers to enable natural ventilation (five percent) [197], retrofitting chillers (five percent), installing third glazing for the windows during refurbishment (five percent), the energy management efforts of tenants (three percent), installing radiative barriers (two percent), and occupant-led ventilation (two percent).

Two of the portfolios of projects started at the end of Phase 1. Five separate energy performance contracts were agreed upon between JCI and the Empire State Building Company. These were to deliver a total of 61 percent of the savings and have a capital cost of $20 million. In addition, the work to improve the energy performance also led to an improvement in the bottom line. The average rent in 2006 was $26.50/sq. ft. The Empire State Building Company began signing new leases averaging between $40/sq. ft. and $60/sq. ft.

Science and engineering-based employees, due to their training, will have a natural tendency to favor the technically driven projects, especially the more complex opportunities described previously. However, implementing these high-risk and high-cost projects would also require knowledge and skill which often straddle across several departmental and/or company boundaries.

Management-based employees, due to their training, frequently do not fully understand the technical details to appraise the merits of technically complex opportunities and prefer opportunities that are quick to implement and carry low risks.

In reality, a combination of all opportunities from simple housekeeping and controls to the technically more complex opportunities is required to give the large resource productivity benefits published by the various studies. Implementing the simpler opportunities first helps reduce the consumption fluctuations and reduce the sizing required, and hence the capital costs and risks involved.

Overcoming the barriers to designing, implementing, maintaining, and sustaining resource productivity not only relies on a good set of improvement opportunities and support from top management but also relies on the cooperation and support of a whole host of people to make it happen. This is the subject for Chapter 7—engaging with other people within the business.

CHAPTER 7

Overcome Corporation's Inertia and Resistance to Change

... an organization's ability to learn, and translate that learning into action rapidly is the ultimate competitive advantage.

—Jack Welch [198]

To deliver resource productivity projects like clockwork, businesses need a large group of people interested in resource productivity, consciously thinking about ways to save resources, making allowances and leeway for the projects to occur, to design, purchase, coordinate timelines, install, test and commission, and operate and maintain the equipment, and then sustaining the improvements made over time.

All of these tasks require interaction and coordination with multiple stakeholders and multiple functions. In a small company, this may be easily arranged. In larger companies, there is a high probability that the projects will be deferred, delayed, and/or delivered partially. Some people immediately attribute this to poor competence, quick to find one or two people as scapegoats, and deem them to be "incompetent," sent for retraining, move to a different role, or removed from the business.

All companies, including yours, are made up of (1) a group of people working together in (2) a defined structure or hierarchy (3) using purposely designed ways of working and processes (4) as informed by its measurements and information to make saleable products and/or services. Remove any of the four components, the business would simply not function or exist. When all four are present, its synergy creates an environment for all elements to function, and organizational culture—a common way of thinking and doing things—emerges.

There is a minimum number of people, drawn from a cross-section in the business, to make resource productivity self-sustaining and drive new projects. This is the concept variously known as *critical mass* or *tipping point*. Depending on which text you follow, this critical mass occurs somewhere when 10 [199] to 20 percent [200] of people are interested and actively engaged in it.

So, coming back to the scapegoat. It may be that he or she is incompetent. It could also be due to a management style that is too focused on data and results thus making the workplace bureaucratic and inhumane. Ultimately, it will affect the human behaviors observed. Frederick Taylor, widely known as the Father of Management by Data, acknowledges the role of human factors:

> *I was a young man in years but I give you my word I was a great deal older than I am now, what with the worry, meanness, and contemptibleness of the whole damn thing. It is a horrid life for any man to live not being able to look any workman in the face without seeing hostility there, and a feeling that every man around you is your virtual enemy.*
>
> —Frederick Taylor [201]

It may also be due to the company's structure, systems, and culture hindering progress. Some examples are manufacturing or sales pressures and/or maintenance pressure soaking up all available attention, poor coordination between departments, people working on a large number of parallel initiatives, people routinely prioritizing a specific task (say production or sales) over other projects, performance measures and appraisals puts other factors (say production or sales) as more important, and a host of other reasons.

> *... The supposition is prevalent the world over that there would be no problems in production or service if only our production workers would do their jobs in the way that they were taught. Pleasant dreams. The workers are handicapped by the system, and the system belongs to the management. ...*
>
> —W. Edwards Deming [202]

... the system that people work in and the interaction with people may account for 90 or 95 percent of performance. ...

—W. Edwards Deming [203]

Pointing fingers to a culprit before looking at the whole business, its culture, and ways of working is a serious attribution error and does not help to prevent future occurrences. To resolve this issue permanently, it is important to distinguish if it is a competency issue or an organizational behavior issue.

The practical choices to addressing organizational issues converge on eight ideas or levers for change: (1) a deliverable and achievable plan, (2) an authentic leadership and management, (3) a defined communication style, (4) a psychologically safe support structure that encourages participation, (5) access to competent personnel, (6) a full awareness of the initiative, (7) a practical opportunity to get involved, and (8) availability of relevant and timely information.

Resolving these issues is a prerequisite for any "behavior change" to occur and stick—the backbone or support infrastructure for tweaking behaviors and change management. Without this glue, organizational research suggests that the application of any well-intended behavior change effort will not result in long-term success [204]. Once these building blocks are in place, you can then look at their effectiveness and assess the applicability of behavioral and organizational culture change techniques.

A Deliverable and Achievable Plan

The first and perhaps, most frequently underestimated, is the availability of a list of credible and achievable plans to save resources. Typically, company leaders declare their resource productivity aspirations, commitments, and goals—perhaps publicly at a shareholders meeting or in the stock market. Strategically and tactically speaking, there is absolutely nothing wrong with declaring the intention publicly. It focuses the attention and efforts of the business on resource productivity and pushes it in that direction.

The problem occurs after that initial statement—when the business frantically tries to decode the commitment and/or finds opportunities to meet its targets—especially when the commitment is based on an often vague idea of initiatives and/or "future technology" that is still not commercially available.

Is there a science-based pathway to achieve the target? Is it based on some future or some emerging technology? How much does it cost? What is its projected reduction? What is the delivery time? What is the detailed implementation plan? How will the declared initiative interact with your core process and with other initiatives, for example, strategy, competition, capacity expansions and/or contractions, capacity increase, new products/services, improving quality, and health and safety? If many initiatives are running in parallel, which ones take priority? How will finance, human resources, time, relevant knowledge and information, and all other resources be budgeted and made available? Have the risks been assessed? What contingencies are in place?

Any chosen objectives and targets must be broken down into smaller tasks or activities and be backed up with data analysis, real and defined projects, and a realistic timeline. This avoids setting the team for failure, thus creating a demotivating environment, a waste of time, and undue stress—especially if the public-stated commitments have to be changed at a later date, along with the customer and market implications. A poorly conceived project may also impact future proposals for improvement.

For these reasons, it may be better to focus on the technical elements of resource productivity first and then link it to the strategy before communicating it publicly. Doing it this way also avoids the need to revise the publicly stated commitments downward due to conflicts with other strategies, declaring an objective that is technically not possible, or having an aggressive plan that is not achievable.

Once the resource productivity plan is in place, like business models and tactical plans, the plan is not "fixed." In some instances, the objective may remain the same, but the individual projects may be accelerated or deprioritized due to changes in business environments, customer expectations, or other unforeseen circumstances. New projects may be added as newer technologies emerge and some existing projects that are no longer feasible or fit-for-purpose withdrawn. If this happens, it is also important to recognize that changes to the interim targets, people, and time requirements may be required.

Authentic Leadership and Management

According to a Gallup poll [205], 85 percent of the workforce are disengaged or disinterested because of a broken psychological and social contact in the workplace—the unsaid behaviors (character traits or attitude) exhibited by top management and replicated throughout the business.

Lane4's [206] "hearts and minds" survey reported that acting with integrity, showing personal interest in people, delivering on promises, and behaving consistently are activities that build trust in the company. Yet, respondents to the same survey suggest their leaders and managers, knowingly or unknowingly, exhibit the exact opposite. A later study by Google (Project Aristotle) between 2012 and 2014 also found the same issues and attitudes hindering team performance and overall performance [207].

This difficulty for leaders and managers to show authenticity has nothing to do with their capability to do their jobs. Except those born with a silver spoon and the revolving door practices for those with silver spoons, leaders and managers are probably very good and very capable in their job. The problem with inauthenticity arises due to behaviors picked up as they climb the ladder—it is a learned behavior. The higher they get up the career ladder, the more inauthentic or "fake" they appear to others.

To explain this, and mentioned at the beginning of this chapter, there are a large number of people working in the business. This also means that there are large variations of character traits. When observing the way professional business leaders [208], doctors [209], athletes [210], and even university students in competitive rowing [211], Kate Ludeman and Eddie Erlandson, and Mark de Rond found that each individual has opposing traits and behaviors within themselves. A person who acts in a controlling manner in a particular job role or situation will be collaborative in other areas. In some areas, an individual may be prescriptive in specific job roles but more flexible in other areas. A shortlist of opposing traits and behaviors is shown in Figure 7.1.

The duality of a person's character traits and behaviors is not a problem per se. Many cultures recognize the duality and the need for balance: the Yin and the Yang, for example. As a person practice more of a particular character trait and were successful, they get rewarded by positional and

Behavioral continuum

Dysfunctional	Functional		Dysfunctional
Cynical	Analytical	Visionary	Narcissist
Inept	Engage	Influence	Coerce
Pushover	Agile	Command	Autocrat
Procrastinate	Consensus	Decisive	Bulldoze
Underperform	Take instruction	Take lead	Expect the impossible
Disinterested	Pragmatic	Creative	Overly opinionated
Lags behind	Near sighted	Farsighted	Ignore near-term needs
Myopic	Reactive	Proactive	Overly critical
Maintain status quo	Conservative	Calculated	Aggressive
Deceit	Accountable	Forthcoming	Manipulate

Figure 7.1 Alpha characteristics

monetary gains. That character traits and its opposite become more pronounced as he/she climbs the corporate ladder. Over time, the brain creates a mental shortcut where leaders and managers automatically act (or react) in *the* way that made them successful—the alpha characteristics emerge. Why is this duality important? What makes them good and successful also creates the opposite which makes them vulnerable. In the context of authenticity, the duality in character traits is seen and perceived as being inauthentic.

An example is investment bankers. They are rewarded for "successful" risks they take to make a profit during the medium to long term. If they make more successful "risks," the higher up in the hierarchy they go and the more bonus they obtain. However, many bankers lead a short-term and instant gratification lifestyle—the complete opposite of what they are at work. Another example is professional team-based sports players such as soccer, football, basketball, and so on. Many professional athletes were spotted and signed from a young age. During training and competitive games, they work well together and deliver their best possible self in the games. Off the pitch, they are given a very high salary, best of health care, transport, food, and accommodation. Many of them behave in a self-absorbed, predatory and entitled manner.

When the manager or a leader takes on the alpha male or alpha female traits, he or she also automatically creates the opposite traits in others. Someone who likes to take initiative expects the rest to follow. If he or she takes on the "superhero" traits, everyone else becomes the "villain." Other traits such as commander–follower, visionary–analytical, and smart–stupid follow the same pattern. Anyone who does not keep in tow "suffers" the consequence. As a result, those being managed build their safety nets, less information is communicated, sugar coating information before it gets channeled upward, and starts to blame others.

Like the bankers and professional sports players, a leader or a manager can become addicted to the "halos"—the attention, status, power, and money the role brings. The symptom of this is easy to find: (1) looking down on others with lower stature, power, and wealth; (2) need to be perceived as "right" in their judgments; (3) doing activities that make him or her the center of attention; (4) constantly pointing out faults and mistakes of others; and/or (5) projecting their faults onto others. Halos lead them to take action based on first impression, gut feel, and previous track record of success, rather than via analysis of data and facts [212]. They become blind to their actions—they see others being the "cause" but cannot see their contribution to the "cause." Social studies suggest that 95 percent of leaders and managers think they are self-aware of their thoughts and actions but only 10 to 15 percent are [213].

A simple solution on how to (re)build leadership credibility, and to reverse the trend of employee disengagement at work, is described in Patrick Lencioni's *The Five Dysfunctions of a Team*, where top management is inclusive and open to others. This means, leaders and managers who are willing to discuss candidly their issues and concerns, collectively making a decision, holding each other to account for their actions and contributions to the overall results, calling out poor behaviors, and a relentless measurement against the intended overall result.

The first and foremost issue for the leadership team is to develop an awareness of their personality preference and emotional and cultural intelligence to sense and adapt to other team members' personality styles and situational needs. There are many personality tests available in the market, including the popular models by Myers Briggs and Daniel Goleman [214]. One of the easiest is William Moulton Marston's DISC model covering four broad personality traits shown in Figure 7.2 and summarized in Table 7.1 [215]. It bears similarities with personality classifications used by the Aztecs, the Chinese, the Romans, and were adapted by Ichak Adize [216], the U.S. Department of Education [217], and Thomas Erikson [218].

The purpose of emotional and cultural intelligence is not to pigeonhole everyone into the personality types but to adapt your style of management and communication to the context and situation. Top management has a large circle of influence in the company and acts as the center of information flows. It makes them an influencer of all initiatives. Without self-awareness and intelligence to sense the needs of others, it is not possible to discuss the issues and concerns of various departments candidly and openly. Holding each other to account and calling out poor

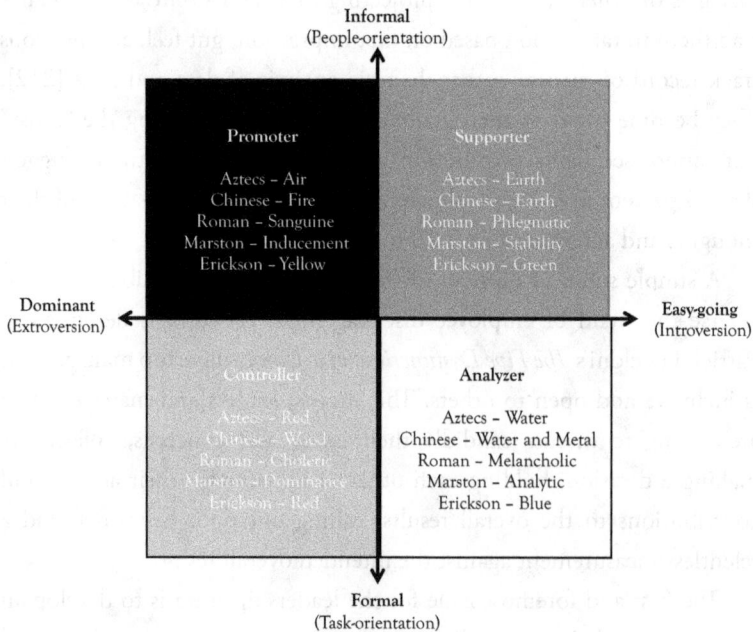

Figure 7.2 *Generic personality traits*

Source: Adapted from [214] and [215]

Table 7.1 Generic description of main personalities and character traits

	Controller	Supporter	Promoter	Analyzer
Behavior pattern	They are quick, strong-willed, and will automatically take control of the situation	They are good listeners, put others at ease, and allow others to initiate things	They are communicative, persuasive, and elevate the mood regardless of who they're with	They are quiet, level-headed, and prefer to solve problems and let others initiate
	They focus on the big picture and make things happen quickly	They focus on the human angle and values of the big picture	They focus on the human angle and values of the big picture	They take a long time to make decisions, especially when there is insufficient data, facts, and concepts
	However, they lack the attention span for minor details	However, they can appear to be wishy-washy and unclear	However, their engaging enthusiasm is blurred with unrealistic possibilities	However, their thorough and systematic analysis can appear cold and slow
	When things get going, they become control freaks, difficult to work with, and repeatedly trample on people's toes	When things get going, the need for consensus makes it difficult to know where they stand, and indecision kills the energy in other people	When things get going, the need for attention won't allow anyone into a conversation, and their stories will reflect reality less and less	When things get going, the speed of action makes them suspect sinister motives and question everyone and everything
Their main strength	Ambitious Competitive Controlling Persistent Decisive Independent Results-oriented Self-confident	Aspiring Considerate Good listener Idealistic Modest People-oriented Thoughtful Trusting	Adaptable Enthusiastic Flexible Innovative Inspiring Tactful Socially skillful Youthful	Analytical Correct Detail-oriented Logical Practical Reflective Reserved Thorough

(Continued)

Table 7.1 *Continued*

	Controller	Supporter	Promoter	Analyzer
Their main weakness	Arrogant Coercive Domineering Forceful Impulsive Impatient Taking excessive risks Unstable	Impractical Gullible Obligated Overcommitted Paternal Perfectionist Self-deprecating Wishy-washy	Afraid of con- frontational Agitated Inconsistent Lacking in conviction Manipulative Short attention span Telling lies Unrealistic	Anxious Critical Dull Moody Pessimistic Slow-moving Socially reserved Uncooperative
Body language	Commanding gestures Large personal space Lean forward Looks down as people Speaks loudly	Small-talk and gestures Neutral personal space Lean backward Friendly eye contact Relaxed	Expressive gestures Small personal space Humorous Friendly eye contact Tactile	Speak without gestures Keep others at a distance Stand or sit still Looks away from people Closed

behaviors will also be impossible as organizational silos and politics will continue to flourish.

The second issue to tackle is the willingness to have an open, candid, and honest discussion among the team responsible for the "overall performance of the company," to appraise the importance of resource productivity and its relationship with the strategic direction, the risks, and opportunities resource productivity presents to the business, and how best to address conflicts and trade-offs alongside the many issues within the company, the overall results required, and each person's contribution.

The third issue is to lead through continual and consistent personal action and through the decisions they make for the business. Being inauthentic is very easy to identify and significantly undo the messages of resource productivity. Telling employees to save energy and water but leaving his or her office lights, fans, and other energy use ON when not in use will detract from the message of authenticity.

Not all initiatives and all projects go smoothly. Conflicts and roadblocks do occur. The fourth issue to contend with is the need to visibly, audibly show that the top team cares for the overall good and overall performance of the business rather than that of a department. Any trade-offs made must be based on overall productivity and benefits. This includes anticipating areas where a potential conflict or barrier may arise, and resolving or arbitrating the conflict promptly. The availability of a safe space for employees to actively volunteer ideas or participate in resource productivity is essential.

When employees continually and consistently see top management that is: (1) focused on overall resource productivity rather than individual functional or departmental performance; (2) the united focus on overall results, it starts to breakdown organizational silos and office politics. Scott Keller and Colin Price's *Beyond Performance* and others also use a similar framework to rebuild company health alongside performance.

Communication Styles

The long-term survival of any initiative in a business, where there are many stakeholders, is not limited to *one-time* communication. According to John Kotter [93], successful companies utilize a variety of methods to communicate and they communicate ten times more often than other companies.

Operational stakeholders are excellent sources of information and your best friend to smoke out issues or identify workarounds. This is because they see the issues and work in the environment every day. Improvement in "their work environment" impacts them more than others. As such, their early buy-in and support and to smoke out potential risks and its resolutions and/or ideas for improvements is paramount to the success of resource productivity projects.

Many people who need to communicate default to creating a presentation and delivering a speech. This is not communication. It is called reading and talking *AT* people. As the saying goes, "communication is a two-way street." Furthermore, many leaders and managers struggle to listen to people and spend a lot of time dominating the conversation, coming up with answers, articulating their views, and showing people "who's the boss."

A good benchmark for communication is to use the 80/20 rule—if you are speaking for 80 percent of the time, you are not communicating— you are talking at people, directing them [219]. Also check in mentally during a "communication" to see if you are listening with the intent to rebut or if you are trying to understand the situation, trying to explore different viewpoints. Again, if you are intent on rebutting, you are not communicating.

Albert Mehrabian [220] found spoken words account for seven percent of the transmitted communication—the rest (ca. 93 percent) is made up of tone of voice, body language, and other nonverbal cues. Stakeholders pick up signs of inauthenticity through nonverbal cues—not words. Using the same DISC model described previously, Table 7.2 shows some ideas on how to communicate with the four different personalities within a business.

Be mindful of your communication style and the authenticity of your words and your actions. As described in the previous section, your actions (leading by example) and the way you speak are louder than the words themselves. Care should also be taken to make sure every opinion has an equal proportion of "air time" and to draw out those that are more silent. Contrary to popular belief, those that didn't speak do not necessarily mean they agree. It could also mean that they disagree or partially agree but there is a "but … ." The effect is called *Abilene Paradox* [221]—situations where people go along with the decision but disagree with it. By identifying them and bringing their views into the fold, it increases their participation and buy-in.

Communication about resource productivity also does not give you a license to use resource productivity jargon within the company. Using the in-company jargon is fine as it is understood. As mentioned in the previous chapters, many of the languages used in resource productivity are scientific or engineering by nature. Words such as "high efficiency," "premium," "eco," "low carbon," "green," and "smart" would be unfamiliar to many stakeholders or have many different interpretations, thus creating confusion and misunderstanding.

Do explore an array of different ways of delivering the message such as workshops, multimedia content, and interactive style of presentation. Verbal updates, the status of projects, and so on can be a good way of giving feedback and/or encouragement. Often, it can also act as a prompt for the need to talk to someone to organize some things or actions.

Table 7.2 Generic communication styles based on personality

	Controller	Supporter	Promoter	Analyzer
What annoys them	Unchallenging and mundane tasks	Sudden change in plans or personnel	Working alone or in the office	Half-baked and poorly conceived plans
	Defining minor details/milestones	Imperfection and poor execution	Surrounded by people with negative attitudes	Insufficient time and space to evaluate data and information
	No one to command or manage	Put on the spotlight (especially when unplanned)	Being told "no"	Making decisions fast
How to talk to them	Be sincere, direct, and argumentative	One-on-one or small group meetings	Be open and amiable to them	Have facts, detailed analysis, case studies, and arguments prepared
	Have the end-goal clearly described	Praise them for their work and contribution	Let them be the center of attention	Check that the facts and analysis is correct, relevant, and applicable
	Make sure additional information are available	Share with them a balanced viewpoint	Let them promote and synthesize the ideas	Make sure additional detailed information are available
	Stay firm with your message	Show them the high-level objectives and plans	Provide them with the details and follow up for a firm commitment	Distinguish the must-have and nice-to-have
How to work with them	Be firm and do not give in	Be firm and ask as a favor/goodwill	Tell him/her the big picture and the benefits of achieving it	Calmly and methodically explain expected from him and why it is important
	Explain the big picture and major steps, and timeline. Allow him/her to take charge	If necessary, ask him/her to lead—don't wait for him/her to volunteer	Let him/her think and feel he/she is doing things on his/her own accord	Point to the big picture and the valid reasons why he/she should go against his/her instincts

(Continued)

Table 7.2 Continued

	Controller	Supporter	Promoter	Analyzer
	Demonstrate the benefits of keeping an eye on the small details	Always present criticism and improvements in private	Know what your message is and the response you need	Provide the necessary data and detailed analysis
	Point out the risks involved in hurrying too much	Allow for routine periods of peace, quiet, and harmony	Do not stop until you get the answer, but always follow up	Allow time for review and decision making
	When issues pop up, explain concisely, and the expected response	Don't apply changes too often and too quickly	Gently, make sure that they honor their words with action	Rushing will lead to further delays

As eluded by John Kotter, awareness and communication should not be a one-time event. People in the business may be competent and are aware of what they need to do. However, they may forget or are unaware of the situation that needed their input. Communicate, communicate, and communicate some more. Use a variety of methods and channels. Add variety and variations to the messaging while making sure the message is consistent.

Case Study: Nissan Motor Company

Nissan Motor Company in the United States has reduced its overall energy consumption by more than 30 percent and saved more than $11.5 million [222]. One of the key tasks behind Nissan's success is the authentic communication on their energy goals and how eliminating waste makes jobs more secure in the highly competitive automotive industry.

These communications are done through a host of channels, ranging from e-mails, intranet, newsletters, interactive message boards in break areas, presentations, staff recognition awards, and ceremonies to larger events such as Energy and Earth Day fairs and energy conferences.

A Psychologically Safe Support Structure

Silo thinking and political turfs in companies are often due to people thinking about business issues such as production, services, sales, energy, water, raw materials, waste, environment, health, and safety in silos, independently from one another, and the strict adherence to departmental or functional boundaries.

The conventional thinking is for an operator to do operations, a technician does maintenance, an engineer does engineering, so on and so forth. Such strict adherence would be fine until there are cross-functional initiatives such as resource productivity, environmental protection, and health and safety, in which everyone is involved and must take part to make it a success. In such initiatives, the innate and unconscious need to pigeonhole the initiative into a department or a function creates siloed thinking and political turfs. Anyone who steps out of bound is seen as a foe, not a friend.

For example, the production department is interested in running the processes and making products. The maintenance department is interested to maintain and ensure the equipment is in the best possible condition. One wants to run it as long as possible while the other wants to stop it from running. Fitting energy, water, and waste into this picture, the work of production, and maintenance significantly impact resource consumption and waste but is typically allocated to the environment department (or similar) whose main function is to control the emissions and pollution after it has been generated by production and/or maintenance. The efficient and effective use of resources does not fit into the traditional view of production, maintenance, or environment. Each department, therefore, prioritizes their job function over that of resource productivity which benefits the overall business.

To get resource productivity done, the environment team "fights" with everyone and every department. Everyone and every department start to pay lip service to resource productivity, doing the absolute minimum to survive the day, and as much as possible blames the other person or function for "not doing their bits." Over time, leaders and managers are seen to act without integrity (saying one thing but doing the other), the continued conflicts tire and people burn out. Commitments to resource productivity wane and deteriorate. This is why 85 percent of the workforce becomes disengaged or disinterested in the workplace [205].

Some companies, realizing a change is required, reorganize or rebrand the company structure or reporting lines. As mentioned previously, frontline employees are best placed to identify problems and improvements. Yet, according to a Gallup poll, less than 70 percent of employees testified that their ideas and opinions are actively solicited and mattered [223]. As such, a reorganization or rebrand does little to disrupt the existing political turfs, thought silos, performance measurement of different functions and departments. It also does nothing to drive resource productivity but delivers more of the same [93].

What is needed is not a change in the organizational structure, but to create psychological safety in the workplace—a work environment where employees feel safe to speak up and voice their opinions, concerns, questions, and ideas without the fear of reprisals, which according to Charles Duhigg is the secret sauce that creates high-performing teams [224].

Reprisal is not limited to the formal performance appraisals and disciplinary actions but extends to include blaming, criticizing, ridiculing, and mocking others. When a psychologically safe environment exists, employees trust and respect each other, feel able to be candid, be open, contribute ideas and issues that are important to them, share information, and report mistakes.

As suggested previously, due care should also be taken to identify and encourage the quieter ones to voice out their thoughts and opinions as *Abilene Paradox* may be at play. It signals that there is additional information and viewpoints that haven't been heard. When a large number of voices have been heard, it allows decision making based on a "fuller" picture and "robust" plans to get things done.

Strong leadership is required to break office politics and organizational silos and to create a psychologically safe environment for issues to be discussed and actioned. This requires leaders and managers to be genuinely interested and committed, be exemplars for the behaviors they want to create and be actively measuring against their policies and goals. They must be seen, heard, felt to be actively contributing toward its resource productivity and taking accountability for the policies and goals it sets.

Then, leaders and managers need to actively and consistently discourage and break down silos, turf wars, and politics and to encourage thinking for the overall good of the business. The use of recognition and rewards coupled with a reprisal-free environment when raising issues or opportunities can and do go a long way in creating a positive and safe environment where ideas flourish. Research on breaking organizational silos recommends that a flatter company structure with fewer titles and slightly overlapping roles and responsibilities works [225].

Even in situations where opinions and emotions are heavily embedded and highly charged, the use of gamified techniques such as Edward de Bono's *Six Thinking Hats* [226] can be used to draw out issues and Edward de Bono's *Six Action Shoes* [227] can be used to draw out recommended course of action under the pretext of a "game."

Competent Personnel

The next component in aligning the company's capability for resource productivity is to ensure the availability of competent people so that they in turn can develop, support, and deliver results. When it comes to competence, businesses tend to think of it from the perspective of hiring someone with specialist training, provision of technical training, or contracting out the technical skills to consultants and service providers.

While some technical knowledge is required to identify, evaluate, champion, and manage the delivery of technical resource productivity projects, it, by itself, is incomplete from the perspective of getting every part of the business (each department and each person) to function like a well-oiled and resource-productive business.

There are other types of competence required to manage resources within a business ranging from tactical planning to the operational controls in different departments and job roles and technical disciplines. Like a clock, if one spring, one pin, or one gear is missing, the clock ticks slower (or faster), or it stops working.

Using *Success Maps* described in Chapter 4 as a basis, how each employee affects resource productivity can be identified. These are the actions that must be controlled to collectively minimize resource consumption. These actions are also the basis for competence to be codified, communicated, trained, and more importantly, embedded into its ways of working.

A series of *Success Maps* can be grouped to identify the roles of supervisory managers and upward to the top management. In some businesses, especially in manufacturing and industrial processes, a select few control the significant proportion of resource consumption. For example, production throughputs or feed could be the authority of the production manager or planning supervisor. As another example, the process manager may be responsible for trialing new procedures that use less energy or water.

In these instances, the decisions and actions of these key managers are crucial in determining the resource productivity in the business. These managers would need additional training to ensure that they are fully aware and appreciate the impact of their decisions and actions on resource consumption, and the knock-on effects on other operational areas and their trade-offs.

At the very apex of the business, the top management, and the board-room, also have external-facing issues from the competition, customer, emerging trends, new products and/or services, technology development, social expectations, legal and regulatory requirements, and their fiduciary duties. The competency needs of top management would need a different type of training to ensure that they are fully aware of, constantly lookout for issues, and appreciate the impact their decisions and actions have on the business, including those of resource productivity.

As such, the detailed roles and responsibilities for each job are different; they must be defined in conjunction and commensuration with the impact their action has on the whole company's resource productivity and with the relevant indicators that would work toward a collective (overall) resource productivity goal. Then, appropriate knowledge and skills can be agreed upon, acquired, and mapped on the business. As to the question of whether the knowledge and skill are obtained through lateral hire, developed internally, or contracted out is a decision top management makes.

Case Study: Bourne Leisure [228]

Bourne Leisure is one of the largest providers of holiday home rentals in the United Kingdom. Established in 1964, employing over 15,000 people, it operates 55 sites with a combined coastal land area of 7,000 acres. Between 2010 and 2015, Bourne Leisure has invested around £8 million to reduce its electricity consumption by 22 percent, natural gas by nine percent, and LPG by 0.6 percent.

In 2015, the company formed an energy team. Reporting directly to the CEO, the team spent seven months auditing 16 representative samples of sites to identify further improvement opportunities. A large number of opportunities were identified and £5.3 million were ring-fenced a month later for implementation over the subsequent three years.

Due to a large number of employees dispersed over a large geographic area, staff engagement and participation is essential in realizing the savings. The very first challenge was to convince top management away from the tried and tested investment-led energy saving to invest in the employees and empower them to make energy savings happen. Unlike the traditional method for top management buy-ins, which is using the evaluation of savings and cost, the business case did not discuss any financials. The discussion centered on what the company needs to do to embed savings as a company ethos, and about doing the right thing for the company and its guests.

Once the funding was approved, instead of buying standard materials from course providers and scheduling people to attend courses externally, time was spent discussing and debating the topics and delivery of the engagement process. It was quickly agreed that the training has to include everyone with a "Site Manager" position, it has to cover all site operations, be hands-on, and everyone walks away with a qualification relevant to the hospitality industry.

In consultation with a hospitality management expert, a draft two-day program was put together to cover all aspects of Bourne Leisure's processes: from basic energy understanding to sharing of Bourne Leisure's data and findings. It covers accommodation, commercial kitchens, swimming pools, sports and leisure facilities, performance venues, bars, cellars and toilets, back of house areas, and external areas. The modules were developed and delivered by a mixture of external and internal subject matter experts according to the overall course design. After the workshop, the attendees will become the sites' champions with an initial 12-month work program and deliverables developed during the workshop.

The next challenge was to coordinate 60+ delegates for the training. There was work needed to identify the availability of workshop spaces within the company's properties, availability for managers to attend the multiday residential workshop, costs to transport the delegates to the site, food and beverage, and team activities. These issues were organized and any issues were resolved. In some cases, first-choice candidates were not available. Rather interestingly, some sites requested more than one delegate.

Of the 62 delegates who attended the workshop, all prepared a three-monthly plan with identified priorities. The plans were signed off by the individual sites' directors for implementation and submitted for grading. Forty-seven reached the level necessary to meet the objectives of the workshop and achieved the qualification. The real show stopper from the workshop was the 12-month monitoring results following the workshop—it recorded a continuous weekly reduction in electricity, natural gas, and water consumption compared to the previous year. It equated to a savings of £2 million. With the cost of the workshop at £70,000, it was money very well spent.

Conscious Awareness of the Initiative

It might sound simplistic, an initial awareness about resource productivity is a fantastic way to kick start a program of works, and by getting the employees to talk about, pique their interest, and jointly own the initiative. It is surprising how many businesses do not do this well or completely relegate this to typing an e-mail or pinning a notice on the board, assigning roles and responsibilities, and specifying expectations for achievements. They assume that everyone will magically know what to do and resource productivity will be done. This step cannot be ignored or taken lightly!

Another common mistake is to treat the awareness activity as a one way—to inform employees of the importance of saving resources and asking employees to do so. Such awareness misses three important points: (1) to engage with employees, they must be invited to participate and contribute; (2) employees must know how their day-to-day work contributes or affects resource productivity; and (3) when they will be expecting to take part or contribute.

The first type of awareness centers on the existence of a resource productivity initiative, the need for it in the business, its urgency for action, and the high-level objective to be achieved. All stakeholders in your business must know why you are pursuing resource productivity, why it matters to the business, and the results to be achieved. If your company has multiple concurrent initiatives, as most companies do, there is also a need to explain how resource productivity fits into the big picture and how would your trade-off energy savings, water savings, raw materials savings, and waste reduction with other initiatives.

As described earlier, many companies report their resource productivity success using one or two overall performance indicators—the one that senior managers use to measure success such as kWh per production volume or m^3 of freshwater per room. While using lagging indicator gives top management information about its relative success, it does little to show how different departments or functions and each employee's work contribute toward resource productivity. The second type of awareness relates to how a successful resource productivity project will be measured, what are the constituent parts of the indicator, how each person in the business can make a difference, and when they are expected to do their part.

As described in *Success Maps* (Chapter 4), Figures 4.1 and 4.2, each level and functions affect resource use and its consumption differently. So, if employees do not understand how their direct actions affect energy, water, and waste, they would be at a loss on how it is relevant to their job. Feedback should be given to all employees on how they are doing on resource productivity. This includes reviews and presentation of performance indicators versus the target, analysis of projects to identify success factors, provide recognition to relevant stakeholders, and celebrate the success. It is also equally important to discuss and identify learnings from completed projects, identify any corrections or corrective actions required, and any arrangements to prevent the recurrence of similar issues.

The third type of awareness stakeholders need to have is the detailed plans to achieve the desired results: the implementation plans, who are the responsible person, what are the roles of each person and/or function to facilitate its delivery, and when these actions are required. Where there are potential barriers, details of its resolution and workarounds, trade-off points and points of escalation are also important.

The plan needs to be realistic, achievable, and deliverable within the various priorities, initiatives, timelines, organizational culture, and constraints. As human beings, we are very adept at picking up nonverbal signals and signs. If a plan is not realistic, not achievable within the timescales or operational constraints, it will be picked up very quickly. It signals that the plan is destined to fail and puts little effort into delivering them. Again, like the other support structure, resource productivity wobbles and the work grinds to a halt.

Lastly, if they identify new opportunities for resource productivity or opportunities to improve or make an existing program even better, they also need to know how they can raise and discuss their ideas in a constructive and psychologically safe manner. The ideas and concerns must be raised in an environment free from reprisals and/or have an impact on their performance appraisals. It may also be an opportune time to use examples from other companies, case studies, and/or site visits to illustrate opportunities, risks, or benefits. The key is not to be pushing ideas to the stakeholders but to pull ideas out through engagement, participation, and consultation.

The collective action of different types of communication described gives rise to the fifth reason for awareness: to remind and refresh stakeholders' memories through regular and consistent messages, thus keeping resource productivity in the active mind of stakeholders. It gives resource productivity more time to embed itself into the culture and ways of working in the business.

Case Study: Arla Employee Engagement

Arla Foods is a farmer-owned, and the UK's largest, cooperative that processes over three billion liters of milk per year across 14 manufacturing sites. Its products include fresh liquid milk, cream, butter and spreads, and cheese packaged under its brand or as a contract manufacturer for major UK brands such as Lurpak, Anchor, Cravendale, Lactofree, and Castello.

As part of its ambitious sustainability strategy, it has invested heavily in new technologies that help to reduce its energy consumption, ranging from more efficient heat exchangers, heat recovery systems, water recovery systems, rainwater harvesting [229], mixed-use refrigerated trucks, and trailers [230] [231].

However, the company also recognizes that employee engagement is paramount to reducing resource consumption and is a firm believer in LEAN manufacturing and continual improvement (CI). It produces a continuous pipeline of posters to inform and encourage employees to reduce water, energy, fuel, and CO_2 impact across its operations.

The key challenge in designing the posters was to transmit big complex numbers in a relevant and fun way. Many of the ideas were generated by employees and are well received by employees and customers alike. The posters also ask employees for their ideas for improvement. All ideas are captured and recorded in each site's CI log, reviewed, and, where possible, allocated for implementation. Any employee who raises an idea receives feedback on their idea and has an opportunity to participate in its implementation [232].

Opportunities to Be Involved

The penultimate piece of the jigsaw puzzle for creating an environment where the business moves as a whole to improve its resource productivity is to identify opportunities for stakeholders to get involved and to contribute.

Nothing is more demotivating than getting employees engaged and having no opportunities to do something about it, or worse still, be reprimanded for it. Two actions are needed: (1) creating opportunities for quick wins through better housekeeping, better scheduling, better controls; and (2) incorporating these new operational controls into normal practice. These short-term wins are also a stopgap for developing long-term wins—opportunities that require a longer time to plan and implement.

You will need to identify and create a constant stream of activities where your colleagues and employees can contribute toward reducing energy, water, and waste. These activities allow them to focus their attention on specific opportunities over some time and reinforce the resource productivity messages and behaviors by integrating them into normal practices.

As described earlier, the use of *Success Maps* can uncover how each person's role and responsibilities can affect resource productivity. The various job roles should, at a minimum, be able to implement the resource productivity requirements at their functions. They should also be provided with the appropriate tools and techniques that facilitate the established operational controls well.

Another idea for involving others is for "technical experts" to delegate less technically demanding tasks or routine controls to operational staff while they focus on the more technically challenging areas. For example, a company might have a campaign on stopping leaks for three months. Then, the focus moves on stopping idle machines, and so on.

In a more "formal" operating environment, it is prudent that operational controls are identified and embedded into procedures, and employees are actively nudged to participate and contribute toward its improvements through the use of job descriptions, training, appraisals, and recognitions.

Case Study: RBS

In 2016, Royal Bank of Scotland (RBS) through its Innovation Gateway piloted an employee engagement initiative using JUMP—a mobile app that raises awareness of environmental and Corporate Social Responsibility (CSR) objectives and enables colleagues to reduce its energy, water, travel, waste, and other in-house sustainability actions.

1,200 employees in 53 sites signed up directly or were referred via the "Refer-a-Colleague" function on the app. The JUMP modules cover the different themes mentioned earlier with five possible improvement actions for each theme. JUMP organizes employees into departmental teams, with a leader board displaying the performance of each team and individual. Employees earn points for simple but effective actions such as better understanding around heating and air conditioning in offices, switching off equipment, and developing a "last person out" checklist to ensure everything was switched off at the end of the day [232].

The top performers collect rewards ranging from wall socket timers for employees to measure their electrical appliances that are usually left on standby at homes, claiming a KeepCup reusable coffee cup or water bottle, and vouchers for outlets such as iTunes and Marks & Spencer (M&S) each month.

The JUMP pilot scheme had a better than average engagement from employees. 80 percent of employees at the trial sites signed up, and the "open rate" for electronic communications was reported to be 44 percent (vs. an industry average of 18 percent), over 2,600 actions were implemented during the year-long pilot, and over 1,000 KeepCups were distributed, which led to the bank removing disposable cups from one of its sites. The bank also reported an overall five percent energy reduction with a 10 percent out-of-hours reduction. This equates to £3 million savings from energy alone or an equivalent of 40,000 tonnes of CO_2 and 200 million liters of water—equating to savings of £7.5M [233].

On March 25, 2017, the JUMP scheme was extended to the remaining sites in the United Kingdom and Ireland, comprising more than 60,000 individuals to coincide with Earth Hour [234].

Case Study: Staff Involvement in GE, Diageo, and 3M

GE, Diageo, and 3M reduce their energy consumption significantly by engaging their employees to tease out opportunities for improvement. These are not limited to energy but also in water, scheduling, waste, production rate losses, and so on.

In the case of 3M, they have completed more than 1,900 employee-inspired and employee-led energy projects giving a 22 percent savings with a financial value of over $100 million [235]. 3M's energy success is based on an Annual Energy Recognition Program that rewards their staff using awards, small gifts, and dining with 3M's top management to drive engagement, continual innovation, and open communication.

On-Time and Appropriate Feedback

The last piece of the jigsaw puzzle is creating and reporting achievements in resource productivity. According to a Gallup poll, only 19 percent reported receiving regular feedback and 83 percent of it was not meaningful [236].

I have seen companies that shy away from reporting their performance comprehensively for fear that it showed results that are contrary to the planned outcome and/or using very fanciful words in reports that could mean different things to different people. I have also seen companies manipulate their resource productivity results (e.g., creating composite KPIs, or benchmarking their KPIs with some obscure benchmarks) to make their results look good or outright lie about their performance.

The primary purpose for reporting performance is to document the initial intent, report the current performance, and compare the intent versus current performance to determine how you are progressing toward your plan for using fewer resources and using them effectively.

Good quality and honest reporting are essential for everyone in the business to understand and determine the right course of action. It could be that the business is (1) on track—in which case, congratulations and continue to do what you've planned; (2) off track—in which case, you need to decide what do you want to do to bring the company back on track by diverting people, time, money, and so on from elsewhere or take some other course of action.

In the postpandemic era, the general public increasingly wants to consume products and services from an environmentally friendly and sustainable business. The younger generations, too, look toward green credentials as one of their employment criteria. Socially responsible investors assess not only the strength of a company's finance but also their long-term strategy, ability to execute, track, and deliver their strategy, and governance systems. As such, the secondary reason for good reporting is to enable and ensure continuing advantage over the competition in business.

As can be seen from the previous chapters and the numerous case studies, resource productivity encompasses many items and making improvements in one resource can impact another. It makes sense for reporting together in an integrated manner rather than treating them separately and as discreet initiatives. Since the turn of the millennium, there has been a proliferation of integrated reporting frameworks, each with varying degrees of success. An emerging and popular reporting framework is the Global Reporting Initiative (GRI), Integrated Reporting Framework (IRF), and the Sustainability Accounting Standards Board (SASB).

As more and more companies use the integrated reporting methodologies, the reporting framework itself can become a source of qualitative benchmark that focuses top managements' attention, to challenge workplace practices and bring about improvements. Two studies at Harvard Business School [237], [238] suggest that companies do take action when they are required to disclose information and subject to being rated. The real winner for reporting can only be that effective actions are taken to improve resource productivity.

Apply Behavior Change Techniques

Without a good support structure described in place, behavior change models and nudges cannot be grafted on and adopted in the workplace. Once there is a structure to engage every part of the business, the next step is to look for opportunities to enhance participation, disarm barriers, and undo unconscious bias toward implementing resource productivity. Even change management techniques popularized by John Kotter [93], Robert Kaplan and David Norton [66], Patrick Lencioni [239], Scott Keller and Colin Price [67], Daniel Goleman, Richard Boyatzis and Annie McKee [214], and Dan Ariely [240] rely on a good foundation to build on.

Behavior change is also not, as some would want you to think, about applying generic staff engagement surveys, awareness training, embedding resource productivity measures into the appraisal processes, and psychologically based techniques such as "nudging," neuro-linguistic programming (NLPs), and others techniques. Those who are familiar with psychology and social science will recognize that there are 93 known behavior change techniques (models) [241] broadly grouped into 26 different mechanisms for initiating change [242]. The models are built for specific users to target a specific behavior change. These models are not scalable as each company, as well as each scenario, exhibits different characteristics.

To understand behavioral change, it is important to understand the concept of unconscious bias and habits. The human brain evolved in a manner where a large amount of decision making is done in a so-called reptilian brain—the first part of the human brain to evolve. It is also the part of the brain that is responsible for the fight or flight responses. The "rational brain" is developed later [243]. As much as we would like to think we are rational beings, science has proven that more than 90 percent of everyday decisions are taken care of by the reptilian brain— our bodily functions, the routine tasks and duties at work, what we choose to eat, and who we are attracted to are pretty much driven by the reptilian brain.

This is important to behavior change because the way the reptilian brain function is a result of a very predictable and self-reinforcing loop. In Charles Duhigg's book, *The Power of Habits*, this loop has a predictable "cue," a trigger that tells the brain to carry out a specific task automatically (or "routine"), which will result in an output. If the output is a negative result (or "pain"), the connection inside the brain to that automatic response diminishes. If it is a "reward," the brain associates that action with the reward. Over time, the brain creates a craving for more rewards and a habit is born.

If you recall your joy when you first rode on a bicycle or took a swim, you can see the reptilian brain at work. That ecstasy from riding a bicycle or swimming motivated you to continue even though you may have a few falls or go under the water a few times. Once you become familiar with it, you no longer think about it, you just "do."

A behavioral issue that inhibits improving resource productivity at work involves the same cue–routine–reward cycle. Employees with conflicting (or competing) instruction placed on them unconsciously taking one course of action over another are due to the cue–routine–reward cycle. In this case, the "reward" can be due to the employee being fearful of reprimand, or being measured on different performance indicators that aren't based on resource productivity. Some examples include financial (e.g., gross margins, opportunity size, unit pricing, margins, time to breakeven, fixed costs, and net present value (NPV) calculations), operational (e.g., end-product quality, throughputs, customer expectations, lead times, and raw materials), maintenance (e.g., runtime availabilities, mean time to failures, mean time between failures, parts quality, and availability), motivational factors (e.g., recognition and rewards by managers and peers), and others (pricing, performance requirements, work in progress, etc.).

Another source of unconscious bias could also stem from employees themselves. For example, an engineer may have done a lot of work on the ventilation, heating, and cooling system to please everyone in the office. He or she may have found a set point that is broadly acceptable for a majority of personnel. An unconscious bias sets in the form of fear if he or she touches the air conditioning system, there will be a lot of work, many complaints, and headaches.

The company's resistance to change may also be a source of unconscious bias. The more successful a business is, the more efficient and effective is the core process in meeting its market demand. The support processes built around its core act as a shield resisting change. It leads people to prejudge changes, especially when the "new" change is unfamiliar, as *bad*, and ultimately hinders its effective and timely implementation.

Develop a picture of how resource productivity opportunities are implemented from idea conception, business case generation, idea championing, conceptual design, detailed design, construction and installation, testing, and commissioning, to benefit realization and operations and maintenance. An example of this end-to-end process is shown in Figure 8.1 and may differ from business to business. It can also differ within the same company depending on the scope and complexity of the project. The important point here is to have a good overview of the end-to-end implementation process and to analyze where the unconscious biases are.

To change the behaviors of a single person or the whole company, you'll need to figure out the specific *cue, routine, and reward* loop. No number of surveys and behavior change actions or nudges will last unless it targets the specific *cue, routine, and reward* that is at play. You will need to identify and understand the predominant *cue, routine, and reward* loop and what is the "reward" for continually doing so. A common list of unconscious biases is as follows:

- *Excessive optimism:* Overly optimistic about the initiative/ projects and underestimating the risks during implementation leading to known and unknown risks far exceeding the savings to be achieved.
- *Overconfidence:* Underestimate the level of knowledge, skills, and experience required to deliver the planned project/initiative. Implementation of the project is met with many obstacles and/or does not fully achieve its intended savings.
- *Confirmation:* Emphasizing evidence that supports a person's personal view, and side-line opposing views, concerns, and evidence.
- *Anchoring:* Evaluating the feasibility of projects/initiatives based on a small set of benefits and/or failing to take into account the overall benefits arising.
- *Assurance:* Preferring to accept the assurance and guarantees provided by a product or service provider instead of doing the analysis based on the overall benefit of the company.
- *Consensus:* Seeking group consensus before making decisions leads to protracted discussions and an inability to take speedy and concrete decisions.
- *Egocentrism:* Believing that resource productivity is a cost burden and time penalty away from making profits—an activity for others lower down the company.
- *Loss aversion:* Not wanting to right-sizing newer and resource-effective equipment "just in case" they might need a bigger capacity in the future.

- *Sunk-cost:* Low confidence that current and future resource productivity opportunities will not amount to much, especially when the previous projects were not as successful as it was initially promoted.
- *Status quo:* Preferring the present ways of working over the changes that resource productivity projects may introduce. This includes the risks from meeting customer demands, product quality, extra efforts, and so on, and the necessary workarounds.
- *Instant gratification:* Valuing the immediate gains from profits versus the value of medium- and long-term success.
- *In-group favoritism:* Showing a liking or preference for people who are comparable and/or share similar values, affiliations, interests, and social standards, thus giving an unsaid preference and influence based on their views.

Ask any person with an addiction, may it be alcohol, drug, prescription medication, shopping, gambling, food, gaming, social media, risky behaviors, sex, and pornography, the solution to overcoming the addiction is to overlay a new, better, or different *cue, routine, and reward* loop over the existing one. Once you have identified the present cue-routine-reward loop, the next step is to identify what action do you need or want employees to take in the future, and the corresponding "reward" or "pain" will motivate employees to choose a different path. The existing loop doesn't go away, it just fades into the background.

Resolving cognitive bias for high-frequency issues such as operational controls, maintenance controls, and routine purchases is to standardize the ways of working into a procedure, incorporating the necessary changes that would bring about the improvements. For infrequent issues such as one-off capital projects and changes to strategy, the use of decision aids, stage gates, or checklists would be in order.

Having done all of the above, there may come a point where the involvement of human resources comes in handy from the perspectives of available tools and techniques to correct the behavior and to minimize the negative impact of such behaviors.

The focus of having the right support structure and behavior changes should be on making the projects go smoothly. According to the *Harvard Business Review*, when companies address the support structure issues, organizational silos and political turfs become irrelevant [117]. The resource productivity project itself also needs careful management to assess it is on track, to nudge it along, or to drag it forward as necessary. This is the coverage of Chapter 8.

CHAPTER 8

Manage the Implementation Program

From the outside, a business can look like a seemingly mindless game of chance at which any donkey could win provided only that he be ruthless. But that is of course how any human activity looks to the outsider unless it can be shown to be purposeful, organized, systematic; that is unless it can be presented as the generalized knowledge of a discipline.

—Peter Drucker [244]

After finalizing and sanctioning the resource productivity projects, most businesses move their focus and attention away to other issues. Their attention comes back to the project when the contractor is ready to hand over the completed project. In the commercial world, more often than not, the attention comes back to hurry the contractor to hand over even if it's not competed or not fully operational.

As mentioned earlier, resource productivity projects, like any other business initiatives and projects, do not magically appear after it is approved. There is a series of activities to bring it to fruition. Someone or some company has to design it, build it, test it, run it, maintain it, and manage it. Figure 8.1 shows the general stages (a.k.a. project phases in some companies) required to deliver a project and some examples of activities that might be required. At each phase, there are many and sometimes differing stakeholders all with an interest in the successful implementation of the project.

The specific steps required will differ from project to project and from company to company. For example, a scheduling change may involve just a reshuffle of orders within a single department and a general update to all scheduling team members. An operational change, on the other hand,

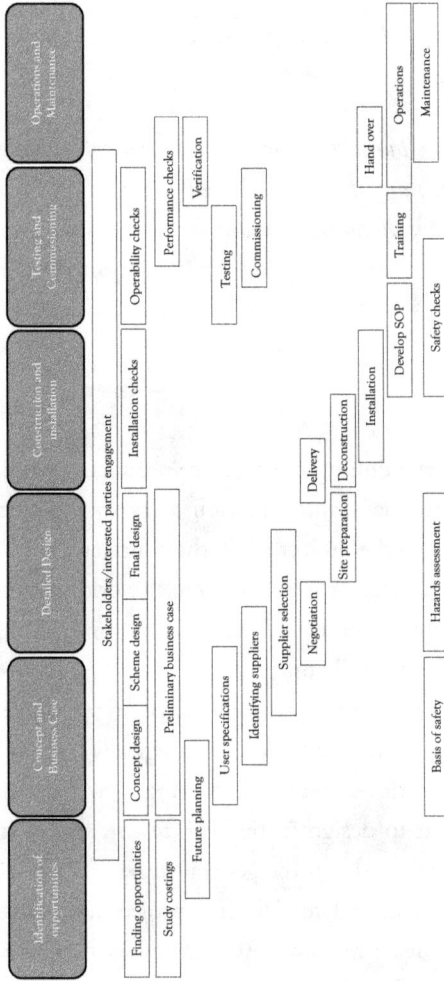

Figure 8.1 End-to-end life cycle of a resource productivity project

may involve an update of the procedure, training, and/or briefing sessions, followed by several spot checks. For retrofitting and/or replacing existing equipment with a more resource-efficient option, it would involve a larger group of stakeholders, each having different interests.

As the type of project becomes bigger, more complex, or carries more risks, the number of stakeholders grows. For example, a project to install a combined heat and power (CHP) plant may start with a concept feasibility stage with minimal involvement from stakeholders. Once approved for detailed design, project staff and operational staff might become involved for constructability details. Health and safety personnel get involved in inherent safety assessment, and so on. The number of stakeholder involvement increases until the project is handed over to operations.

It is essential to manage every project, and the associated risks, from its conception through to beneficial use: different components of the project are brought up to speed or deferred to the right time such that all parts come together on time and at the right space; declared resource performance is achieved and delivered at the budgeted cost. In general, the risks that arise may be related to the customer, technical, financial, logistical, health and safety, psychological, and geopolitical.

Without managing the projects, conflicts and issues that arise may delay the project significantly or indefinitely. It may also operate at a performance level that is less than the designed or marketed performance leading to all stakeholders blaming the other for faults. All of these are bad practices in project management, can lead to significant cost overruns, and more critically, can be avoided.

Depending on the size and complexity of the project and the company, there may be a designated manager to lead and execute the project or multiple managers executing specific parts of projects. Regardless of how each project is assigned, it will involve project planning, budgeting, scheduling, allocating appropriate resources (internal and/or contracted resources), identifying and managing risks, and delivering the project for beneficial use.

The knowledge and skill of project management and project controls are outside the scope of this book. Should you want to read about best practices in project management, there are many good books on this topic. To ensure a fit-for-purpose project and reap the maximum resource productivity benefits, there are nonproject management-related activities that cannot be delegated to project managers as your company's input is paramount. This chapter describes these activities.

Concept Design

The purpose of a concept design is to consolidate the ideas and features for the resource productivity opportunity into a "user requirement" and conceptual model that will deliver the lowest possible resource consumption. This is also equally applicable to major renovation and refurbishment of buildings, plants, and machinery.

Having access to resource productivity benchmarks and Best Available Technique (BAT) information will help pick the right process, plants, and machinery and define the expected performance required. If the concept design is modeled after an existing core process, this is also a great time to add in operational and maintenance experience by incorporating necessary design changes. The output from a concept design is a definitive "user requirement" for development into the detailed specifications and detailed designs.

In a manufacturing environment, the core process input and outputs, production speed, key material and equipment selection, and resource productivity features (e.g., variable speed drives, heat recovery, and thermal storage) need to be specified. In a built environment, the building orientation, information on the weather pattern, key architectural features, building layout, useful floor spaces, the purpose of building, occupancy, resource productivity features (e.g., windows film PV, rainwater harvesting, and building fabric selection), and key decorative features (e.g., water feature and sculpture) need to be specified.

Traditionally, a project scope details the full design with an intent to build everything in one go. It may be decided to have a modular approach to the overall implementation. For example, the bottom half of the building is completed with the view to build the top half in the future. As another example, two boilers or chillers were installed with an allowance to expand the system up to a maximum capacity of 10 as the business needs grow. This type of design flexibility allows the business to function without committing to finance the unneeded capacity. Technology obsolescence is also less of an issue. However, the facilities to expand the infrastructure must be built into the design and these would need to be discussed and incorporated at this stage.

All of the aforementioned needs to be done before approving the design for the next step. This is because this design affects resource consumption and productivity over its lifetime. Making design changes past this point or the need to retrofit the facility at a later date is more costly and/or is sometimes not possible. Carrying out design reviews, also known as design qualification in some companies, puts a formalized framework to ensure that the essential design features address resource productivity needs.

Scheme Design

The purpose of scheme design is to convert the user requirement into preliminary design options based on the supplier information and quotations for major equipment and components. The scheme design allows the business to confirm if the design is fit for its purpose and make changes before it is constructed. It also allows modeling and predicting the performance of resource productivity features, and confirming its feasibility. The outputs from a scheme design range from general arrangements drawings, building or process diagrams, major equipment schedules, and datasheets, operating and maintenance philosophies, options for construction, the detailed business case for funding approval, and basic monitoring and metering plans.

Apart from the above, other stakeholders are also involved. In this stage, getting inputs from people that would eventually operate, maintain, and inspect it is paramount to resolve or overcome current operational issues. If it is a hospital, getting the medical consultants, surgeons, general practitioners, nurses, and facilities team on board will make the design usable. If it is a production plant, getting the operators and maintenance inputs will help to design out issues.

The legal compliance team may be interested to ensure all the relevant legal requirements are on the right side of the law. The health and safety teams may be involved to ensure all stages of the design, construction, and operations are safe. The resource productivity teams would also need to ensure that the equipment is modeled as a system rather than as individual equipment. At the end of the day, the suppliers are supplying their equipment and can only ensure their equipment functions as specified; the company is responsible for it to function as a system within the company's processes.

For a new build, complex, high prestige, or high-cost projects, it is highly likely that there will be multiple iterations of this step to optimize the design. This should be encouraged rather than making fundamental changes at a later time but has to fall within certain limits. The growing use of Building Information Modeling (BIM), Computer Fluid Dynamic (CFD) modeling, and 3D visualization tools may allow this work to involve building a virtual model which can be reviewed in depth before committing to physical construction.

When not managed, spending over 10 times the value of the project at this step is not uncommon. Any changes made at this phase incur lower costs compared to making changes later in the project lifecycle. In real life, a lack of discipline leading to major re-engineering or corrections during the construction step or installation step has been observed. All of these come at very high costs.

Case Study: Bradagh Interiors [245]

Based in Derry, Northern Ireland, Bradagh Interiors is a medium- and large-scale interior construction and installation company. As part of John Lewis Partnerships supply chain requirements, Bradagh Interiors assessed its overall resource productivity performance.

They have found that engaging with design teams early enables certain client design requirements and specific walls to be built without first overengineering the prefabricated frames and walls and subsequently trimming them, thus providing significant savings through reduced energy and waste, material costs, and labor costs.

Based on the analysis, the benefit of engaging with the client at design stages could provide a resource savings of over £500 thousand a year, raw material reduction of 170 tonnes/year, waste reduction of 25 tonnes/year, and a CO_2 emission savings of over 500 tonnes/year.

Detailed Design

The purpose of a detailed design is to develop all the details for construction and/or fabrication. That would include all the civil and structural drawings, mechanical drawings, electrical and instrumentation drawings, bill of materials, project resourcing, project finance, cost planning, project scheduling, installation and commissioning checklists, and so on.

If the previous steps have been followed, any changes, at this stage, should be minor. Typically, it may be down to reorienting specific equipment or plumbing, adding or removing small items such as valves, and so on.

Your involvement in this stage is typically limited to a detailed review of all drawings, specifications, general layout arrangements, and bill of materials to ensure detailed design and materials are "fit for purpose" from an operational, maintenance, and health and safety perspective and incorporate all items discussed and approved previously, and that all resource productivity features have been incorporated into the design.

Once the detailed design is "approved," it is common to "freeze" the design so that no further change can be entertained, thus avoiding scope creep. It serves as a reference to the final build and is used for fabrication and construction. The procurement, installation, testing, and commissioning are carried out to this set of drawings and specifications. There may be long lead items that may be prioritized for early procurement. Any major changes after this point will become very costly due to the costs of equipment, materials, and manpower.

Procurement

Procuring the specified equipment and manpower for the project is the next phase. While this is relatively straightforward, two things could and frequently go wrong.

The first is that the equipment specified, for whatever reason is not available or could not be available within the required time, and an alternative has been offered. For example, the design may require a chiller with a minimum turndown of 10-to-1, but the one offered required a longer lead time or the manufacturer offered an alternative with a lower turndown of 4-to-1. The alternative offer would consume more energy, which would defeat the purpose of the project.

The second is that someone decided to purchase a piece of equivalent equipment that is cheaper, from their preferred supplier rather than as specified, or that the preferred supplier shipped to wrong equipment than the one purchased. Using the same chiller example, for whatever reason, a chiller made by another manufacturer was purchased instead of the one specified in the design. This alternative chiller may, in the majority, have similar features to the specifications, but some features are incompatible with the design and required performance, thus impacting its future operating costs.

While the chiller example above portrays the negative impact on resource productivity, it could also be a positive impact—the chiller might be more energy efficient. Alternatively, while the chiller may be more efficient, it may have a different installation requirement, thus increasing the installation costs or doesn't fit with the existing design thus making the system inefficient, or that it has specific operating requirements which limit the operational flexibility of the chiller.

The important thing is to check all equipment procured and delivered conforms to its design specification before installation. All deviations from the specifications should be incorporated into the concept design and scheme design model to determine how the changes impact resource productivity as a system. A decision can then be taken to accept the replacement or insist on having it as per the design specification.

For this reason, some companies request for and some equipment suppliers provide two separate tenders: a technical tender and a financial tender. This enables the tenders to be evaluated by the technical personnel and financial personnel separately.

Construction and Installation

The purpose of the construction and installation is rather straightforward but is also one that is fraught with errors and issues that impact resource productivity. Issues relating to this phase frequently occur due to one or a combination of the following scenarios:

1. The loading, offloading, and handling of major equipment and machinery were not done according to the manufacturer's guidelines, which invalidates the manufacturer's warranties.
2. Construction and installation of all equipment and control systems were not done according to the detailed design and manufacturers' instruction, limiting the accuracies and operating performance of the equipment.
3. A cost-overrun leads to the purchase of a lower cost or off-specification equipment to complete the project.
4. A time-overrun leads to skipping the installation of key components that affect resource productivity being left out.
5. Access to the equipment for, say, maintenance, inspection, or calibration could require additional work.
6. Shut down or space limitations may constrict the periods when construction and installation work can take place.

There is a need to ensure that the loading, offloading, and handling of major equipment and pieces of machinery are according to the manufacturer's guidelines. In addition, all construction and installation of all equipment and control systems are as per the detailed design and manufacturers' instructions. Like in procurement, any deviations should be analyzed according to the scheme design model and any negative deviations rectified and/or reinstated before the next step.

During this step, the business should start to think about creating a time slot for its people to learn and familiarize themselves with the new plant, develop draft procedures, and plan for employee training.

Testing and Commissioning

Once the design, procurement, and installation are complete and correct, the next step in the project life cycle is testing and commissioning. If all of the steps have been followed diligently, issues in this step are primarily due to the design being wrong or the equipment is not able to deliver the resource productivity stated in the design. Any issues should be resolved between the designer and the equipment manufacturer before the next step.

The commissioning parameters and results are frequently used to finalize the draft procedures and put the training plan in motion. If the company has a formal training program, the theory portion can be delivered at this stage and the hands-on portion in the next step.

Start-Up and Handover

Officially, at the end of the testing and commissioning step, the project is handed to the business for normal operation. However, the period between successful testing and commissioning and operations and maintenance is not a clear-cut step. This step has many names and differs by industry. Some call this step the start-up and handover, while others call this the soft landing.

This step allows for overlap between construction, testing, and commissioning to fix issues, operations and maintenance teams proof the new building and equipment, and for training its employees on the new ways of working. This period can be extended especially for projects that do not strictly follow the project life cycle steps described, or there is a long list of items to be fixed.

Some companies have performance guarantee contracts with the designer and/or equipment supplier. This period would be used to demonstrate the declared performance over a longer time compared to that afforded by the testing and commissioning step. If this is the case, then this period is also sometimes called the operational qualification step.

More often than not, especially in the commercial environment, issues are never fully fixed. It is important to ensure that all issues are fixed and the actual resource productivity performance compared to its designed performance. The root cause of any negative deviations has to be identified and its impact modeled against the scheme design model. A satisfactory resolution to the "unfixable" or "very costly fix" issues must be resolved before accepting the "key" as any resource productivity issues have an operational impact over its planned life.

Operational and Maintenance

This step, operation and maintenance is what most companies are familiar with. During this step, it is essential to ensure that the resource productivity features are incorporated into the procedures and that everyone is competent to operate and maintain the equipment.

Suffice to say, if the business does not operate and maintain the new equipment following its procedures and as designed, its resource productivity results will also suffer.

At periodic intervals, it is also essential to review the design and equipment to confirm if it still functions as per the design, resource productivity performance is still as expected, and to review if there is any advancement in the technology and best practices. These should be collated for adoption either as a modification or as part of future projects.

Decommissioning and Disposal

The last step in a project life cycle is decommissioning and disposal. For most companies, this is usually an afterthought. Decommissioning and disposal are also applicable when modifying, refurbishing, and revamping an existing facility where some parts of the building or process are decommissioned and/or disposed of.

In some countries, and for companies that want to embrace a closed-loop economy, thinking about how to decommission and dispose of the building and equipment at its end of life is essential. It may also influence the material selections, core process selection, and design decisions.

For an operating core process, decommissioning, in the main, would be about making the building and installation safe. That means isolating the section from other operational parts, de-energizing all machinery and equipment, and safely draining all liquids and gases. It may also include identifying opportunities to reuse, recycle, and repurpose leftover materials and equipment.

In some businesses that have grown organically over many years, it is not uncommon to find "legacy" plant and machinery laying around—all of which clogs up space and make the workplace congested. As a good practice, when an asset is no longer in beneficial use, all of the assets and associated plumbing and cables should be removed.

As such, thinking about the general framework and methods of decommissioning and disposing the asset at its end-of-life should be done as early as possible, preferably at the concept design step. However, it can also be developed during the operation and maintenance step, especially as part of the asset life planning.

Case Study: Designing "Green" Luxury Hotels [246]

"Green" design and construction practices in the hotel sector not only address environmental concerns by saving energy, water, and resources but is also expected to improve guest satisfaction, making them want to return and to recommend the hotel—all of which are important factors in the hospitality industry.

However, there is a perception that pursuing environmental concerns are in direct conflict with guest satisfaction and comfort in luxury hotels. This perceived conflict arises because many people think that "modern, functional, and resource-productive hotels" are not compatible with the needs of "luxury hotels." They have a perception that modern and resource-productive hotels have smaller prefabricated spaces; use nonexotic, recycled, and low-cost furnishing; use cool and hard lighting; and have aerated water taps. They also associate luxury hotels with spacious interiors, use plush or exotic materials for furnishing, use warm and soft lighting, and have bathrooms with large bathtubs and multiple showerheads.

However, this need not be the case. Proximity Hotel (Greensboro, NC) and Bardessono Hotel (Yountville, CA) are two luxury hotels that have been designed and constructed as "green" hotels and have achieved the highest LEED Platinum rating while providing their guests with a comfortable and luxurious environment. A green building relies upon a "whole building" approach that covers the entire project lifecycle from design, construction, operation, and eventual demolition.

Opened in 2007, Proximity Hotel is an AAA Four Diamond Rating hotel with 147 rooms, a restaurant, and 5,000 ft.^{2} of conference, meeting, and event facilities. To achieve their goals of green building, luxury, and long-term economic viability, the design implemented over 70 green building practices and was the first LEED Platinum awarded to a hotel.

Opened in 2009, Bardessono Hotel, a boutique luxury hotel features 62 luxury rooms, a spa with four treatment rooms, a 75-foot-long rooftop infinity pool, a fine-dining restaurant, and a meeting space. The hotel was also awarded the LEED Platinum certification.

Both the Proximity and Bardessono projects were initiated by private developers, both of whom combined a passion for sustainability with the desire to provide luxurious and comfortable accommodation to their guests. The developers of both hotels emphasized the importance of the concept design step by articulating clear project goals (sustainability, cost, the level of the quality, etc.) and assessing the trade-off between luxury and sustainability using the cost-premium benefit principles—namely the premiums paid by both hotels to incorporate green practices.

At the concept design step, both hotels assembled an integrated team that has experience in hotel management and green building design. The integrated team was led by a team leader who is accountable for the design process. The team assessed many possible green building strategies and technologies to jointly come up with a design concept that satisfies the hotels' aspirations and criteria.

In the scheme design step, the ideas and concepts were transformed into a set of buildable documents. The teams developed a "design model" that incorporated the requirements for a luxury hotel and green building opportunities. This model showed energy, water use, and related costs. For example, energy models were used to determine the impact of the Heating, Ventilation, and Air Conditioning (HVAC) system selected on operation costs and to identify any potential indoor air quality issues related to acoustics, procurement costs, and life cycle costs.

The project teams for both hotels also examined and chose materials and resources used for construction, including reusing and recycling of materials, sourcing for local and regional construction materials furnishings. These choices help to reduce construction waste, unnecessary transportation, and disposal. When the output from this step was approved, it was further transformed into drawings and specifications in the detailed design step.

Both project teams constructed and installed the agreed green practices as designed. Erosion and sedimentation control plans, construction waste management plans, and indoor air quality management were implemented to minimize site pollution and potential contaminants in the construction site.

Testing and commission included the monitoring and verification of green practices on both projects. During the operation and maintenance step, both hotels monitored their energy and water consumption to verify their performance is as per the designed specification.

Both hotels have also raised awareness among their employees on sustainability and their roles in continued sustainability performance and improvements. Both hotels also raised awareness on the sustainability features of the hotels and the role of green building designs and construction to their guests. Sixty-seven percent of Proximity hotels' guests described their stay as exceeding their expectations of a luxury hotel, with 23 percent meeting their expectations. The Bardessono hotel was recognized as one of the top relaxation hotels by Travelers' Choice in 2011.

In terms of return for investment using the cost-premium benefit principles, the green features were expected to pay for themselves in a few years due to cost savings achieved and tax incentives.

CHAPTER 9

Celebrate, Learn, and Repeat

... Achieving a goal, accomplishing a task, or resolving a problem often evoked great pleasure and sometimes elation. Even making good progress towards such goals could elicit the same reactions.
—Teresa Amabile, 2011 [247]

Having gone through the pain of putting in a new way of working that incorporates resource productivity and identifying and implementing a series of resource-saving projects, many companies take a step back assuming that the system would run itself.

At this point, while the resource productivity projects may be complete, the *Strategy-to-Execution Premium* itself is still not self-sustaining—it is missing one last element, that is, closing the loop and renewing the efforts. This is an important step to ensure that the initiative is not a one-off effort and that the culture and practice will continue.

Before closing the loop, it is important to take a moment to look back at what had been achieved, celebrate the success, learn lessons from any mistakes and success, and bring that lesson forward into the next round of the resource productivity cycle.

Celebrate, Now!

No matter the size of the project or the significance of each person's contribution, acknowledging everyone and their contribution, and celebrating their achievements is a must. This is, perhaps, one of the things that get the least attention and the most resistance from the leadership and management alike.

Many leaders and managers either feel that celebrating success is a waste of time and money or think that "it's part of the employees' duty and responsibility—they are paid to work. As such, there is no need to celebrate." Rather interestingly, those who take this attitude would also be quick to blame others when things go wrong—precisely the sort of activities that break trust and psychological safety at work.

Like leaders and managers, employees need to feel good about a job well done and their efforts count. Teresa Amabile and Steven Kramer, psychologists and organizational dynamics gurus attest to the fact that happy people make good products or services and they in turn generate satisfied customers.

Acknowledgment and appreciation need not be an expensive and elaborate occasion. It can also simply be an honest and heartfelt congratulation or a pat on the shoulder. When delivered authentically and sincerely, it creates an infectious positive attitude and encourages further successes not only in the company's initiatives [247] such as resource productivity but also in the company's purpose and core process [67].

Many attribute this to Abraham Maslow's hierarchy of needs theory [248] and Frederick Herzberg's two-factor theory [249]. Maslow's theory postulates that when lower-level needs, such as physiological, safety, security, and loving relationship needs are met, people move on to higher-level motivational activities, such as creating self-esteem and learning, social belonging, actualizing personal aspirations, and altruism.

Adding to Maslow's theory, Herzberg posits that when lower-level needs (also known as hygiene factors e.g., status, job security, salary, benefits, work conditions, and vacations) are fulfilled, the motivational level diminishes. The presence of higher-level needs (also known as motivation factors e.g., challenging work, recognition, responsibility, meaningful work, and involvement in decision making) increases motivation level. Herzberg calls for a need to simultaneously maintain lower-level "hygiene factor" and to increase the "motivation factor" at work.

So, assuming the lower levels needs are in abundance (or why would people come to work?), the cumulative effects of a clear, believable, and achievable vision; ability to contribute and take part in cocreating a resource-productive environment; knowing that their work and contributions matters; and the eventual celebration works the higher-level motivational needs. Remembering Charles Duhigg's book, *The Power of Habits*, the act of celebration is the "rewards" part of the habits equation and will reinforce the brain to do more. In this case, do more resource productivity!

Checking the Effectiveness of Actions

Chapter 4 reviewed the measurements and benchmarking necessary for evaluating the resource productivity of the business. When the successful implementation generates good results, the success is not due to the projects on their own. As demonstrated by this book, there is a multitude of activities within the business—ranging from leadership, planning, operational, engineering, and management—culminating in the delivery of the various components of a project.

A measurement of management progress is needed to assess the relative effectiveness of each contributing component. This is where audits come in to assess—the degree of alignment between the company's strategic intent and its policies and objectives; the results achieved; the effectiveness of the *Strategy-to-Execution Premium* in delivering planned results; if corrections, corrective, and preventive actions are effective; and if further improvement opportunities exist.

In this regard, companies tend to do superficial audits by themselves (e.g., internal), preferring to check the straightforward bits and close an eye (or both eyes) on the more complicated bits, especially when they are auditing other departments or higher authorities in the business. Real and consequential issues are usually picked up by second parties (e.g., customer or supplier audits) or by third-party auditors (e.g., regulator, certification body, or rating agencies). Relying on second- or third-party auditors to identify issues with the company's *Strategy-to-Execution Premium* is a bad strategy and bad practice, and it should be avoided for three reasons.

Firstly, empirical evidence from Michael Toffel and his team [238], [250] found that companies receiving a negative performance report respond and improve promptly, whereas companies receiving positive performance bask in the glory while their competition catches up and exceeds their performance. They are also finding a worrying behavior from good performing companies—companies are spending more time finding and/or creating new categories or subcategories where they can remain on top rather than finding ways to continually improve. Companies lagging are also less likely to engage with and subject themselves to a third-party audit [251] unless they are made to do so.

Secondly, third-party audits carry out their audits based on a minimum set of "mandatory" information. The third-party auditors then sample the available documentation and generate an overall impression of performance. This is akin to sampling an already small subset of information to assess overall performance. However, any issue identified by a third-party auditor may result in a regulatory fine and/or the certifications withdrawn. Apart from the regulator audits, the objectivity of certification body audits and rating agency audits were also in question as the company pays for the audit [252].

Thirdly, the need and practice of second-party audits are usually limited to businesses where there are high risks of information asymmetry from third-party audits or when the reputation risks are unacceptable to the clients of the company. Similar to the third-party audits, any issues identified may result in the contract of supply being withdrawn. In practice, except for a small number of industries such as pharmaceuticals, aviation, automotive, and some very large companies, most companies will defer to third-party audits rather than carrying out second-party audits.

Internal audits are the best option to minimize business risks and should act as the first line of defense against poor execution and poor management. Empirical evidence from Michael Toffel and his team [237] reports companies that self-police and self-report have better conformity rates, improve their *Strategy-to-Execution Premium* performance, and have systems to reduce errors and prevent undesired outcomes. As such, internal audits should be more rigorous and thorough compared to other audit types. Empirical evidence also suggests that companies subscribing to supply chain audits are less susceptible to nonconformities and respond to any deficiencies faster than third-party audits [252].

Renewing the Efforts

After going through the *Strategy-to-Execution Premium*, the business environment may have changed. Some competitors might have gone, and new complementary products and/or services might have emerged. Technology will have matured and moved on, and their costs would probably have been reduced.

A resource productivity initiative that is "fit for purpose" must continue to be consistent with the company's overall strategy and its core process; the resource productivity projects are reinforcing the overall strategy, are optimizing the performance of the whole company, and are implemented efficiently and effectively. The next agenda to close the loop, per se, lies in top management having an open, honest, and candid review of the efforts about its strategic intent, business aspirations, and the needs of the business in the next planning cycle.

Similar to the process for evaluating the external and internal issues forming the strategic direction of your company in Chapter 1, the type of questions to ponder over during a leadership meeting includes elements that are strategic and externally focused and elements that are execution and internally focused. Some examples of the external and internal elements to consider are shown in Table 9.1.

The decisions from closing the loop may come in the form of:

- Reaffirming the same course of action and continuing as planned
- Level up the resource productivity initiative from the initial starting point described in Chapter 3 to the next level of complexity and its corresponding reward
- Expanding the *Strategy-to-Execution Premium* to include additional elements such as quality, health, and safety, environmental impacts, social and welfare of the local community, and so on
- Restrategizing and rolling out revisions to the plan
- Applying corrections and corrective actions to existing plans
- Redoubling the existing efforts to speed up implementation and
- Renewing and refreshing the efforts with new ideas for improvements

Table 9.1 *External and internal issues for consideration during the renewal process*

External issues	Internal issues
• Would our external stakeholders and interested parties care if we manage and improve our resource productivity? • What value (financial and nonfinancial) are we gaining from managing and improving our resource productivity? • How did we fare against our competition? Did our competition take notice of our efforts? How did they respond? • Would the high-level objectives set meet the expectations of our external stakeholders and our aspirations? • Are there any emerging trends that we need to monitor (or potentially) that impact our resource productivity targets? • Are there any changes to the high-level objectives required? Do we need to make it tighter? Do we need it to achieve it more expediently?	• Does the existing program of works meet and exceed our high-level objectives? • Are there any longer-term planning and contingencies in place to meet longer-term resource productivity objectives? • Are there any projects in the plan that would open up or limit emerging opportunities? • What is the current status and trajectories of resource productivity results and planned improvements? Is it likely to meet and exceed the high-level objectives? • Is the existing resourcing adequate to achieve our high-level objectives? Are they competent to deliver the high-level objectives? • How effective are projects implemented? Were they primarily smooth and as planned? Were there a lot of unexpected issues and rework? • Were there a lot of corrections and corrective actions? • Are there any issues and conflicts that we need to monitor and resolve? • Are there any opportunities to improve the existing management and delivery of resource productivity projects? • If there is an opportunity to start the resource productivity journey from scratch or all over again, what and how would we do differently?

Case Study: Amanco [253]

Amanco is a Latin American producer and marketer of plastic pipes and fittings for transporting water. It is among the market leaders in Colombia, Ecuador, Brazil, and Mexico. Its' vision is to be recognized as a leading industrial group in Latin America operating with ethics, eco-efficiency, and social responsibility.

As a corporation, it practices triple bottom line and is recognized as one of the most admired and best places to work. While Amanco is a respected sustainability leader, its strategy and its journey to this position haven't been a smooth and single-step exercise.

Amanco's first triple bottom line scorecard was introduced in 2000. The corporation defined three high-level objectives which were translated into detailed objectives and action plans for each operating unit. Resources were allocated, and results were reviewed quarterly between top-, middle-, and front-line management.

Roberto Salas, the then Chief Operating Officer, felt that the sustainability scorecard and initiatives didn't represent its triple bottom line aspirations, but were merely a reclassification of existing initiatives. Between 2002 and 2003, its strategy and scorecard were redesigned to align and explain how each of the activities relates to its triple bottom line aspirations. This helped the company communicate its strategy and objectives clearly and consistently.

New issues continue to be uncovered. In the main, the sustainability efforts had no predefined owner and its sustainability objectives had multiple and differing interpretations at national and business unit levels. Most business units continue to have a budget-based and financial performance-driven culture. The information available at that time indicated that national and business units needed more hands-on coaching to live the triple bottom line vision, and also linked the achievement of the scorecard to compensation.

However, by 2005, the new way of working was still slow and had only 70 employees included in the new compensation system. Amanco's triple bottom line and scorecard continue to develop and adapt according to market conditions, business needs, and issues uncovered.

Using Competitive Advantage

Chapter 1 covered the importance of a home for resource productivity in the strategic direction of the business and the idea of identifying the options for using improved resource productivity as a competitive advantage. Another loop to close and to realize the benefits of a competitive advantage that resource productivity brings lies in taking the actions to implement the competitive advantage and using that competitive advantage. It is through the use of the advantage that matters. Without executing the competitive advantage, it is merely an academic exercise and consigned to the bookshelves.

Except for monopolies, all business environments are dynamic, and any competitive advantage will diminish over time as other competitors catch up. In which case, any resource productivity gains will disappear. Only you and your company will be able to understand the value of your competitive advantage, and how long the advantage will be in effect.

Case Study: Graham Packaging

Founded in 1970, Graham Packaging designs and manufactures customized sustainable packaging solutions for a wide range of industries including food and beverage, personal care, automotive, chemical, household, and health care industries. The company began with the design of the first plastic motor oil container. Over the last 50 years, they have continued to innovate in all areas, including sustainable packaging.

During the manufacturing process, many polyethylene terephthalate (PET) bottles are rejected for scratches and scruffs, that is, cosmetic reasons. Taking over 30 years, Graham Packaging developed the reusable and refillable PET bottle (REFPET Generation III)—a unique bubble texture design that reduces the appearance of cosmetic defects by 75 percent while allowing the bottles to be reused 25 times before disposal [254].

Many extrusion-molded PET and high-density polyethylene (HDPE) bottles are formed through a uniform extrusion thickness giving the same mechanical strength from all parts of the bottle. From the customer perspective, the process is not only more costly to produce due to the additional material and energy consumed but also costly to transport and store. Graham Packaging's light-weighting initiatives have resulted in AccuStrength—extrusion molding process that uses vertical bands that can be adjusted for no-load bearing areas giving rise to bottles that are up to 11 percent lighter [255].

Recently, the company completed trials of manufacturing food-grade and nonfood-grade plastic bottles with varying degrees of recycled plastic of up to 100 percent ocean-bound plastics (OBP) [256]. The company is in the process of commercializing this product.

Design innovations can have a significant impact in terms of consumer preferences and long-term resource productivity. This need not be a single-step innovation. The innovation can take the form of continual improvements that matures over time.

These activities—celebrating success, renewing the efforts, and applying competitive advantage while simple—are essential to make resource productivity a self-enforcing and self-sustaining initiative. A thorough and candid discussion of these external and internal elements allows top management to close the *Strategy-to-Execution Premium* loop, by returning the initiative to where we started in this book, back to Chapter 1.

From a business perspective, restarting from Chapter 1 makes sense. The technologies for resource productivity are continually evolving. The legal and environmental requirements can change. So as the business environment—customer preferences, competition, cost of goods and services, new and alternative technologies, and organizational learning. All of these create new opportunities and/or change the attractiveness of existing opportunities.

It drives itself through a new cycle of planning of what you want to do; doing what you planned; checking that you still want what you have planned and what you are doing will achieve your plan; make the necessary corrections and adjustments to achieve it; and review and refresh the efforts. Without this, resource productivity becomes a one-off activity as there is nothing to regenerate the initiative.

Chapter 10 pulls all 10 elements of the *Strategy-to-Execution Premium* together from an implementation perspective.

CHAPTER 10

Implement a Strategy-to-Execution Premium

*I hear you say "Why?" Always "Why?" You see things, and you say
"Why" But I dream things that never were, and I say "Why not?"*
—George Bernard Shaw, 1921 [257]

In the quest for achieving long-term and sustainable resource productivity in a business, we have introduced 10 elements shown in Figure I.5 and we have explored each element briefly in the various chapters. We have also described a need to "close the loop" depicted in Figure 2.2, whereby the 10 elements form a chain of activities that are self-driving and self-sustaining and are also rooted in a company's strategy and aspirations.

But … How do we implement such a *Strategy-to-Execution Premium*? Where do we begin? Technically, as it is a closed-loop, as long as all 10 elements are implemented, the exact sequences to which they are done do not matter! The key to the decision lies in what makes sense to you and your business.

Unless you are starting a brand-new company from scratch, you would already have bits and pieces where you can adopt, improve on, and also the new bits that would need to be built. In essence, you could follow this book chapter by chapter. You could start with leadership and follow the steps as shown in Figure 2.2. You could also start the leadership and technical analysis in parallel and bring them together to form the whole strategy.

This chapter describes the implementation of a functional *Strategy-to-Execution Premium* in ten steps as shown in Figure 10.1. This plan is an inclusive plan where all key stakeholders from the top to the shop floor are involved—allowing everyone to cocreate the resource productivity initiative. There are two companions to this book—a playbook and a blueprint—which you may find helpful.

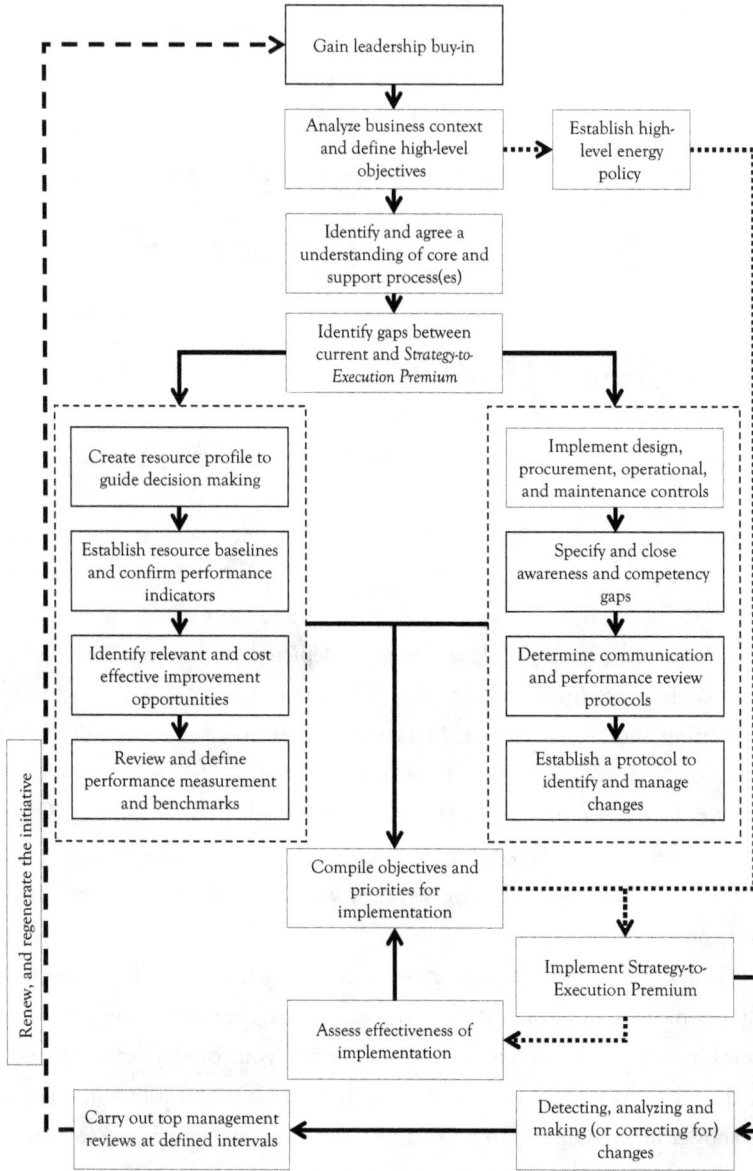

Figure 10.1 Indicative Strategy-to-Execution Premium implementation

Step 1: Understand *Strategy-to-Execution Premium* and Gain Top Management Buy-In

The very first step is to understand what forms a closed-loop *Strategy-to-Execution Premium*. The aim is to understand the principles behind the premium, the 10 elements (or leverage points) making up the premium, the issue it is resolving, and the value it brings.

Think of it as preparing a business case for implementing a long-lasting resource productivity. Why does your company need a framework for driving improvements? What benefit would it bring to your business that doesn't already exist? If there are no benefits and do not present opportunities, then this *Strategy-to-Execution Premium* is useless.

The motivation for a business to implement a *Strategy-to-Execution Premium* differs from one to another. The key to gaining senior leadership buy-in lies in determining what would attract their attention. This reasoning may be obscured, particularly to those lower down the company, but it can be guessed through your company's vision, mission, values, and policy statements—providing it is not a copycat copy that is.

While senior team buy-in is essential, it does not have to start at the top. As shown in Chapter 2, this is a myth—one that is perpetuated by those who have no experience in operations or running businesses. Middle management and the shop floor can be the seed for resource productivity to flourish. This is typically grown via his/her network of peers until a high-level sponsorship is secured.

Step 2: Analyze Business Context and Define High-Level Objectives

As described in Chapter 1, the second step is to define the strategic direction of your company, analyze the external and internal issues the business faces, and determine a range of strategic themes your company needs (and wants) to progress. Then, identify how resource productivity messages are related to the strategic direction and strategic themes of your company.

When analyzing the strategic direction, senior executives are very adept at identifying the needs of the customer and its competition. The senior team should look at a wider set of external issues that affects the operability of the business in the long run, so as not to be tunneled into a customer-only mindset. The wider external issues can be summarized into an acronym PESTLE—Political stability, Economic conditions, Societal expectations, Technology innovation, Legal requirements, and

Environmental protection. These external issues will affect your company's ability to meet its present and future needs and should be addressed. Some of the common themes are quality, environmental impacts, health and safety, resource productivity, and resilience.

For companies with a disciplined practice to scan the operating environment and review its strategy, these issues may be picked up and analyzed regularly. For others, this knowledge may be outdated or, perhaps, be lost due to staff turnovers.

When planning to address the external issues, senior executives need to look inwards at the internal capabilities of the business to address the identified external issues—their strengths, weaknesses, opportunities, and threats for delivering the strategic direction. This is where organizational structure, alignment, culture, competence, performance measurements, and so on come into play.

Care should be exercised when identifying issues as there are more stakeholders affecting the business than just customers, competition, and employees. Some other stakeholders are regulators, suppliers, contractors, and local communities. Care should also be exercised to distinguish between the parties that have a direct effect or impact on your business and those who are "interested to know."

For a business to operate efficiently and effectively toward its strategic direction (purpose, vision, mission, and values), a set of high-level strategic themes, objectives, and targets needs to be developed, defined, and agreed, thus setting in stone a *True North* or what James Collins, Jerry Porras, and Jim Collins called *Big Hairy Audacious Goals* (BHAG) [Tom Peter calls this *Clear and Compelling Audacious Goal* (CCAG)]—where activities and detailed plans can be developed, prioritized, mobilized, and measured against.

Case Study: MIT Sloan Business School [258]

In 1914, the MIT Sloan School of Management was formed as part of its engineering administration curriculum. In 1925, it started to offer a master's degree in management. The scope and depth of the school grew steadily in line with the advances in management theory and practice. By 2000, management became the second-largest undergraduate major at MIT.

Operating out of building E52, conference rooms were small, too few, and chronically overbooked. There were insufficient breakout rooms for study groups, student collaborations, and interviews. Research groups, integral to the school, were housed in satellite buildings, which erode collaborations and cohesion. Office spaces were also in short supply which resulted in some faculty members using the converted storerooms and washroom spaces. The cafeteria was also undersized, offering limited choices with very long lines.

At that time, in need of additional facilities and teaching infrastructure, the school's Department of Facilities pressed for a new, sustainable, and "green" MIT Sloan building. The dean of the school, Richard Schmalensee, had many external and internal factors to consider before making the final decision.

A new building will increase the capacity and space for the school to deliver quality education. It also presented an opportunity for the school to differentiate itself from other business schools. Being a "green" and sustainable building, it would be the first top business school to do so and required a good grasp of the current and future needs.

Pursuing the "green" building proposal promised lower environmental impact, energy costs, and operating costs. At that time, "green" building consisted of limited known technologies and improvements and also new and emerging technologies for which neither the school nor MIT had any experience. At that time, some of the emerging "green" technologies also had a very bad reputation or had value propositions that were difficult to quantify due to the lack of installations in commercial buildings. All of these increased the investment risks and uncertainties over the costs and benefits. It also placed a lot of effort for the MIT facilities department to learn, and any mistakes could be costly and permanent.

Choosing a new building also raised a lot of "internal politics" as the competition for space within MIT is intense. The views and projections for student numbers and hence space requirements may not be shared by the other schools and the Board of Trustees. Furthermore, the faculty, staff, students, alumni, recruiters, and potential donors would have strong and sometimes opposing views on how the new building should look and function. MIT repairs and maintenance, as the ultimate custodian of the building, also had a strong interest and were wary of the new and emerging technologies to be incorporated into the design. Balancing all of these required substantial political and negotiation capital.

MIT's board wanted the Sloan school to be close to its Engineering school to maintain its close collaboration between science and engineering with business and commercialization. However, the school wanted to be close to economics and social science. Regardless of where the new building is to be built, due to the lack of space, several schools and departments would be impacted. Temporary space would have to be identified and renovated to be fit-for-purpose; some schools would have to move into temporary (multiyear) spaces; a new building would have to be built; after moving into the new building, the old building would have to be refurbished for use by others.

Some in the university's board and administration were in favor of hiring famous architects to deliver a bold and futuristic building which would add a significant burden on the financial costs. Others do not, due to another star architect-designed building in MIT, the Strata Center, which was plagued by several late scope changes, significantly behind schedule, and hundreds of millions over budget. That building also had many design and construction flaws including pervasive leaks, cracks, and drainage problems leading to protracted lawsuits.

Built over three years, building E62, the Sloan School of Management's new home was completed in 2010. It was also the "greenest" building at MIT with sustainable features such as a high-performance building envelope with operable windows in office areas, light-sensitive window shades, a green roof, low-wattage lighting, demand-based ventilation, occupancy sensor controls, water-based terminal heating and cooling units, and an irrigation system that minimizes water use by responding to changes in weather [259], [260].

Step 3: Identify and Agree on the Core and Support Process

The third step is to develop and agree on a visual representation of the company's core process and support process. The idea here is not to redesign the processes but to identify the various steps in transforming the inputs into the products and/or services your company provides its customers.

There are many ways to develop the core process and support processes and to integrate resource productivity into the processes. Among all of the tools available, the process maps (or flow charts) and Supplier-Inputs-Process-Outputs-Customer (SIPOC) are very popular in companies. Value stream maps and swim lane diagrams are, strictly speaking, not tools that map out the detailed process but can serve as an initial discussion on identifying the core and support processes and their interdependencies.

Having an agreed process is essential as it is the process that consumes raw materials, energy, and water. It is also the process that creates waste. On the subject matter of quality, environmental impact, and health and safety risks, it is still the process that generates the issue that needs to be handled. As such, it is important to understand the process and its requirements, before mapping its resource productivity.

While the aim is not to redesign the process, it can be a source of prolonged discussions and disagreements, "Why are we doing this?" "What is the purpose of this process?" "Since when this was introduced?" "Why are we reworking so many times?" "Why is this process the bottleneck?" and so on. They are opportunities for learning and for optimizing the process.

Every stage in the process life cycle—from design, procurement, installation, commissioning, operations, maintenance, refurbishments, and eventual disposal—also needs to be controlled to minimize resource consumption and resource productivity over its life cycle. You may find having an "owner" for each of the processes or stages beneficial in coordinating between the distinct process steps.

From an internal auditing perspective, it is also the process that needs to be audited as they are also the sources for resource productivity deviation.

Step 4: Identify Gaps in Current Operations and Determine Implementation (Project) Plan

The fourth step, perhaps after rereading this book, is to understand what activities are necessary to implement a closed-loop *Strategy-to-Execution Premium*. The aim is to translate the principles, tools, and techniques into the company's lingo and carry out an analysis of which activities meet or exceed the description and which activities fall short of the description.

There are several pitfalls in this step; the most common one is to confuse an ability to regurgitate the principles of a *Strategy-to-Execution Premium* with the specific step-by-step implementation of the premium. The ability to regurgitate what you have read may form part of your learning process. Until it is assimilated, and successfully applied, it remains as a set of principles, tools, and techniques. The aim here is to identify the scope of works required and generate a project plan and the resources needed to implement a balanced *Strategy-to-Execution Premium*.

A good key to unlock this is to ask, "What are the specific steps I must do to implement this principle, tool, or technique?" This should be followed by, "Would a person unfamiliar with the book, reading what I've written down, know what he or she needs to do? Is taking just one step or doing one activity achieve what is required?" If the answer is "No" or not an immediate and resounding "Yes" to both questions, then you'd probably need to break down the task into more steps or develop a detailed scope of works document to go with it.

You will also need to distinguish between a high-level summary for top management approval, budgeting, and progress tracking, and a more detailed plan for day-to-day or week-to-week monitoring and management of the implementation program. Whether this is one overall Gantt chart with supplementary detailed scopes of works or multiple detailed Gantt charts is a matter of choice.

The second pitfall is to assume that a perfect *Strategy-to-Execution Premium* has to be identified before implementing the premium. The company's strategic intent and operating environment are dynamic and constantly changing. It is not a static ecosystem. There are also many levels of interactions and pinch points. Due to the dynamic and multivariable nature of business, perfection only exists in hindsight when all the planning, execution, and monitoring come together with a large pinch of luck and experience. As the *Strategy-to-Execution Premium* is a closed-loop construct, as long as all elements are available, the premium is good to go with continual improvements and tweaking along the way.

The third pitfall is the thinking that the whole *Strategy-to-Execution Premium* has to be designed and implemented in one go. Unless there is a legal or competitive reason to do so, the premium can be implemented in one single sweep or multiple stages (phases or modular). The choice for speed and coverage is entirely within the prerogative and aspiration of your company. You may decide to implement the whole system in the whole of your company one go. You may decide to implement the whole system in part of your company and roll it out later. You may also decide to implement the premium by the chapters in this book leading to the whole closed-loop at the completion date.

Once the program is developed, do make sure to identify the key people or teams responsible for the tasks, and present it to top management for approval and buy-in. Tools such as project charter, project-on-a-page, RACI, or RASCI matrix come to mind. When this is done, the plan is ready to communicate and launch.

Step 5: Technical Activities

The next step covers all of the technical concepts from measurement and benchmarking (Chapter 4), profiles and baselines (Chapter 5), and identifying opportunities for improvement (Chapter 6). This step and Step 6 can be implemented in parallel or series. The technical activities are grouped because the tools and techniques are interlinked and some iteration may be involved before a good set of accurate, repeatable, and reliable findings can be made.

All technical assessment starts with an analysis of resource productivity data concerning the inputs and outputs of its process. If you are starting from scratch, you may find analyzing energy and water invoices, raw material invoices, and waste invoices a good place to start.

Using the output from Step 3, map out how each resource is consumed or generated at each of the process steps. You may also find indicating all relevant and existing measurement points and meters on the same map beneficial. It may be necessary for you to take additional spot measurements or submetering before you can quantify resource consumption. Where a new measurement is required permanently, that new measurement can be added to the action plans for implementing the *Strategy-to-Execution Premium*.

After this, you need to use the data collected and analyzed to develop a profile of where and how much each resource is consumed by the process and establish a baseline of how the consumption varies with the activity levels of the process. A good profile will help to show where resources are consumed. Good baselines will help to show if the resource consumption is as expected or in excess. There are many regression analysis and statistical analysis tools available. Regardless of which ones you use, look at the data and the analysis to ensure that you do not fall into the trap of "garbage in, garbage out" syndrome.

Next, you'll need to establish resource productivity indicators for your process. A good place to start may be to look at some examples and Internet searches for performance indicators. Calculate the performance indicators for your process and compare them with the benchmark indicators. This set of performance indicators, when it is fully understood and agreed upon, can be used to measure and track your company's progress and to sustain its improved performance.

Following on from the previous activity, you'll need to identify a good range of ideas for improving the resource productivity of your process. This may be aided by the process mapping discussions and from the analysis and benchmarking of data. The technical and economic feasibility of these opportunities must be assessed, and the recommendation is prioritized according to your company's economic thresholds.

While there are many frameworks and standards for identifying improvement opportunities, and there is no prescription on who can carry out resource productivity audits, very often, a fresh pair of eyes is beneficial to challenge existing practices. The external resource will purely be a fresh pair of eyes and hands; they are not your enemy. Do not set out to fight their recommendations. Work with them throughout the audit and provide additional insights as it allows them to generate better recommendations.

Needless to say, external resources cannot be your resource productivity champion, change your process, or be expected to be familiar with your company's ways of workings and practices. So, you or someone in your company will need to work with the external resource, understand the opportunities, take charge of the recommendations, and champion them within the business.

As the business learns more about its core process and its patterns of resource consumption, new information and improved information may render some of the assumptions and technical analysis invalid. As such, it will be necessary for you to review the profile, baseline, and performance indicators routinely.

Step 6: Managerial Activities

Like Step 5, the managerial activities include several topics concerned with aligning the company, from top to bottom, to enable, facilitate, accelerate, and sustain resource productivity. A graphical illustration of alignment is shown in Figure 10.2.

A good place to start is to review the outputs from top management in terms of your company's strategic direction described in Chapter 1. If the business does not have a formalized strategy analysis function, you will need to find a way to convince top management to define the purpose, vision, mission, and values of the business based on a strategic analysis of the business environment and future needs.

Resource productivity may not be an explicit high-level objective in the strategic direction but is hidden beneath the details making up the high-level objectives and targets. Your next task will be to identify how resource productivity fits in with the strategic direction. The more leverage you can identify, the better. They become your tick box when preparing business cases for resource productivity.

With this complete, then it is time to align the rest of the company or risk creating confusion, conflicting messaging, and competing intentions within the company. As discussed in Chapters 2 and 7, the activities include creating an open and psychologically safe environment for participation; building awareness of the initiative; frequent and authentic communication; ensuring the necessary competence is defined, acquired (developed in-house, training, contracting, outsource, partnerships, etc.), and maintained within the company; operational controls; and knowledge management.

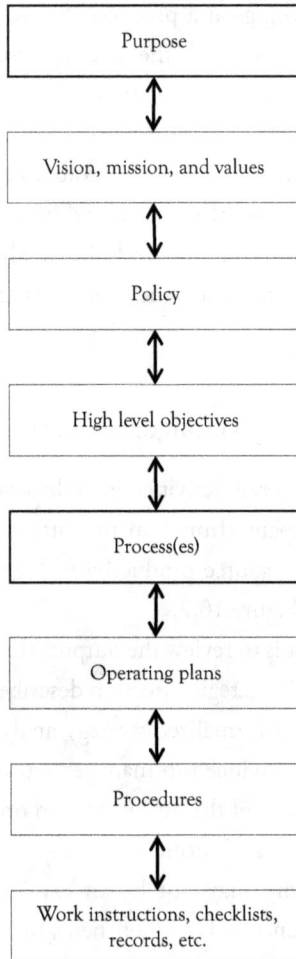

Figure 10.2 Alignment between the company's purpose, systems, and processes

On the topic of competence, many immediately think it is about specifying a relevant university education in a relevant subject, the number of years of experience, membership of a relevant professional institution or association, or attending a training. Contrary to this, the very first task is to define the specific resource productivity knowledge, skills, and behaviors required for the different job roles in your company. Different job roles affect resource productivity differently. Training everyone to the same level of knowledge is not only a waste of time and money, the knowledge and skill will not be utilized by everyone and will be forgotten in no time.

Using tools like *Success Maps*, job analysis, and RACI matrix is a good way to uncover the specific ways in which each job role and responsibilities affect resource productivity, and also what are the specific knowledge and skills required for them to play their part. Without this definition, it would be difficult for you to source for training course offerings or identify the appropriate external resource.

The next task will be to decide how you will acquire that knowledge and skills: develop in-house, acquire, collaborate with others, or contract as necessary. Finally, you'll also need to decide how to make sure the knowledge and skill are up-to-date and retained within the company. As you can see, there is a lot more than merely specifying a degree, number of years of experience, and attending training.

Moving on to awareness and communications, everyone must be aware of your resource productivity initiative and projects and their specific role in helping to deliver this in your company. There is a tendency for top management, managers, and technical personnel to communicate less than is needed for the message to stick. Every time you or anyone communicates resource productivity messages, make sure that it is authentic, consistent, targeted, based on facts, and free from reprisals and occurs regularly. If in doubt, communicate 10 times more.

As mentioned in the previous chapters, the effectiveness of a *Strategy-to-Execution Premium* lies in a thorough understanding of the company's process and in making sure the core is as efficient and effective as possible. This is achieved by establishing and implementing design, procurement, installation, operational, and maintenance controls that incorporate the conditions for optimal resource productivity. There are two types of activities that need operational controls: ones that are routine and frequent and ones that are nonroutine and infrequent.

Techniques like standard operating procedures or work instructions, control charts, and single-point lessons are only good for routine and frequent activities. Incorporating the new ways of working into any existing initiatives in your company, for example, Kaizen, Six Sigma, 5S, Lean, business excellence models, designs of experiments, theory of constraints, and a host of other productivity tools, is a good idea. You will need to determine the resource productivity requirements for each of your company's processes such as the way to operate and maintain the equipment.

Techniques such as stage gates and checklists work for nonroutine and infrequent activities—these would be things that are carried out a few times a year or less. You will still need to establish what activities need to be done to make sure resource productivity decisions are made consistently. The decision may be to create a new or modify an existing checklist or stage-gate for the particular activity.

Another important but frequently neglected task is the creation and management of documentation. Documentations are created for two purposes: a communication tool and a record of achievements. Policies, objectives, and procedures are documented so that they can be communicated consistently and allow an ability to compare eventual results against the intention. It also serves as a record for managing the history of actions and potential learnings.

For these reasons, you will need to ensure that appropriate documentation is created and that it remains legible with the appropriate revision controls, and outdated documentation removed from easy access and day-to-day use. You may find a procedure to create, approve, distribute, use, modify, retain, and dispose of documentation beneficial.

One final task that falls into the managerial category is the management of change. You will need to identify deviations and delays in projects versus the overall project plan, measure the achieved improvements versus intended savings, assess the implication of changes, and draw relevant learnings and insight. This could take the form of project meetings, regular scans of changes and updates, and critical pathway analysis. The use of contingent allowance can also help to smooth out the plans.

The management of change also extends to changes in the business environment and strategic intent. This may take the form of changes in your company's strategic intent, changes in operating plans, unexpected events and/or demand, natural staff turnovers, and so on. For these events, a process that focuses on detecting, analyzing, and managing the consequences of these changes is in order. This could be an additional agenda item in the management review.

Step 7: Compile Objectives for Approval, Prioritize Action Plans, and Do, Do, and Do Some More

Step 7 acts as a funnel for all actionable items from Step 1 to Step 6. In this step, you will be collecting and collating all of the actions required for implementing your *Strategy-to-Execution Premium*, prioritizing the actions, putting them on a program, and identifying the appropriate resources required.

This is also an opportune time to compare the outcome of the individual activities to see if it is deliverable according to the high-level objectives and targets set by top management and to determine if any adjustments to the timelines and resourcing are required. Equally as important, where there is a shortfall, to determine additional actions required to close the gap.

Some technical projects do not have an interdependent relationship with other parts of your process while others do. Some projects require something else to happen before they can be implemented. A good example is the use of combined heat and power (CHP) plant. When sized based on pre-energy savings loads, it may result in it not being able to operate optimally when other energy savings are implemented (or blocks future energy-saving projects due to a need to pay back the CHP investments). When the CHP is sized for postenergy saving loads, a smaller CHP plant will result in lower capital costs and allow other energy-saving projects to prosper.

When planning for technical projects, you must carry out a sensitivity analysis to identify a way to stack or group the projects in a manner that maximizes the savings while minimizing costs as described in Chapter 6.

It is also important for you to identify not just the person doing the work but also the various stakeholders and their needs during the implementation phases described in Chapters 7 and 8. This creates a project plan and objectives that are realistic and relatable to the stakeholders, thus minimizing the risk for disappointments and conflicts at a later date.

Once the detailed objectives, targets, and project plans are in place, it is a good time to check that the program is what George Doran calls SMART: Specific to an area for improvement, Measurable via at least one indicator for progress, Assignable to someone to act, Realistic within the available resources, and Time-bounded for its delivery on-time and in-full [261].

The last task is to get the plan approved by the leadership team. Implementation is key to realizing resource productivity benefits. Depending on the size and capabilities of your company, it may be beneficial to use external resources to deliver the technical project according to Chapter 8 while you focus on the activities to implement your *Strategy-to-Execution Premium*. This will give you the ability to focus on the larger picture and to monitor and track all components against the overall benefits.

Step 8: Analyze the Risks (of the Aforementioned Activities) and Prepare an Internal Audit Program

Step 8 turns the focus from implementation to risk management, that is, what are the risks for the agreed objectives and projects (Step 7) to either (1) slow down or stop in its track; (2) deviate from the original intent; and (3) for technical projects to be delivered late, over budget, and/or less than budgeted benefit.

The first task is to identify applicable risks that are present in your company, quantify the controllable risks, and recognize those risks that are naturally uncontrollable, for example, changes to customer specifications, economic conditions, or global crisis. It is also important to recognize risks can be of external origin and can also be of internal origin ranging from the leadership team down to the shop floor. Identification of comprehensive risk factors and incorporating the risks into an internal audit program will help to detect, correct, and/or mitigate the effects of these risks on resource productivity.

There are many methodologies for risk assessments in companies with the two most popular methods being qualitative and/or quantitative risk registers and composite risk matrixes. Risk registers are qualitative by nature and documents known risks and their resolution in a tabular format. Risk matrixes attempt to qualitatively rank "risks" using multiple criteria using 2 × 2, 3 × 3, 4 × 4, or 5 × 5 matrixes. Naturally, larger matrixes afford the business an ability to differentiate the various risk categories appropriate to their operations. Some companies introduce a third dimension (frequency) to the matrix, enabling the computation of risk, frequency, and severity separately.

Once all of the risks have been analyzed, it would be possible to compile an internal audit program. An example framework for using an integrated risk assessment matrix to arrive at audit frequency is shown in Table 10.1, Table 10.2, and Table 10.3. The way risks are incorporated into an internal audit program is shown in Figure 10.3. Formally, an

Table 10.1 Consequence category guide diagram

Severity level	Worst case consequence if SOP is *not* carried out and/or carried out wrongly							
	Safety	Environment	Waste	Health	Quality	Maintenance	Action by regulator	Media attention
Catastrophic	...	...	...	...	...	...	...	...
Extreme	...	...	...	...	...	...	...	...
Major	...	...	...	...	...	...	...	...
Serious	...	...	...	...	...	...	...	...
Minor	...	...	...	...	...	...	...	...

Table 10.2 Frequency category guide diagram

Category	Frequency of SOP carried out
A	Once or twice per year
B	A few times every quarter
C	A few times per month
D	A few times per week
E	Once or a few times per day

Table 10.3 Audit prioritization guide diagram incorporating risk analysis

Consequence descriptor						
	Catastrophic	Quarterly	Monthly	Monthly	Weekly	Weekly
	Extreme	Yearly	Quarterly	Monthly	Weekly	Weekly
	Major	Yearly	Yearly	Quarterly	Monthly	Monthly
	Serious	Yearly	Yearly	Yearly	Quarterly	Monthly
	Minor	Yearly	Yearly	Yearly	Yearly	Quarterly
		A	B	C	D	E
		Frequency descriptor				

```
┌─────────────────────────────┐
│ Compile all core and support│
│     processes described     │
└─────────────────────────────┘
              │
              ▼
┌─────────────────────────────┐
│   Assess the frequency and  │
│ consequence for each process to│
│ potentially deviate from intent│
└─────────────────────────────┘
              │
              ▼
┌─────────────────────────────┐
│ Use the results to prepare an│
│    internal audit program   │
└─────────────────────────────┘
              │
              ▼
┌──────────────────────┐   ┌──────────────────┐   ┌──────────────────┐
│ Carry out audits making up the│→│ If applicable, apply│→│ Verify correction and│
│   whole audit program│   │ corrections and │   │ corrective action is│
│                      │   │ corrective actions│   │     effective     │
└──────────────────────┘   └──────────────────┘   └──────────────────┘
              │
              ▼
┌──────────────────────┐   ┌──────────────────┐
│ Review the outcome of audits and│→│ Report performance│
│ any corrections and corrective│   │ to top management│
│        action        │   │                  │
└──────────────────────┘   └──────────────────┘
              │
              ▼
┌─────────────────────────────┐
│ Review the overall outcome of│
│ internal audits program and │
│     adjust as necessary     │
└─────────────────────────────┘
```

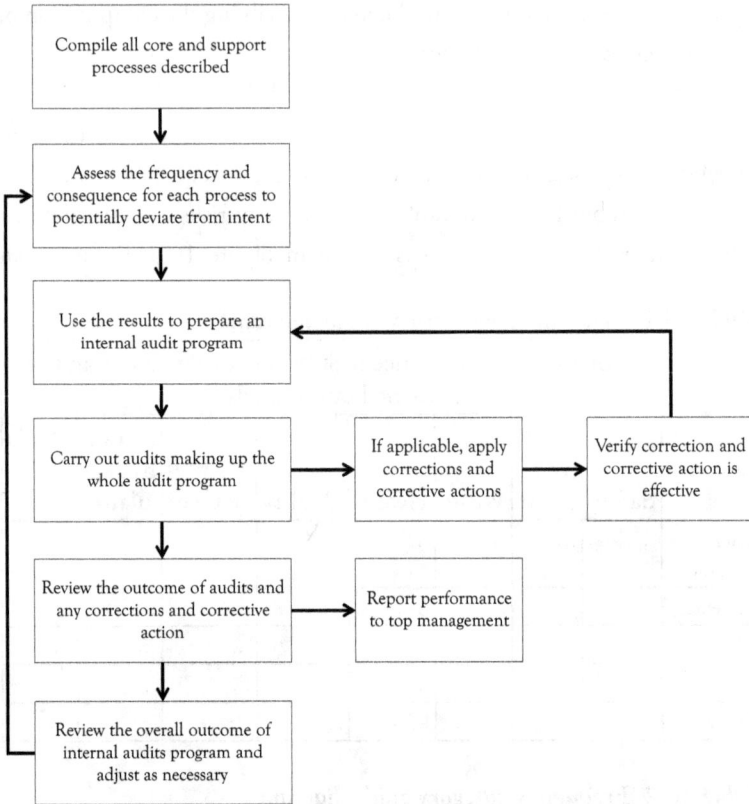

Figure 10.3 *Incorporating risks into an audit program*

internal audit program consists of (1) a description of the activity to be audited; (2) the frequency (or schedule) for the audit; (3) the specific area or element to be audited; (4) the audit method and sampling criteria; (5) the criteria for which an internal auditor would make a judgment against; and (6) the selection of internal auditor(s).

Some of the items to be audited, particularly lower frequency items or small and simple projects, have lower risks, hence would afford a low frequency of checks, say, once a year or once every couple of years. Some of the items carry higher risk, particularly operational controls for projects where errors cannot be detected easily or high repercussions would need to be checked very frequently.

Naturally, the risk evaluation should form just the first pass audit schedule. As time progresses, the audit findings should also act as a guide to refine the risk analysis pushing down the audit frequencies for those that continually exhibit conformity and pulling up the audit frequencies for those with more nonconformities.

Step 9: Carry Out Reviews at Defined Intervals

Step 9 involves carrying out reviews of the *Strategy-to-Execution Premium* at defined intervals. While reviews are parked in this location, the actual reviews need not be limited to this step. Many types of reviews take place within a business.

Your reviews can be anything ranging from operational meetings, planning meetings, project meetings, management meetings, strategy meetings, and many other meetings. Reviews should include monitoring the resource productivity performance as described in Step 5 as it provides a numerical measurement to track project progress, track the implementation of *Strategy-to-Execution Premium*, and track resource productivity results.

The trick is to discuss the relevant activities at the right levels. So, at an operational level, the review might include scheduled projects and/ or audit activities for the day or week. At a planning meeting, the review might discuss the various projects and initiatives—issues concerning scheduling.

Internal audits (Step 8) are also part of your arsenal of reviews. An internal audit reviews the relevant documentation, observes specific action in question, discusses with the relevant personnel, and analyzes performance. Internal auditors compare this objective evidence with the specified objectives and targets. A state of play on resource productivity in the company will emerge from the internal audit. If there are deficiencies in the expected performance and plans, the root cause will be analyzed and resolved so that the plan can be brought back on track and in line with the strategic intent of your company. Figure 10.4 shows some examples of causes for deficiencies in resource productivity performance and their resolution.

As the internal audit will involve judgment by the auditor, the competence and independence of the auditor are important to the internal audit program. Research by Jodi Short, Michael Toffel, and Andrea

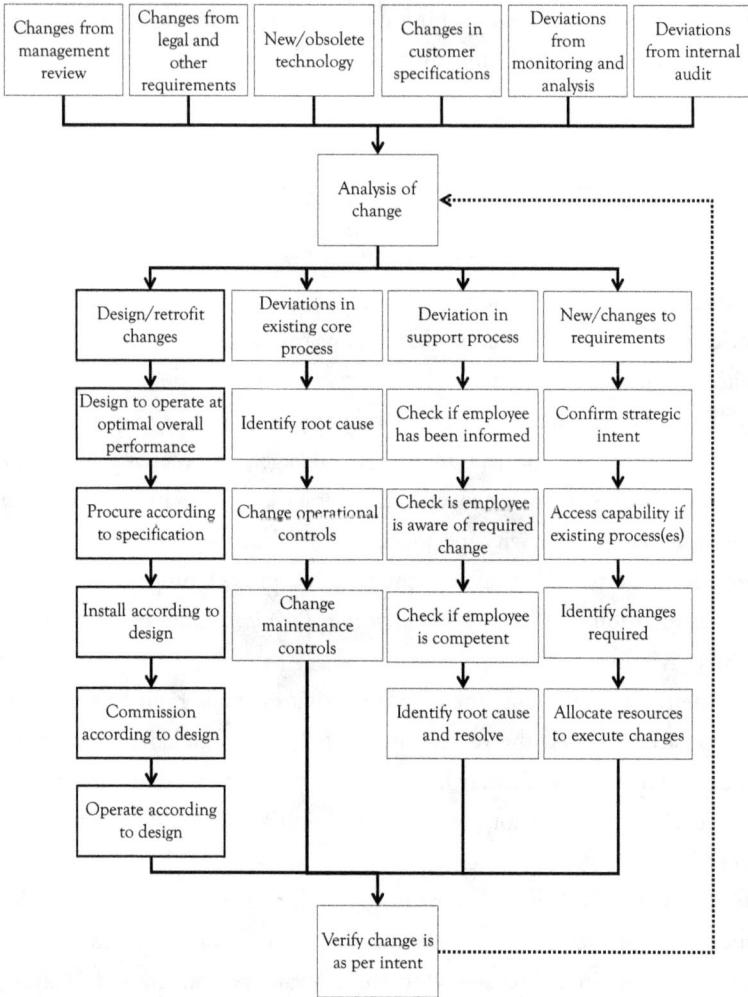

Figure 10.4 Typical sources of deviation and its resolution

Hugill [262] suggests that audit results are most dependable, accurate, and repeatable when the auditors are less familiar with the audit area. If necessary, external auditors can be engaged to act as independent auditors.

More interestingly, the research also found increased dependability, accuracy, and repeatability when the audits were carried out, or paid for, by the customer (in a supply chain) instead of by the company. So, in addition to internal audits, you may want to consider inviting your customers to audit your company's resource productivity.

At the highest levels of the business, your leadership team's review will include taking all of the available information internal to the company and making an appraisal as to its suitability, adequacy, and effectiveness.

Step 10: Renew and Regenerate the Initiative

Finally, Step 10, as mentioned in Chapter 9, is the most crucial of all steps to achieve a self-driving and self-sustaining *Strategy-to-Execution Premium*. If this step is not done, the resource productivity becomes a one-off initiative ... until the issue reappears on your top managements' radar in the future.

What is clear is that improvement can be made over time because the business environment and external issues of your company are dynamic and constantly changes. What is cost-prohibitive now may become cheaper in the future. You may also gather more data and insights from your company's process which makes certain opportunities applicable and relevant. New technologies and trends may open up new avenues for improvements that were initially thought impossible.

As such, it is important to set aside some time and resources to celebrate successes (even tiny ones) and renew the initiative. Some companies repeat the steps described in this book immediately, perhaps when supplemented with new team members who bring a fresh pair of eyes. Some companies repeat the cycle at a preset timeframe or when there are changes, modifications, and refurbishments to your company's process.

While this book has focused on resource productivity, and enrolling you to implement your resource productivity opportunities, this framework can be used to integrate many other issues that are of interest to the business. As suggested throughout the book, issues around quality, health and safety, environmental impact, and social and welfare of the local community are some elements for consideration. The majority of the tools and techniques will remain the same, and only some of the tools and techniques will need to be replaced. An example of a different set of tools for integrating quality, health and safety, and environmental impact is shown in Table 10.4.

Table 10.4 Ideas for tools that can be used in conjunction with
Strategy-to-Execution Premium

	Quality	Health and safety	Environmental
Chapter 5	Failure Mode Effect Analysis (FMEA) Root Cause Analysis (RCA) Six Sigma, etc.	Hazards Identification (HazID) Risk assessment, etc.	Environmental scan Environmental aspects Environmental impact Source–pathway–receptor analysis, etc.

Case Study: IKEA Supplier Audits

Founded in 1943 by Ingvar Kamprad at 17 years of age at Elmtaryd village in Agunnaryd (Sweden), IKEA grew from its beginnings as mail-order catalog furniture to become a €28.5 billion company with 345 stores in 43 countries. It had a growth strategy to double its worldwide sales by 2020 in a balanced and sustainable way while producing products at lower prices [262].

While IKEA had the vision to be sustainable, it relied heavily on third-party suppliers. In 2013, they manufactured 25 percent of particle boards it consumed and 15 percent of its furniture. IKEA relies on a mix of own-operated and contractor-operated distribution centers and warehouses to meet its demands. IKEA also relies on a small number of franchisees to retail its products in 17 countries. All in, IKEA works with approximately 1,000 primary and 18,000 secondary suppliers [263].

To maintain and build on a strong brand image and values, there is a need to ensure all IKEA products and service providers live and breathe the same IKEA standards and values. In 2002, IKEA introduced an IKEA Way (IWAY) supplier scorecard. It was originally developed to ensure a sustainable supply of wood and forestry products, it was expanded in 2010 to include energy, raw material performance, water, waste, transport, materials handling, and other criteria such as health and safety, social welfare, and business ethics [263], [264].

This concept of supply chain management works because the majority of its suppliers and contractors are located in economically developed countries that have a common understanding and aspiration toward increasing resource productivity, increasing quality, reducing costs, and maintaining long-term partnerships [265]. IWAY includes a mandatory list of activities that is a prerequisite to becoming a supplier and/or contractor with IKEA. In addition to the must-haves is a list of continual improvement requirements.

To ensure all IKEA suppliers and contractors fulfill its "must-haves" and continual improvement conditions, it employs a pool of internal auditors to audit new suppliers within nine months of the initial contract and every two years thereafter (in the case of some countries, every year). Violation of any "IWAY must-haves" will result in immediate termination of the contract. For continual improvement conditions, IKEA works with the supplier to bring it back on track within three months. If the situation persists, it will result in IKEA phasing out the said supplier. As of 2016, the average number of years IKEA has with a supplier is 11 years [266].

Case Study: BMW Group Sustainability Management [267], [268], [269]

Through the years, BMW Group's aspiration to protect the environment has taken on many forms. In 1993, the group published its environmental guidelines based on the ICC Charter for Sustainable Development and Agenda 21. In 1995, BMW Group implemented an Environmental Management System (EMS) to manage its environmental risks and impacts in all of its manufacturing facilities. All of the facilities were certified to ISO 14001 and the sites in Europe also attained the Eco-Management and Audit Scheme (EMAS) certification.

In 1999, the group began to look at ways to gain more value from their EMS efforts and decided to integrate the management and decision making of the business, environmental, and social issues into a single system. It was hoped that the initiative would facilitate BMW Group's commitment to implement the United Nations Global Compact's human rights, labor, and environmental principles. DesignWorks/USA was chosen as the pilot site for the integrated "sustainability" management system.

Founded in 1972, DesignWorks/USA (a now wholly owned subsidiary of BMW Group) provides design and engineering services to internal and external clients. DesignWorks/USA continues to serve half of its clients outside the group, including customers in the car, articulated vehicles, rail, construction equipment, mobile phones, cameras, personal computers, ski goggles, and sunglasses.

DesignWorks/USA was chosen for three specific reasons: (1) the design function has high leverage on sustainability issues over its entire planned life of a plant or machinery; (2) the employees at DesignWorks/USA, owing to the nature of their work, can bring creativity into developing, implementing, and resolving issues within the integrated management system; and (3) the length of time for each project or assignments is relatively shorter than other BMW Groups businesses; as such, the integrated management system can be rapidly stress-tested and scaled up in shorter time scales.

The first task was to develop an integrated management system framework that consists of business, environmental, and social issues BMW Group wants to address. The framework, Sustainability Management System Guidance, defines sustainability as, "a state of balance among the environment, society, and economy, achieved by creating a sense of shared organizational and personal responsibility for all future environmental, economic, and social impacts of the organization, which become the basis for actions calculated to meet the needs of the organization without compromising the future ability of others to meet their needs."

The guidance requires DesignWorks/USA to:

- Create a sustainability policy
- Identify business, environmental, and social issues having an impact on the operations

- Establish objectives and targets to address the risks and improve on the current situation
- Identify legal requirements related to business, environmental, and social aspects of its operations
- Develop programs to achieve the objectives and targets
- Develop education and training to ensure awareness and competence
- Regularly interact with external stakeholders such as regulators and the general public
- Evaluate progress via periodic audits and management review

DesignWorks/USA began its implementation phase in 2001 with the formation of a steering committee consisting of the Director of Finance, Director of Operations, and representatives from each department. A policy was developed to set out commitments to meet and exceed all health and safety requirements and be responsible for the resource use, environmental protection, and social issues both internally and externally with its suppliers and customers.

Each department was asked to assess and develop a comprehensive inventory of environmental, social, and economic issues. Environment issues include solid wastes, emissions, effluents, and resource use, as well as issues associated with the design, manufacture, and end-of-life disposal of products designed for clients. Social aspects included items such as employee retention, turnover, optimal working conditions, gender and racial equity, workload and sufficient staffing, building evacuation, first responder training, indoor air quality, and general environmental, health, and safety awareness. Economic aspects included items such as increasing revenue by increasing sales to niche customers interested in sustainability, reducing various business risks, improving employee productivity, and reducing operating costs.

There were some more creative aspects identified in the process. It includes opportunities to improve the workflow, incorporating opportunities to suggest environmental criteria to clients in the design process, opportunities around moving toward a life cycle impact of designs, expanding the environmental and sustainability thinking of clients, child or forced labor, and human rights screening criteria applied to suppliers and vendors, and the dissemination of information and idea generation by teaching at local schools and universities.

All of the identified issues were assessed and prioritized on seven criteria on a five-point scale: the probability of occurrence; intensity; duration; legal and regulatory; stakeholder concerns; leadership potential; and level of control. Each department then developed objectives, targets, and action plans on issues with the highest scores. Individuals were assigned the responsibility for meeting the set targets. Having said that, the plans do change and were revised following each department's weekly sustainability meeting.

For example, there was a need to replace one offices' roof. The typical process involves removing the existing tar, which is often landfilled, and new tar is used. Working with contractors, a new coating system was used which encapsulated the existing tar in situ, removing the need for landfill, reducing the noise, dust, and fumes, and reducing heat losses/gains through the roof.

An example of the social issues is the development of a formal compensation assessment program that determines the salary structure of a person based on education and experience, thus debiasing against gender, race, and sexuality. Another example is seeking permanent resident status for its key employees.

Examples of working with clients on sustainability issues are twofold: those that are open and welcome sustainability recommendations and those that are not interested or skeptical. For clients who are not interested or skeptical, the designers recommend the use of high quality and environmentally friendly materials by highlighting other attributes of the material or design without focusing on the sustainability features.

Examples of working with suppliers and contractors include sending questionnaires to gather information and gain commitments on some environmental, labor, and human rights practices; writing to its contractors to inform them about DesignWorks/USA sustainability management initiative; informing them that all future tenders must include descriptions of the measures the contractors taken to protect the environment throughout the project; and inviting suppliers and contractors to their annual "open house" where sustainability management messages are reinforced.

Internal audits were carried out annually to ensure that business operations and decision making throughout DesignWorks/USA conform to the integrated sustainability management system. The audit team, consisting of volunteers from several departments, examines the policy, sustainability issues, objectives, targets and action plans, compliance with legal requirements, and the extent to which each department applies sustainability to internal and external activities.

Based on the results of DesignWorks/USA, BMW Group committed to rolling out the initiative to all of its production facilities from 2003. Moving forward by 10 years (2013), it is possible to observe the integrated sustainability management in practice in BMW Groups' manufacturing sites and in the products BMW sells.

Internally, BMW Group reduced its consumption of resources and emissions by 35.7 percent per vehicle manufactured in 2012 against the base year of 2006. They are targeting a further 45 percent reduction by 2020. The share of renewably sourced energy had increased from 36 to 48 percent. The use of secondary or recyclable raw materials has also increased. As of 2008, 85 percent of BMWs are reusable and recyclable at their end-of-life—seven years ahead of the legal requirement in European Union.

From a product perspective, BMW Group pursued a strategy to develop combustion engine technology (Efficient Dynamics), electric (i series) and hybrid (Power eDrive) drivetrains, and light-weighting cars through the use of high quantities of aluminum, magnesium, and carbon fibers.

BMW Group is also investing in a suite of mobility websites or apps to promote sustainable mobility in an urban environment. DriveNow allows users to find, hire, drive, and park vehicles in different locations within a city. ParkNow allows users to identify available parking spaces in partner and roadside spots. ChargeNow allows users to identify available charging points for electric vehicles.

References

1. Henderson, R., and P. León Baridó. 2009. "Environmental Management at IBM (A): Making Sustainability Sustainable Through Passion and Process." Cambridge: MIT Sloan Management.

2. Beder, S. 2012. *Suiting Themselves: How Corporations Drive the Global Agenda*. Earthscan.

3. The Business Roundtable. 1997. "Statement on Corporate Governance." Washington, DC: The Business Roundtable.

4. Hill, T. October 07, 2020. "Fossil Fuel Gains Falling Short of 2C Mark Despite Net-Zero Pledges, Investor Group Warns." BusinessGreen. [Online]. Available: www.businessgreen.com/news/4021261/fossil-fuel-giants-falling-short-2c-mark-despite-net-zero-pledges-investor-group-warns (accessed April 20, 2021).

5. Pinko, N. October 29, 2020. "ConocoPhillips, ExxonMobil, and Chevron Climate Pledges and Actions Fall Short." Union of Concerned Scientists. [Online]. Available: https://blog.ucsusa.org/nicole-pinko/conocophillips-exxonmobil-and-chevron-climate-pledges-and-actions-fall-short (accessed April 20, 2021).

6. Harper, D. November 21, 2017. "Starbucks Falls Short on Environmental Commitments." Sierra. [Online]. Available: www.sierraclub.org/sierra/starbucks-falls-short-environmental-commitments (accessed April 20, 2020).

7. Laville, S. April 22, 2020. "Coca-Cola and Pepsi Falling Short on Pledges Over Plastic – Report." *The Guardian*. [Online]. Available: www.theguardian.com/environment/2020/apr/22/coca-cola-pepsi-falling-short-pledges-over-plastic-tearfund-report (accessed April 20, 2021).

8. Naidu, R. September 27, 2019. "Nestle, P&G Say they will Miss 2020 Deforestation Goals." Reuters. [Online]. Available: www.reuters.com/article/us-consumer-goods-deforestation-idUSKBN1WC1WC (accessed April 20, 2021).

9. Eavis, P., and C. Krauss. April 13, 2021. "What's Really Behind Corporate Promises on Climate Change?." The New York Times. [Online]. Available: www.nytimes.com/2021/02/22/business/energy-environment/corporations-climate-change.html (accessed April 20, 2021).

10. Dietz, S., B. Bienkowska, D. Gardiner, N. Hastreiter, V. Jahn, V. Lomar, A. Scheer, and R. Sulliwan. 2021. "TPI State of Transition Report 2021." London: Transition Pathway Initiative.

11. Greenhouse, S. August 03, 2019. "Yes, America Is Rigged Against Workers." *The New York Times*, www.nytimes.com/2019/08/03/opinion/sunday/labor-unions.html (accessed November 12, 2021).

12. Semuels, A., and M. Burnley. August 22, 2019. "Low Wages, Sexual Harassment and Unreliable Tips. This Is Life in America's Booming Service Industry." *Time Magazine*, https://time.com/5658442/tipped-restaurant-workers-american-economy/ (accessed November 2021).

13. Beer, T. April 02, 2021. "More than 50 Major U.S. Corporations-Including Nike and FedEx-Paid No Federal Taxes Last Year." *Forbes*, www.forbes.com/sites/tommybeer/2021/04/02/more-than-50-major-us-corporations-including-nike-and-fedex-paid-no-federal-taxes-last-year/?sh=6b773e5c21d3 (accessed November 26, 2021).

14. Majid, A. 2021. "Amazon's Profit have Soared—But Its Tax Bill Hasn't." *New Statesman*, https://newstatesman.com/business/economics/2021/06/amazon-s-profits-have-soared-its-tax-bill-hasn-t (accessed November 26, 2021).

15. Gupta, A., A. Raghunath, L. Gula, L. Rheinbay, and M. Hart. 2019. "The Decade to Deliver: A call to Busiiness Action. THe United Nations Global Compact-Accenture Strategy CEO Study on Sustainability 2019." United Nations Global Compact and Accenture Strategy.

16. World Commission on Environment and Development. 1987. *Our common future*. Oxford: Oxford University Press.

17. Elkington, J. June 25, 2018. "25 Years Ago I Coined the Phrase "Triple Bottom Line." Here's Why It's Time to Rethink It." *Harvard Business Review*.

18. Wackernagel, M., L. Hanscom, P. Jayasinghe, D. Lin, and A. Murthy. 2021. "The Importance of Resource Security for Poverty Eradication." *Nature Sustainability*.

19. BP plc. 2017. "BP Statistical Review of World Energy." BP plc, London.

20. *David Attenborough: A life on our planet*. 2020. Directed by Fothergill, A., J. Huges, and K. Scholey. [Film]. United Kingdom: Silverback Films and WWF Productions.

21. *Breaking Boundaries: The Science of Our Planet*. 2021. Directed by Clay, J., United Kingdom: Silverback Films.

22. Sud, M. 2020. "Managing the Biodiversity Impacts of Fertiliser and Pesticide Use. Overview and Insights from Trends and Policies Across Selected OECD Countries – Environment Working Paper No.155." Paris: Organisation for Economic Co-operation and Development.

23. Bowcott, H., L. Fomenko, A. Hamilton, M. Krishnan, M. Mysore, A. Trittipo, and O. Walker. 2021. "Protecting People from a Changing Climate: The Case for Resilience." *McKinsey & Company* https://mckinsey.

com/business-functions/sustainability/our-insights/protecting-people-from-a-changing-climate-the-case-for-resilience (accessed November 24, 2021).

24. Rockström, J., W. Steffen, K. Noone, A. Persson, F.S.I. Chapin, E. Lambin, T. Lenton, M. Scheffer, C. Folke, Schellnhuber, HJ, B. Nykvist, C. de Wit, T. Hughes, S. van der Leeuw, H. Rodhe, S. Sörlin, P. Snyder, R. Costanza, U. Svedin, M. Falkenmark, L. Karlberg, R. Correll, V. Fabry, J. Hansen, B. Walker, D. Liverman, K. Richardson, P. Crutzen, and J. Foley. 2009. "Planetary Boundaries: Exploring the Safe Operating Space for Humanity." *Ecology and Society* 14, no. 2.

25. Steffen, W., K. Richardson, J. Rockström, S. Cornell, I. Fetzer, E. Bennett, R. Biggs, S. Carpenter, W. de Vries, C. de Wit, C. Folke, D. Gerten, J. Heinke, G. Mace, L. Persson, V. Ramanathan, B. Reyers, and S. Sörlin. 2015. "Planetary Boundaries: Guiding Human Development on a Changing Planet." *Science* 347, no. 6223.

26. Economist Intelligence Unit. 2013. "Sustainability Insights: Learning from Business Leaders." London: Economist.

27. Cullen, J.M., J.M. Allwood, and E.H. Borgstein. 2011. "Reducing Energy Demand: What are the Practical Limits?." *J Environ Sci & Technol* 45, no. 4, pp. 1711–1718.

28. Enkvist, P., T. Naucler, and J. Riese. April 2008. "What Countries Can Do About Cutting Carbon Emissions." *McKinsey Quarterly*.

29. Burchardt, J., P. Gerbert, S. Schonberger, P. Herhold, C. Brognaux, and J. Paivarinta. 2018. "The Economic Case for Combating Climate Change." The Boston Consulting Group.

30. IEA. 2019. "Energy Efficiency 2019." Paris: International Energy Agency.

31. Leung, H. June 03, 2019. "Southeast Asia Doesn't Want to Be the World's Dumping Ground. Here's How Some Countries Are Pushing Back." [Online]. Available: https://time.com/5598032/southeast-asia-plastic-waste-malaysia-philippines/ (accessed July 20, 2021).

32. Heubl, B. August, 2021. "Why Britain Needs a New Approach for Plastic Waste." *Engineering & Technology* 16, no. 7, pp. 42–45.

33. FAO. 2019. *The State of Food and Agriculture 2019. Moving Forward on Food Loss and Waste Reduction*. Rome.

34. Ambrose, J. November 04, 2021. "US Oil Giants Top Lists of Lobby Offenders Holding Back Climate Action." *The Guardian*, www.theguardian.com/business/2021/nov/04/us-oil-giants-top-list-lobby-offenders-exxonmobile-chevron-toyota (accessed November 26, 2021).

35. Boren, Z., A.C. Kaufman, and L. Carter. September 28, 2020." Revealed: BP and Shell Back Anti-Climate Lobby Groups Despite Pledges." *Huffington Post*, www.huffingtonpost.co.uk/entry/bp-shell-climate_n_5f6 e3120c5b64deddeed6762 (accessed November 26, 2021).

36. Clarke, M, 2021. "Resource Sector Lobbies Hardest on Climate Change, While Net Zero Backers 'Disengaged'." *ABC News*, www.abc.net.au/news/2021-09-09/climate-change-lobbying-mostly-fossil-fuel-companies/100445112 (accessed November 26, 2021).

37. Jacquet, J. March 14, 2021. "The Meat Industry is Doing Exactly What Big Oil does to Fight Climate Action." *The Washington Post*, www.washingtonpost.com/outlook/the-meat-industry-is-doing-exactly-what-big-oil-does-to-fight-climate-action/2021/05/14/831e14be-b3fe-11eb-ab43-bebddc5a0f65_story.html

38. Milman, O. November 26, 2021. "Apple and Disney Among Companies Backing Groups Against US Climate Bill." *The Guardian*. www.theguardian.com/us-news/2021/oct/01/apple-amazon-microsoft-disney-lobby-groups-climate-bill-analysis (accessed November 26, 2021).

39. Krugman, P. 2021. Corporate America Is Lobbying for Climate Disaster. The New York Times. 2 Sep 2021. https://www.nytimes.com/2021/09/02/opinion/corporate-taxes-biden-spending-bill.html (accessed November 26, 2021)

40. Vaughan, A. 2021. European airlines have been lobbying against EU climate plans. New Scientist. 9 Jun 2021. https://www.newscientist.com/article/2280172-european-airlines-have-been-lobbying-against-eu-climate-plans/ (accessed November 26, 2021).

41. McCarthy, N. March 25, 2019. "Oil And Gas Giants Spend Millions Lobbying To Block Climate Change Policies." *Forbes*, www.forbes.com/sites/niallmccarthy/2019/03/25/oil-and-gas-giants-spend-millions-lobbying-to-block-climate-change-policies-infographic/?sh=72fda9917c4f (accessed November 26, 2021).

42. Gans, A. 2021. Oil and gas spending steady ahead of U.N. climate change conference. Open Secrets. www.opensecrets.org/news/2021/10/oil-and-gas-spending-steady-ahead-un-climate-change/ (accessed November 26, 2021).

43. Adam, K; Stevens, H. November 08, 2021. "Who has the Most Delegates at the COP26 Summit? The Fossil Fuel Industry." *The Washington Post*. www.washingtonpost.com/world/2021/11/08/cop26-glasgow-climate-summit-fossil-fuel/ (accessed November 26, 2021).

44. Berg, P., D. Feber, A. Granskog, D. Nordigården, and S. Ponkshe. January, 2020. "The Drive Toward Sustainability in Packaging—Beyond the Quick Wins." *McKinsey Quarterly*.

45. Lavery, G., G. Pennell, S. Evans, and S. Brown. 2013. "The Next Manufacturing Revolution: Non-Labour Resource Productivity and its Potential for UK Manufacturing." London: Lavery/Pennell.

46. Hundertmark, T., K. Lueck, and B. Packer. May 2020. "Water: A human and business priority." *McKinsey Quarterly*.

47. Scharmer, O., and K. Kaufer. 2013. *Leading from the Emerging Future: From Ego-System to Eco-System Economies.* San Francisco: Berrett-Koehler Publishers.

48. InfluenceMap. 2019. "Corporate Carbon Policy Footprint 2019: The 50 Most Influential Assessed." InfluenceMap.

49. Harvard Business Review Analytical Service. 2011. "Global Business and the Dawn of a New Energy Reality." *Harvard Business Review.* Boston.

50. Financial Times. 2014. "Combining Profits and Purpose: A New Dialogue on the Role of Business in Society." London: Financial Times.

51. Norton, D. 2007. "Strategy Execution: A Competency that Creates Competitive Advantage, A Palladium White Paper." Palladium Group.

52. Green Monday, 2011. "Energy Efficiency White Paper." Green Monday.

53. Reiny, S. January 04, 2018. "NASA Study: First Direct Proof of Ozone Hole Recovery Due to Chemicals Ban." NASA's Earth Science News Team. [Online]. Available: www.nasa.gov/feature/goddard/2018/nasa-study-first-direct-proof-of-ozone-hole-recovery-due-to-chemicals-ban (accessed June 13, 2021).

54. Hayward, R., J. Lee, J. Keeble, R. McNamara, C. Hall, and S. Cruse. 2013. "The UN Global Compact-Accenture CEO Study on Sustainability 2013. Architects of a better world." UN Global Compact and Accenture.

55. Rigby, D., and B. Bilodeau. 2018. "Management Tools and Trends 2018." Bain & Company Inc.

56. Bloom, N., C. Genakos, R. Martin, and R. Sadun. 2010. "Modern Management: Good for Environment or Just Hot Air?." *The Economic Journal,* no. 120, pp. 551–572.

57. Matteini, M. 2011. *Why ISO 50001 and Energy Management for Industry of Developing Countries and Emerging Economies.* Vienna: United Nations Industrial Development Organization.

58. Therkelsen, P., R. Sabouni, A. McKane, and P. Scheihing. 2013. "Assessing the Costs and Benefits of the Superior Energy Performance Program." *2013 ACEEE Summer Study on Energy Efficiency in Industry.* New York, NY: American Council for an Energy Efficient Economy.

59. Leinwand, P., and C. Mainardi. 2013. "What Drives a Company's Success?." *Harvard Business Review.*

60. Marr, B., M. Bourne, M. Kennerley, M. Franco, M. Wilcox, C. Adams, and S. Mason. 2003. "Business Performance Management: Current State of the Art." Cranfield: Cranfied School of Management and Hyperion.

61. Knoster, T. 1991. "Model for Managing Complex Change. Presentation in The Association for Severely Handicap (TASH) Conference." Washington, D.C.

62. Everett, R. 1962. *Diffusion of Innovations.* New York, NY: The Free Press.

63. Bernow, S., J. Godsall, B. Klempner, and C. Merten. July 2019. "More than Values: The Value-Based Sustainability Reporting that Investors Want." *McKinsey & Company*.

64. Zinkin, J. 2019. *Better Governance Across the Board: Creating Value Through Reputation, People, and Processes*. Boston: Walter de Gruyter.

65. Bresnahan, K. 2019. "THE PURPOSE DEBATE Back to the '80s: Business Roundtable's 'Purpose' Statement Redux." [Online]. Available: www.directorsandboards.com/articles/singlepurpose-debate-back-%E2%80%9880s-business-roundtable%E2%80%99s-%E2%80%9Cpurpose%E2%80%9D-statement-redux (accessed March 18, 2020).

66. The Business Roundtable. 2019. "Statement on the Purpose of a Corporation." Washington, DC: The Business Roundtable.

67. Handy, C. 2002. "What's a Business for?" *Harvard Business Review*.

68. Orlitzky, M., F. Schmidt, and S. Rynes. 2003. "Corporate Social and Financial Performance: A Meta-Analysis." *J. Organization Studies* 24, no. 3, pp. 403–441.

69. Kaplan, R., and D. Norton. 2008. *The Execution Premium: Linking Strategy to Operations for Competitive Advantage*. Boston: Harvard Business School Publishing.

70. Keller, S., and C. Price. 2011. *Beyond Performance: How Great Organizations Build Ultimate Competitive Advantage*. New Jersey, NJ: John Wiley & Sons.

71. Edlich, A., H. Heimes, and A. Watson. October 2016. "Can You Achieve and Sustain G&A Cost Reductions?." *McKinsey Quarterly*.

72. Murray, A. May 16, 2019. "The 2019 Fortune 500 CEO Survey Results are In." *Fortune*.

73. Eccles, R., I. Ioannou, and G. Serafeim. 2014. "The Impact of Corporate Sustainability on Organizational Processes and Performance." *Management Science* 60, no. 11, pp. 2835–2857.

74. McKinsey & Company. 2020. "Purpose: Shifting from Why to How." *McKinsey Quarterly*.

75. Montgomery, C. January 2008. "Putting Leadership back into Strategy." *Harvard Business Review*, no. 1, pp. 54–60.

76. Tilles, S. July 1963. "How to Evaluate Corporate Strategy." *Harvard Business Review*.

77. Jones, B. 2016. "The Difference Between Purpose and Mission." *Harvard Business Review*.

78. Hayes, R., and W. Abernathy. July–August 2007. "Managing Our Way to Economic Decline." *Harvard Business Review* 58, No. 4, p. 6777.

79. Heskett, J. 2011. *The Culture Cycle: How to Shape the Unseen Force that Transforms Performance*. London: Pearson Financial Times Press.

80. Pedley, M. July–August 2018. "Five Fords Energy Park." *The EMA Magazine,* pp. 18–20.

81. Morris, S. June 13, 2012. "Welsh Water Unveils £1bn Investment Programme." *The Guardian.*

82. Newing, R. 2006. "Case study: Welsh Water." [Online]. Available: www.ft.com/cms/s/2/837994d6-6f28-11bd-ab7b-0000779e2340.html (accessed April 12, 2015).

83. Dŵr Cymru Welsh Water. 2015. "Dŵr Cymru Welsh Water business plan: 2015 - 2020." Cardiff: Dŵr Cymru Welsh Water.

84. Braga, T. 2009. "What Does it Take to Get Projects Off the Ground? Johnson & Johnson Capital Relief Funding for CO2 Reduction Projects." WWF Climate Savers and IMD.

85. K. Holland. September 23, 2007. "'In Mission Statements, Bizspeak and Bromides.' Job Market: Under New Management." *New York Times (New York ed.),* p. 317.

86. Collis, D., and M. Rukstad. April 2008. "Can You Say What Your Strategy Is?." *Harvard business review 86,* pp. 82–90.

87. Lencioni, P. 2002. "Make Your Values Mean Something," *Harvard Business Review* 80, no. 7, pp. 113–117.

88. Bové, A., D. D'Herde, and S. Swartz. 2017. "Sustainability's Deepening Imprint. McKinsey Global Survey results." McKinsey & Company.

89. Ulrich, D., and N. Smallwood. June 2004. *Capitalizing on Capabilities.* Harvard Business Review.

90. Willard, B. 2004. "Teaching Sustainability in Business Schools: Why, What and How." In *Teaching Business Sustainability Volume 1: From Theory to Practice,* pp. 261–81. Sheffield, Greenlead.

91. Kaplan, R., and D. McMillan. February 03, 2021. "Reimagining the Balanced Scorecard for the ESG Era." *Harvard Business Review.* [Online]. Available: https://hbr.org/2021/02/reimagining-the-balanced-scorecard-for-the-esg-era (accessed March 10, 2021).

92. Abu Dhabi National Oil Company. 2017. "Global Energy Management System Implementation: Case Study. Abu Dhabi National Oil Company (ADNOC)." Clean Energy Ministerial.

93. Zamzam, M. 2014. "Planning and Implementing Energy Efficiency Improvements. A Presentation at the 10th Engineering Excellence Forum, Abu Dhabi Men's Technical College on 18 Mar 2014." Abu Dhabi.

94. Garrett, J. Spring/Summer 2016. "Sustainability Lessons We Can Learn from the Car Industry." *Output,* pp. 18–19.

95. Cassell, P., I. Ellison, A. Pearson, J. Shaw, A. Tautscher, S. Betts, and A.F.M. Doran. 2016. "Collaboration for a Closed-Loop Value Chain: Transferable Learning Points from the PEALCAR Project. A Circular

Economy Case Study." Cambridge: Cambridge Institute for Sustainability Leadership.

96. U.S. Senate Committee on Homeland Securities & Governmental Affairs. May 21, 2010. Conscience and Courage: Honoring the Legacy of Senator Margaret Chase Smith, www.hsgac.senate.gov/media/minority-media/conscience-and-courage-honoring-the-legacy-of-senator-margaret-chase-smith (accessed November 24, 2021).

97. Kotter, J. 2007. "Leading Change: Why Transformation Efforts Fail?" *Harvard Business Review* 86, pp. 97–103.

98. Bhattacharya, C. May 2020. "Taking Ownership of a Sustainable Future." *McKinsey Quarterly.*

99. Lencioni, P. 2020. *The Motive: Why so Many Leaders Abdicate their Most Important Responsibilities.* New Jersey, NJ: Jossey-Bass.

100. Kishan, S. July 20, 2021. "BlackRock Voted Against 255 Directors for Climate Issues." Bloomberg. www.bloomberg.com/news/articles/2021-07-20/blackrock-voted-against-255-directors-for-climate-related-issues (accessed November 12, 2021).

101. Interface Inc. n.d. "The Interface Story." [Online]. Available: www.interface.com/EU/en-GB/sustainability/our-history-en_GB (accessed June 19, 2020).

102. Bryant, S., and K. Wong. 2017. "Gravity Payments: Setting the World or Itself on Fire?" *Journal of Case Research and Inquiry* 3, pp. 13–27

103. Moye, D. April 14, 2021. "CEO hits back at Fox News after they derided him for Offering $70,000 minimum salaries." *Huffington Post,* www.huffingtonpost.co.uk/entry/dan-price-gravity-payments-cut-salary_n_60760cebe4b001befb6d8b9f (accessed November 26, 2021).

104. Entrepreneur en Espanol, April 20, 2021. "The CEO Who Gave his Employees a Minimum Wage of $ 70,000 says his company's revenue tripled." *Entrepreneur Europe,* www.entrepreneur.com/article/369908 (accessed November 26, 2021).

105. Campbell, D., J. Case, and B. Fotsch. June 09, 2020. "Run your Business So You'll Never Need Layoffs." *Harvard Business Review,* https://hbr.org/2020/06/run-your-business-so-youll-never-need-layoffs (accessed November 26, 2021).

106. Makower, J. 2016. "Inside Interface's Bold New Mission to Achieve 'Climate Take Back'." [Online]. Available: www.greenbiz.com/article/inside-interfaces-bold-new-mission-achieve-climate-take-back (accessed June 19, 2020).

107. Unilever. n.d. "Unilever Sustainable Living." [Online]. Available: www.unilever.com/sustainable-living/ (accessed June 19, 2020).

108. Wenzel, W. 2020. "20 C-Suite Sustainability Champions for 2020." [Online]. Available: www.greenbiz.com/article/20-c-suite-sustainability-champions-2020 (accessed June 19, 2020).

109. Porter, M., and C. der Linde. 1995. "Towards a New Conception of the Environment-Competitiveness Relationship." *Journal of Economic Perspectives* 9, no. 4, pp. 97–118.

110. Barham, K., and C. Heimer. 1998. *ABB - The Dancing Giant: Creating the Globally Connected Corporation.* Pitman Publishing Ltd.

111. British Airways. September 07, 2021. "BA Better World." British Airways. [Online]. Available: www.britishairways.com/en-us/information/about-ba/ba-better-world (accessed September 14, 2021).

112. Hamel, G. July–August 2000. "Waking Up IBM: How a Gang of Unlikely Rebels Transformed Big Blue." *Harvard Business Review.*

113. Miller, P., and T. Wedell-Wedellsborg. 2013. "The Case for Stealth Innovation." *Harvard Business Review* 91, no. 3, pp. 90–97.

114. Dutton, J., S. Ashford, and R. O'Neill. 1997. "Reading the Wind: How Middle Managers Assess the Context for Selling Issues to Top Managers." *Strategic Management Journal* 18, no. 5, pp. 407–425.

115. Accenture. 2010. "Understanding Consumer Preference in Energy Efficiency: Accenture End-Customer Observatory on Electricity Management 2010." Accenture.

116. Bonini, S., and T. Bové. 2014. "Sustainability's Strategic Worth. McKinsey Global Survey results." *McKinsey & Company.*

117. Gromet, D., H. Kunreuther, and R. Larrick. 2013. "Political Ideology Affects Energy Efficiency Attitudes And Choices." *Proceedings of the National Academy of Science of the United States of America* 110, no. 23, pp. 9314–9319.

118. Aknin, L., E. Dunn, and M. Norton. 2012. "Happiness Runs in Circular Motion: Evidence for a Positive Feedback Loop Between Prosocial Spending and Happiness." *J Happiness Studies* 13, pp. 347–355.

119. Reyna, E., J. Hiller, C. Riso, and J. Jay. 2012. "The Virtuous Cycle of Organizational Energy Efficiency: A Fresh Approach to Dismantling Barriers." *2012 ACEEE Summer Study on Energy Efficiency in Buildings.*

120. Braga, T., A. Ionescu-Somers, and C. Billington. 1986. "What Does it Take to Get Projects Off the Ground? Johnson & Johnson Capital Relief Funding for CO_2 Reduction Projects." In *WWH Climate Savers Innovation Case Stud* , pp. 31–41. WWF.

121. Siemens. 2020. "Decarbonization." [Online]. Available: https://new.siemens.com/global/en/company/sustainability/decarbonization.html (accessed July 10, 2020).

122. Koller, T., R. Nuttall, and W. Henisz. November 2019. "Five Ways that ESG Creates Value." *McKinsey Quarterly.*

123. Delevingne, L., A. Gründle, and S. Kane. February 2020. "The ESG Premium: New Perspectives on Value and Performance." *McKinsey Quarterly.*

124. Harvard Business Review Analytic Services. 2019. "Testing Organizational Boundaries to Improve Strategy Execution." *Harvard Business Review.* Boston.

125. Mankins, M., and R. Steele. 2005. "Turning Great Strategy into Great Performance." *Harvard Business Review* 2607.

126. Cook, R., S. de Raedemaecker, J. Fabianowicz, and A. Fantoni. 2017. "Holding a Mirror to the Management System: How Mature is it?." *The Work of Leaders in a Lean Management Enterprise,* pp. 52–59.

127. Lamach, M. October 2017. "How our Company Connected our Strategy to Sustainability Goals." *Harvard Business Review.*

128. Charles, A. 2017. "Global State of Process Excellence 2017." Process Excellence Network.

129. Van Zyl, R. 2013. *Making Energy Savings a Reality. Saldanha Works – A Case Study. Presentation at African Utility Week: Delivering Beyond Tomorrow.*

130. UNIDO. 2013. "Introduction and Implementation of an Energy Management System and Energy Systems Optimisation." Case Study: AcelorMittal Saldanha Works, South Africa.

131. Kotter, J. 2014. *Accelerate.* Cambridge: Harvard Business Review Press.

132. Kotter, J., and H. Rathgeber. 2006. *Our Iceberg is Melting: Changing and Succeeding under any Conditions.* London: Macmillan.

133. Hinde, T. 2012. *The Economist's Guide to Management Ideas and Gurus.* London: Economist Books.

134. Matteni, M. 2015. *UNIDO Presentation at ISO/TC242 Energy Management plenary meeting in Merida, Mexico.* Merida: UNIDO.

135. US Department of Energy. 2012. "Improving Steam Systems Performance: A Sourcebook for Industry." DOE/GO-102012-3423, 2 ed. Washington DC: US Department of Energy.

136. IEA. 2007. "Tracking Industrial Energy Efficiency and CO2 Emissions." Paris: IEA.

137. Fraunhofer Institute for Systems and Innovation Research. 2013. "Analysis of a European Reference Target System for 2030." Karlsruhe: Coalition for Energy Savings.

138. Jevons, W. 1865. *The Coal Question. An Inquiry Concerning the Progress of the Nation, and the Probable Exhaustion of Our Coal Mines.* London: Macmillan and Co.

139. The Dearborn Independent. 1922. *Ford Ideals: Being a Selection from "Mr Ford's Page".* Michigan: The Dearborn Publishing.

140. Herring, H. 2006. "Energy Efficiency: A Critical View." *Energy* 31, no. 1, pp. 10–20.

141. ISO. 2018. "ISO 50001 Energy Management Systems - Requirements with Guidance for Use." Geneva: ISO.

142. Broad, L. 2013. "Dawn Meats Uses Space Technology to Achieve Thermal Energy Reduction." [Online]. Available: www.2degreesnetwork.com/groups/2degrees-community/resources/dawnmeats-uses-space-technology-achieve-thermal-energy-reduction/ (accessed December 30, 2013).

143. Coca-Cola Hellenic Bottling Company. 2010. "Energy and Climate Change." [Online]. Available: www.coca-colahellenic.com/sustainability/environment/energyandclimate/ heat_and_power_plant (accessed May 08, 2013).

144. Brown, D. 2013. "Driving Down Carbon Through the Supply Chain." Cambridge: Cambridge Institute for Sustainability Leadership.

145. Goldberg, A., E. Holdaway, J. Reinaud, and S. O'Keeffe. 2012. "Promoting Energy Savings and GHG Mitigation through Industrial Supply Chain Initiatives." Institute for Industrial Productivity.

146. Burchardt, J., M. Frédeau, M. Hadfield, P. Herhold, C. O'Brien, C. Pieper, and D. Weise. January 26, 2021. "Supply Chains as a Game-Changer in the Fight Against Climate Change." [Online]. Available: www.bcg.com/publications/2021/fighting-climate-change-with-supply-chain-decarbonization (accessed February 10, 2021).

147. Chanel, G. 2011. "High Yields from Sustainable Supplies." *T Magazine,* no. 5, pp. 26–29.

148. Pepsico UK. December 07, 2020. "We're Cutting Carbon Emissions by Bringing Potatoes Full Circle." Pepsico UK [Online]. Available: www.pepsico.co.uk/news/stories/cutting-carbon-emissions (accessed April 20, 2021).

149. GlaxoSmithKline. 2013. "GSK Corporate Responsibility Report 2012." London: GlaxoSmithKline.

150. Werbach, A. 2009. "Strategy for Sustainability: A Business Manifesto." Boston: Harvard Business Review Press.

151. Unilever. 2012. "Sustainable Living: Water Use by Consumers." [Online]. Available: www.unilever.com/sustainable-living-2014/reducing-environmental-impact/water-use/water-use-by-consumers/? (accessed June 17, 2014).

152. Braungart, M., and W. McDonough. 2002. *Cradle to Cradle: Remaking the Way We Make Things.* New York, NY: North Point Press.

153. Groupe Renault. 2017. "Renault, Actively Developing Circular Economy Throughout Vehicles Life Cycle." [Online]. Available: https://group.renault.com/en/news/blog-renault/renault-actively-developing-circular-economy-throughout-vehicles-life-cycle/ (accessed January 29, 2019).

154. Kollau, R. 2014. "Upcycling: Discarded Airline Materials are Upcycled into Sports Gear, Soccer Balls and Handbags." [Online]. Available: www.airlinetrends.com/tag/upcycling/ (accessed April 03, 2020).

155. Verbeek, J. February 2015. "Closing the Loop, Adding Value." *The Chemical Engineer*, pp. 34–36.

156. Posnett, D. December 2017. "Buses Full of Beans." *The Chemical Engineer*, pp. 35–37.

157. McCartnet, T. March 2018. "Rubbish roads." *The Chemical Engineer*, pp. 43–45.

158. Smithers, R. April 28, 2018. "Raise a Toast! New Beers Made from Leftover Bread Help to Cut Food Waste." *The guardian*.

159. Re:newcell. 2019. "Re:newcell - We Make Fashion Sustainable." [Online]. Available: https://renewcell.com/. (accessed April 03, 2020).

160. Braw, E. July 15, 2014. "Southwest Airlines Upcycles 80,000 Leather Seats Into Bags, Shoes and Balls." *The Guardian*.

161. Emirates Press Office. 2017. "Emirates Introduces Sustainable Blankets Made from 100% Recycled Plastic Bottles." [Online]. Available: www.emirates.com/media-centre/emirates-introduces-sustainable-blankets-made-from-100-recycled-plastic-bottles/ (accessed April 03, 2020).

162. Lichtenstein, B., J. Carroll, C. Page, J. Laur, and P. Senge. 2008a. "Materials Pooling (A): Opportunity and Potential of the Sustainability Consortium." *MITSloan Management Case 08-057*.

163. Lichtenstein, B., J. Carroll, C. Page, J. Laur, and P. Senge. 2008b. "Materials Pooling (B): Challenges to a Collaboration for Sustainability." *MITSloan Management case 08-058*.

164. Carbon Trust. 2013. "Tesco - Supply Chain Carbon Management." [Online]. Available: www.carbontrust.com/our-clients/t/tesco/ (accessed January 17, 2019).

165. EPOS. 2014. "Enhanced Energy and Resource Efficiency and Performance in Process Industry Operations via Onsite and Cross-Sectorial Symbiosis." [Online]. Available: www.spire2030.eu/epos (accessed January 17, 2019).

166. UNIDO. 2019. "Industrial Resource Efficiency Division and Circular Economy." Vienna: UNIDO.

167. Lee, D., and L. Bony. 2009. "Cradle-To-Cradle Design at Herman Miller: Moving toward Environmental Sustainability Case 9-607-003." Cambridge: Harvard Business School.

168. Miller, H. May 12, 2021. "Mirra chair." Wikipedia. [Online]. Available: https://en.wikipedia.org/wiki/Mirra_chair (accessed September 16, 2021).

169. Hiemstra, G. April 24, 2013. "Herman Miller Mirra 2: Berlin's Studio 7.5 Redesigns the Michigan Furniture Maker's Classic Office Chair." Cool Hunting. [Online]. Available: https://coolhunting.com/design/herman-miller-mirra-2-chair/ (accessed September 16, 2021).

170. Neave, H. 1991. "Deming speaks to European Executives." London: British Deming Association.

171. Hammer, M. Spring, 2007. "The Seven Deadly Sins of Performance Measurement [and How to Avoid Them]." *MIT Sloan Management Review*.

172. Kelvin, W. 1883. *Electrical Units of Measurement. Lecture to the Institution of Civil Engineers on 3 May 1883*. London: Institution of Civil Engineers.

173. US Energy Information Administration. 2012. "Commercial Buildings Energy Consumption Survey (CBECS)." [Online]. Available: www.eia. gov/consumption/commercial/data/2012 (accessed March 2017).

174. Kannan, R., and W. Boie. 2003. "Energy Management Practices in SME – Case Study of a Bakery in Germany." *Energy Conversion and Management* 44, pp. 945–959.

175. Barnard, P., T. Darkins, B. Earl, and K. Adeyeye. 2014. "Retrofitting for Water Efficiency: A Hotel Case Study." *Proceedings of the Water Efficiency Conference 2014, 9-11 September 2014*. Brighton, UK.

176. Envirowise. 2008. "Bakery improves resource efficiency. Case Study CS823." Harwell: HMSO.

177. ISO. 2014. "ISO 50002 Energy Audits - Requirements with Guidance for Use." Geneva: ISO.

178. Oung, K. 2013. *Energy Management in Business: The Manager's Guide to Maximising and Sustaining Energy Reduction*. Farnham: Gower Publishing.

179. Murray, S. 2011. "Unlocking the Benefits of Energy Efficiency: An Executive Dilemma." *Economist Intelligence Unit report*. London: The Economist.

180. Hancock, G. 2009. "How GE's 'Treasure Hunts' Discovered More than $110m in Energy Savings." [Online]. Available: www.greenbiz.com/ blog/2009/05/13/how-ges-treasure-hunts-discovered-more-100m-energy-savings?page=full (accessed January 01, 2009).

181. Dougherty, K., and H. Mikytuck. n.d. "GE's eco Treasure Hunt Checklist." GE Capital.

182. Roos, G. 2010. "GE Energy Treasure Hunt Yields $2.1m Energy Savings at NY Hospital." [Online]. Available: www.environmentalleader. com/2010/07/ge-energy-treasure-hunt-yields-2-1m-energy-savings-at-ny-hospital (accessed January 27, 2019).

183. Dunn, M. 2013. "GMS Irvine – Energy Efficiency." Amsterdam.

184. CMR Consultants. 2014. "CMR Consultants' Energy Kaizen: Accelerated Energy and CO2 Savings Programme." [Online]. Available: www.energ-group. com/media/570098/energy_kaizen_brochure.pdf (accessed April 15, 2014).

185. ABB. January 2018. "Plastic Bottle Maker Benefits from Motor-Drive Package." *Energy world*, p. 21.

186. ABB. 2016. "Case PrimePac Limited: SynRM Investment Leads to 30% increase in Bottle Production." ABB.

187. Costa Coffee. 2013. "Behind the Beans." [Online]. Available: www.costa. co.uk/behind-the-beans (accessed April 15, 2020).

188. Gosnell, G., J. List, and R. Metcalfe. 2017. "A New Approach to an Age-Old Problem: Solving Externalities by Incenting Workers Directly. Centre for Climate Change Economics and Policy. Working Paper No. 296." University of Leeds and London School of Economics and Political Science.

189. Iberia Airlines. 2014. "Does a Plane's Paint Job Affect Fuel Consumption?." [Online]. Available: https://love2fly.iberia.com/2014/01/airplane-paint-fuel-consumption (accessed March 21, 2020).

190. BASF, Lufthansa Cargo AG, Lufthansa Technik. May 03, 2021. "Lufthansa Group and BASF Roll Out Sharkskin Technology." Joint News Release. BASF, Lufthansa Cargo AG, and Lufthansa Technik. [Online]. Available: http://sharkyear.com/2021/lufthansa-group-and-basf-roll-out-sharkskin-technology.html (accessed May 31, 2021).

191. Kingsley-Jones, M. 2010. "Airbus Details A380's New, More Efficient Heathrow Departure Procedures, Flightglobal." [Online]. Available: www.flightglobal.com/news/articles/airbus-details-a380s-new-moreefficient-heathrow-departure-procedures-339067 (accessed July 21, 2013).

192. ISPE. 2011. 2011 FOYA Category Winners. https://ispe.org/facility-year-awards/winners/previous/2011 (accessed July 21, 2013).

193. Heathrow Airport. n.d. "Airbus A380 New Departure Procedures. Sustainability Case Study." [Online]. Available: www.heathrowairport.com/about-us/community-and-environment/ sustainability/case-studies/airbus-a380-new-departure-procedures (accessed June 06, 2013).

194. Logistics Middle East. 2009. "Emirates Uses Weather to Reduce Fuel Burn." [Online]. Available: www.logisticsmiddleeast.com/article-1758-emirates-uses-weather-to-reduce-fuel-burn (accessed May 25, 2020).

195. Sugimoto, S. 2016. "The ANA Group's Circular and Environment Strategy." *Towards a Circular Economy: Corporate Management and Policy Pathways,* pp. 43–58.

196. Aflaki, S., and P. Kleindorfer. 2010. "Going Green: The Pfizer Freiburg Energy Initiative. 03/2010-5680." Fontainebleau: INSEAD Social Innovation Centre.

197. US Department of Energy. 2010b. "Success Story: Ingersoll Rand Discovers Hidden Savings with a Three-Tiered Energy Audit Model," US Department of Energy Industrial Technologies Program.

198. Sultana, K. 2018. "A Roadmap for Industry to Increase Energy Efficiency." [Online]. Available: www.smartindustry.com/blog/smart-industry-connect/a-roadmap-for-industry-to-increase-energy-efficiency/ (accessed September 01, 2018).

199. Baczko, K., A. Malkin, I. Campbell, R. Quartararo, and A. Lovins. 2009. "A Landmark Sustainability Program for the Empire State Building: A Model for Optimizing Energy Efficiency, Sustainable Practices, Operating Expenses and Long Term Value in Existing Buildings." Jones Lang LaSalle.

200. Shaw, J. March–April 2012. "A Green Empire: How Anthony Malkin'84 Engineered the Largest 'green' Retrofit Ever." *Harvard Magazine.*

201. Shaw, J. March–April 2012. "Green Engineering." Harvard Magazine.

202. Slater, R. 1998. *Jack Welch and the GE Way: Management Insights and Leadership Secrets of the Legendary CEO.* McGraw Hill.

203. Xie, J., S. Sreenivasan, G. Korniss, W. Zhang, C. Lim, and B. Szymanski. 2011. "Social Consensus through the Influence of Committed Minorities." *Physical Review E* 84.

204. Gladwell, M. 2000. *The Tipping Point: How Little Things Can Make a Big Difference.* Little Brown.

205. Brown, J. 1963. "The Social Psychology of Industry." Penguin.

206. Deming, W. 1982. "Out of the Crisis." Cambridge: Massachusetts Institute of Technology, Center for Advanced Educational Services.

207. Scholtes, P., B. Joiner, and B. Streibel. 2018. *The Team Handbook.* 3 ed. Mathuen: Goal/QPC.

208. Grant, R. 2012. *Contemporary Strategy Analysis.* 8th ed. John Wiley & Sons.

209. Gallup Inc. 2017. "State of the Global Workplace." New York, NY: Gallup Press.

210. Lane4. 2010. *A Question of Trust: A Current Look at Trust in Leadership.* Buckinghamshire: Lane4.

211. Rozovsky, J. 2015. "The Five Keys to a Successful Google Team." [Online]. Available: http://rework.withgoogle.com/blog/five-keys-to-a-successful-google-team/. (accessed October 10, 2018).

212. Ludeman, K., and E. Erlandson. 2006. *Alpha Male Syndrome.* Boston: Harvard Business School Publishing.

213. de Rond, M. 2017. *Doctors at War: Life and Death in a Field Hospital - The Culture and Politics of Health Care Work.* New York, NY: Cornell University Press.

214. de Rond, M. 2012. *There is an I in Team: What Elite Athletes and Coaches Really Know About High Performance.* Boston: Harvard Business Review Press.

215. de Rond, M. 2008. *Last Amateurs: To Hell and Back with the Cambridge Boat Race Crew.* London: Icon Books.

216. Rosenzweig, P. 2007. *The Halo Effect ... and the Eight Other Business Delusions that Deceive Managers.* New York, NY: The free press.

217. Eurich, T. October 18, 2018. "Working with People who Aren't Self-Aware." [Online]. Available: https://hbr.org/2018/10/working-with-people-who-arent-self-aware. (accessed October 18, 2018).

218. Goleman, D., R. Boyatzis, and A. McKee. 2013. *Primal Leadership: Unleashing the Power of Emotional Intelligence.* Boston: Harvard business review press.

219. Marston, W. 1928. *Emotions of Normal People.* Taylor & Francis Ltd.

220. Adizes, I. 2004. *Management/Mismanagement Styles: How to Identify a Style and What to do About it.* Santa Barbara: The Adizes Institute Publishing.

221. Sayers, S. 1978. "Leadership Styles: A Behavioural Matrix." Portland: Northwest Regional Educational Laboratory, US Department of Education.

222. Erikson, T. 2019. *Surrounded by Idiots: The Four Types of Human Behaviour (or, How to Understand Those Who Cannot Be Understood).* London: Vermilion.

223. Ferrari, B. February 2012. "The Executive's Guide to Better Listening." *McKinsey Quarterly.*

224. Mehrabian, A. 1971. *Silent Messages.* 1st ed. Wadsworth: Belmont.

225. Harvey, J. 1988. "The Abilene Paradox: The Management of Agreement." *Organizational Dynamics* 17, no. 1, pp. 17–43.

226. US Department of Energy. 2010a. "Nissan Showcases the Results of an Energy-Wise Corporate Culture. Industrial Technologies Program. May 2010." Washington, DC: Energy Efficiency and Renewable Energy Centre, US Department of Energy.

227. Herway, J. 2017. "How to Create a Culture of Psychological Safety." [Online]. Available: www.gallup.com/workplace/236198/create-culture-psychological-safety.aspx (accessed May 07, 2020).

228. Duhigg, C. 2016. *Smarter Faster Better: The Secrets of Being Productive in Life and Business.* New York, NY: Random House.

229. Majchrzak, A., and Q. Wang. September–October 1996. "Breaking the Functional Mind-Set in Process Organizations." *Harvard Business Review.*

230. de Bono, E. 1985. "Six Thinking Hats: An Essential Approach to Business Management." Little Brown & Company.

231. de Bono, E. 1991. *Six Action Shoes.* Longman Higher Education.

232. Arje, S. March–April 2018. "1 Dedicated Team, 47 Keen Candidated, £2 Million Saving." *The EMS Magazine,* no., pp. 6–9.

233. WRAP. 2014. "Case Study: Motivating Employees to Save Water." WRAP.

234. ENDS. 2012. "One-of-a-King Combination Trailer and Tanker Hits the Highways." ENDS.

234. Transport Engineer. December 2012. "Innovative engineering." *Transport Engineer,* pp. 8–11.

235. Lynch, M. 2017. "RBS Innovation Gateway Trial Report: JUMP." JUMP.

236. Ogleby, G. 2017. "RBS Eyes £3m Energy Savings Through Employee Engagement Scheme" [Online]. Available: www.edie.net/news/7/RBS-rolls-out-national-employee-engagement-competition (accessed May 24, 2020).

237. Barton, T. 2017. "RBS Rolls Out Sustainability Engagement Scheme." [Online]. Available: employeebenefits.co.uk/issues/april-online-2017/rbs-rolls-out-sustainability-engagement-scheme-across-the-uk-and-ireland/ (accessed May 24, 2020).

239. US Department of Energy. 2010. "3M's Model Rewards and Recognition Program Engages Employees and Drives Energy Savings Efforts. Industrial Technologies Program." Washington, DC: Energy Efficiency and Renewable Energy Centre, US Department of Energy.

240. Adkins, A., and B. Rigoni. 2016. "Managers: Millennials Want Feedback, But Won't Ask for it." Gallup Inc.

241. Toffel, M., and J. Short. 2011. "Coming Clean and Cleaning Up: Does Voluntary Self-Reporting Indicate Effective Self-Policing." *Journal of Law & Economics* 54, no. 3, pp. 609–649.

242. Doshi, A., G. Dowell, and M. Toffel. 2013. "How Firms Respond to Mandatory Information Disclosure." *Strategic Management Journal* 34, no. 10, pp. 1209–1231.

243. Lencioni, P. 2012. *The Advantage: Why Organizational Health Trumps Everything Else in Business.* San Francisco: Jossey-Bass.

244. Ariely, D. 2009. "Predictably Irrational: The Hidden Forces that Shape our Decisions." Harper Colins.

245. Michie, S., M. Richardson, M. Johnston, C. Abraham, J. Francis, W. Hardeman, M. Eccles, J. Cane, and C. Wood. 2013. "The Behavior Change Technique Taxonomy (v1) of 93 Hierarchically Clustered Techniques: Building an International Consensus for the Reporting of Behavior Change Interventions." *Annals of Behavioral Medicine* 46, no. 1, pp. 81–95.

246. Michie, S., R. Carey, M. Johnston, A. Rothman, M. de Bruin, M. Kelly and L. Connell, "From Theory-Inspired to Theory-Based Interventions: A Protocol for Developing and Testing a Methodology for Linking Behaviour Change Techniques to Theoretical Mechanisms of Action." *Annals of Behavioral Medicine* 52, no. 6, p. 501–512.

247. Kahneman, D. 2011. *Thinking, Fast and Slow.* London: Allen Lane.

248. Magretta, J., and N. Stone. 2002. *What Management Is: How it Works and Why it's Everyone's Business.* London: HarperCollins Publishers.

249. Resource Efficient Scotland. n.d. "Early Engagement at Design Stage May Make Material Savings of Over £500 ka Year for Bradagh Interiors." [Online]. Available: https://energy.zerowastescotland.org.uk/case-study/early-engagement-design-stage-may-make-material-savings-over-%C2%A3500k-year-bradagh-interiors (accessed June 01, 2020).

250. Ahn, Y., and A. Pearce. April 2013. "Green Luxury: A Case Study of Two Green Hotels." *Journal of Green Building,* no. 1, pp. 90–119.

251. Amabile, T., and S. Kramer. 2011. *The Progress Principle: Using Small Wins to Ignite Joy, Engagement, and Creativity at Work.* Harvard Business Review Press.

252. Maslow, A. 1954. *Motivation and Personality.* New York, NY: Harper and Row.

253. Herzberg, F., B. Mausner, and B. Snyderman. 1959. *The Motivation to Work*. 2nd ed. New York, NY: John Wiley.

254. Chatterji, A., and M. Toffel. 2008. "How Firms Respond to Being Rated." *Strategic Management Journal* 31, no. 9, pp. 917–945.

255. Marquis, C., M. Toffel, and Y. Zhou. 2016. "Scrutiny, Norms, and Selective Disclosure: A Global Study of Greenwashing." *Organization Science* 27, no. 2, pp. 483–504.

256. Short, J., M. Toffel, and A. Hugill. 2016. "Monitoring Global Supply Chains." *Strat. Mgmt. J.* 37, pp. 1879–1897.

257. Kaplan, R., and R. de Pinho. 2008. *Amanco: Developing the Sustainability Scorecard (9-107-038)*. Cambridge: Harvard Business School.

258. Graham Packaging. April 28, 2021. "Get More Use Out of a Single Bottle." Graham Packaging. [Online]. Available: www.grahampackaging.com/solutions/reusable-packaging (accessed April 28, 2021).

259. Graham Packaging. April 28, 2021. "Redefining Sustainability and Design. Pinpoint Where Material is Placed Throughout Your Container or Bottle." Graham Packaging. [Online]. Available: www.grahampackaging.com/solutions/lightweighting/accustrength (accessed April 28, 2021).

260. Lingle, R. March 03, 2020. "Graham Packaging's Deep Dive into Sustainable Packaging." Plastics Today. [Online]. Available: www.plasticstoday.com/packaging/graham-packagings-deep-dive-sustainable-packaging (accessed April 28, 2021).

261. Shaw, G., Writer. 1921. *Back to Methuselah, The Serpent, Part 1: In the Beginning, Act 1 Where the Serpent Says these Words to Eve*. [Performance].

262. Sterman, J., A. Kaulberg, and B. Patten. 2019. "Is it Easy Being Green? MIT Sloan Considers the Opportunities and Threats of Sustainable Building. MIT Sloan Case Study." Boston: MIT Sloan Sustainability Initiative.

263. MIT Capital Projects. 2010. "MIT Sloan School, Building E62." [Online]. Available: https://capitalprojects.mit.edu/projects/mit-sloan-school-e62 (accessed June 12, 2020).

264. MIT Sloan. 2010. "E62: The heart of MIT Sloan." [Online]. Available: https://mitsloan.mit.edu/buildingthefuture/about-e62.php (accessed June 12, 2020).

265. Doran, G. 1981. "There's a S.M.A.R.T. Way to Write Management's Goals and Objectives." *Management Review* 70, no. 11, pp. 35–36.

266. Rangan, V., M. Toffel, V. Dessain, and J. Lenhardt. 2015. "Sustainability at IKEA Group (Case Study 9-515-033)." *Harvard Business School*.

267. Apte, S., and J. Sheth. 2017. *The Sustainability Edge: How to Drive Top-Line Growth with Triple-Bottom-Line Thinking*. Rotman/UTP Publishing.

268. IKEA. 2011. *The IKEA Approach to Sustainability: How We Manage Sustainability in our Business.*

269. Sandybayev, B. 2017. "Strategic Supply Chain Management Implementation: Case Study of IKEA." *Nobel International Journal of Business and Management Research* 1, no. 1, pp. 5–9.

270. Inter IKEA Systems B. V. 2016. "Our Business in Brief." Malmo: Inter IKEA Systems B. V.

271. Toffel, M., and N.M.K. Hill. 2003a. "Developing a Management Systems approach to Sustainability at BMW Group (Part 1 of 2)." *International Journal of Corporate Sustainability* 10, no. 2, pp. 29–38.

272. Toffel, M., and N.M.K. Hill. 2003b. "BMW Group's Sustainability Management System: Preliminary Results, Ongoing Challenges, and the UN Global Compact (Part 2 of 2)." *International Journal of Corporate Sustainability* 10, no. 3, pp. 51–60.

273. Blunck, E. 2016. "Germany BMW's Sustainability Strategy of Evolution and Revolution Towards a Circular Economy." In *Towards a Circular Economy: Corporate Management and Policy Pathway. ERIA Research Report 2014–44, eds.* V. Anbumozhi and J. Kim, pp. 75–92. Jakarta: ERIA.

274. Ford, H. May 08, 1928. Interviewee, *N.Y. American.* [Interview].

275. Janda, K. 2009. "Buildings Don't Use Energy: People Do." In *26th Conference on Passive and Low Energy Architecture.* 22 – 24 June. Quebec City.

276. CEMEX. 2012. "CEMEX's Position on Climate Change." [Online]. Available: www.cemex.com/MediaCenter/Files/CEMEX_POSITION_on_Climate_ Change.pdf (accessed June 17, 2014).

277. Grayson, D., M. McLaren, and N. Exter. 2014. "Combining Profit and Purpose: A New Dialogue on the Role of Business in Society." Cranfield University School of Management and Financial Times.

278. Hopkins, M. 2009. "What Executives Don't Get About Sustainability (and Further Notes on the Profit Motive)." *MIT Sloan Management Review* 51, no. 1.

279. Beshears, J., and F. Gino. May 2015. "Leaders as Decision Architects." *Harvard Business Review 44,* no. 3.

280. Halvorson, H., and D. Rock. July 2015. "Beyond Bias." *Strategy + Business.*

281. Maslow, A. 1970. *Motivation and Personality.* New York, NY: Harper & Row.

282. Porter, M., and M. Kramer. December 2006. "Strategy and Society: The Link Between Competitive Advantage and Corporate Social Responsibility." *Harvard business review* 84, no. 12, pp. 78–92.

283. Willard, B. 2005. *The Next Sustainability Wave: Building Boardroom Buy-In.* New society publishers.

284. ISO Focus. November–December 2013. "Energy Boooooost for Costa Coffee." *ISO Focus* 101, p. 46–47.

285. Holdings, A. 2005. "Product Backgrounder." Cambridge: Arm Holdings.

286. Hammer, M., and K. Somers. 2014. *Resource-Productive Operations: Five Core Beliefs to Increase Profits through Leaner and Greener Manufacturing Operations.* Brussels: McKinsey & Company.

287. "Apple Mac Arm M! Competitive Trafe-offs." Stephen Smith's Blog, November 13, 2020. [Online]. Available: https://smist08.wordpress.com/2020/11/13/apple-mac-arm-m1-competitive-trade-offs/ (accessed June 29, 2021).

About the Author

Kit Oung is a Principal Consultant and coach on health and safety management, environmental management, and Operational Excellence with a specialism in energy and resource productivity. His work helps managers maximize their energy and resource productivity; identify the minimum investment cost pathways; reduce the often complex and technical messages into a clear, meaningful, and simple-to-understand business case; enable them to engage with senior executives; disarm barriers for performance improvement; and bring about its implementation safely and healthily.

He brings with him 25 years of hands-on and practical experience from working with a range of small-to-medium-sized, blue-chip commercial, industrial, governmental, and nongovernmental organizations across five continents in design, operations, management, consulting, policy design, corporate governance, and executive education. As such, he can understand technical and managerial challenges, work with multiple stakeholders, cultural sensitivities, manage multidisciplinary projects, and personnel development.

Kit also trains new and aspiring professionals in good governance, particularly on understanding, implementing, maintaining, and auditing ISO14001, ISO45001, ISO50001, and Integrated Management Systems at British Standards Institution (BSI). He speaks and writes engagingly and in a jargon-free manner on business sustainability, energy and resource efficiency, and integrated management.

In a voluntary capacity, Kit serves as IChemE congressman, IChemE Energy Community of Practice, and as a judge on IChemE annual awards (energy, sustainability, and water category) and the annual Global Energy Management Leadership Awards. He is also one of the U.K.'s principal experts in developing standards in the field of environmental management, energy management, circular economy, and integrated use of management systems. He leads the development of European (EN16247-3) and International (ISO 50002) standards for energy auditing, International standard for managing water impacts (ISO 14002-2), and the U.K.'s lead energy assessor competency (PAS51215).

Index

Concise and Applied Business Books